PHYSICAL EDUCATION
IN ENGLAND
SINCE 1800

PHYSICAL EDUCATION IN ENGLAND SINCE 1800

by

PETER C. McINTOSH

B.A. (Oxon), M.A. (B'ham)
Diploma of Physical Education, Carnegie College
Senior Inspector of Physical Education
Inner London Education Authority

REVISED & ENLARGED
EDITION

BELL & HYMAN
London

Published by
BELL & HYMAN LIMITED
Denmark House
37–39 Queen Elizabeth Street
London SE1 2QB

First published in 1952 by
G. Bell & Sons Ltd
Revised and enlarged 1968
Reprinted 1972, 1974, 1979

ISBN 0 7135 0689 X

Printed in Great Britain by
The Camelot Press Ltd, Southampton

Acknowledgements

MY most longstanding debt of gratitude when I first wrote this book was to Mr. M. L. Jacks who from my schooldays onwards was a constant source of inspiration, help and encouragement. Unhappily he was no longer alive when I came to revise my work but Mrs. Jacks kindly gave me information and access to his papers.

Mr. A. D. Munrow and Professor E. A. Peel contributed valuable criticism while the book was in course of preparation. Many friends and colleagues in education and in physical education have supplied me with information, some of it hitherto unpublished, on the recent history of physical education. In particular I wish to thank Miss C. Cooke, Mr. H. P. Crabtree, Mr. A. H. Gem, Mr. G. W. Hedley, Mr. E. G. Holland, Mr. E. Major, Mr. D. D. Molyneux, Mr. G. W. Murray, Mr. A. E. Syson, Mrs. P. Tebbitt, Miss L. Ullman, Mr. S. H. Woollam and Mr. S. Wilson. The Rev. J. D. E. E. Firth and Mr. L. Warwick James kindly gave me access to documents at Winchester College and Marlborough College. I am indebted to the Warden and Fellows of Winchester College and to the Master and Council of Marlborough College for permission to use extracts from documents in their possession.

Mr. J. May, Mr. G. W. Hedley, Mr. G. W. Murray and

Mr. K. L. Woodland have not only helped me with the revision of the book but have contributed valuable appendices. Mr. J. T. R. Graves read the original typescript most carefully and made many helpful corrections and suggestions. The librarian and staff of the Physical Education Association of Great Britain and Northern Ireland helped me with advice and information on many occasions.

Contents

The Plates

between pages 160 and 161

The Figures

List of Abbreviations

E.D. Education Department of the Committee of Council on Education.

J.S.P.T. 'Journal of Scientific Physical Training.' In 1922 the title was changed to 'Journal of School Hygiene and Physical Education'. From 1944 the title was 'Journal of Physical Education' and from 1955 'Physical Education'

J.P.E. 'Journal of Physical Education' (see above).

L.E.A. Local Education Authority.

N.P.F.A. National Playing Fields Association.

N.C.S.S. National Council of Social Service.

R.B.E. Annual Reports of the Board of Education.

R.C.M.O. Annual Reports of the Chief Medical Officer of the Board of Education. After 1922 they were published under the title 'The Health of the School Child'.

R.E.D. Annual Reports of the Education Department.

R.P.S.C. Report of the Public Schools' Commission 1864 (Clarendon Commission).

R.S.I.C. Report of the Schools' Inquiry Commission 1868 (Taunton Commission).

S.S.P.E.A. Secondary Schoolmasters' Physical Education Association.

CHAPTER 1

Introduction

DURING the 19th century there grew up in England two distinct traditions of physical education. While each had its origin in earlier days neither had grown beyond the embryonic stage by 1800. In the Public Schools 'organised games' began to appear early in the century. At first games were the spontaneous recreations of the boys and were for the most part disapproved of by masters. However, as the century wore on, 'organised games' came to be recognised by authority and were regarded as a powerful force in the education of the sons of the middle and upper classes. They became a feature of all Public Schools, old and new, great and small. Outside the Public Schools a different type of physical education grew up, springing from several roots—military drill, callisthenics, and gymnastics. From them grew the system of physical training which, at the end of the century, was being adopted in the public elementary schools.

The games which came to form the major part of physical education in Public Schools were the team games of football and cricket together with rowing at those schools which were situated on a navigable river. These sports were indigenous. Gymnastics, on the other hand, were of foreign extraction. Gymnastics were not unknown in England in earlier centuries and one of the earliest treatises on vaulting was written by William Stokes and published in London in 1652; nevertheless the gymnastic systems which found favour in the 19th century were in the main derived from either Sweden or Germany. Systems inspired by the work of P. H. Ling in Sweden tended to emphasise free standing exercises without apparatus, while those from Germany made use of poles and ropes, horizontal and parallel bars. It was the so-called Swedish system which, at the end of the century, predominated and formed the basis of the system which was later sponsored by the medical department of the Board of Education.

At the beginning of the 20th century there were, therefore, two systems of physical education in vogue in England, the Public School system of organised games and the elementary school system of physical training. The one concentrated on character training and the other on discipline and the physiological effects of systematised exercise. Each system had been developed to meet social as well as physical needs and for that reason alone it would have been difficult for any two-way traffic in physical education to have taken place between Public and public elementary schools. Other factors, however, added to the difficulty. The two types of school catered for entirely different age ranges, and while it was possible for boys at Public Schools to play games suitable for the physique of adults, these games were unsuitable without modification for elementary schoolboys. Elementary schools moreover were always faced with the problem of maximum numbers in minimum space—a problem that never seriously worried Public Schools except those which, like Merchant Taylors', were situated in the City of London. A more serious obstacle was the distinction which grew up between training and recreation, first officially stated by the Board of Education in 1910 but still persisting in the title of the

Physical Training and Recreation Act of 1937. Physical training attached to itself a peculiar educational significance and moral value which its protagonists tended to deny to games. An almost puritanical idea was commonly held that games were recreative, pleasurable and of less educational value than physical training. It was often assumed too that physical training could be made enjoyable and popular only by the most skilled and enthusiastic teachers. However that may be, the dichotomy within physical education between training and recreation was sharp at the beginning of the 20th century. It has become less sharp as the century has worn on, just as the distinctions between social classes frequenting Public Schools and other schools have become less clear-cut.

In blending the two traditions of physical education important parts have been played by secondary grammar schools and by the Girls' High Schools and Public Schools. The grammar schools, many of them of ancient foundation, were incorporated in a comprehensive system of secondary education as a result of the Balfour Act of 1902. Their physical education derived both from Public Schools and from elementary schools. The Girls' High Schools, many of which were founded in the second half of the 19th century, incorporated physical education in their curricula early in their career. While some of their physical education was inspired by current practices in boys' Public Schools, their concern for the social accomplishments and for health led them to introduce dancing, callisthenics and, late in the century, Swedish drill. During both the 19th and the 20th centuries institutions and organisations outside the school system also exerted an influence upon the development of physical education. While it is not easy to assess the part played by such bodies as the Amateur Gymnastic Association or by the Boy Scout movement they have undoubtedly affected both theory and practice.

The fusion of the two traditions of physical education into a national system has been by no means complete, and depends as much upon the provision of adequate facilities for games and sports for the whole population as upon an appreciation of the real value of systematic physical training and its place in education.   The purpose of this study is to trace and try to account for the growth of two traditions of physical education in the 19th century, and to examine how far they have become fused in the 20th century.

CHAPTER 2

Games in Early 19th-Century Public Schools

THE famous statement that the battle of Waterloo was won on the playing fields of Eton seems to have been first attributed to the Duke of Wellington three years after his death by Count Charles de Montalembert in a book *De l'avenir politique de l'Angleterre*, and is probably spurious.[1] When, however, at the end of the century Père Didon, the French educationist, visited Eton and remarked that the boys who learned to command in games there were learning to command the Indies his statement was recorded by the Royal Commission on Physical Training for Scotland.[2] He was speaking little less than the truth and was certainly voicing a view of the value of organised games in school life that was generally accepted. The 19th century witnessed a growth of Athleticism in Public Schools remarkable alike for its technical developments and for its social significance. At the beginning of the century, cricket and golf alone of our modern popular games were both organised and played under a generally accepted code of laws. The prize ring was to some extent organised and the rules drawn up by Jack Broughton in the 18th century were still observed, but the Queensberry rules were still far in the future. Pedestrian contests too were well publicised and were attended by large crowds, but were quite unlike the formalised competitions of modern track and field athletics. Rowing was still 'boating', football and hockey were tests of strength rather than games of skill, and lawn tennis had not been invented. In the second half of the century, all these games and sports and many others besides were organised under national associations. On the initiative of old Public School boys, refinements were introduced and laws for the conduct of the sports were codified and accepted throughout the British Isles and beyond. Socially, the cult of athleticism was closely bound up with the rise of a new middle class to educational privilege and political power. It will be the purpose of the next three chapters to trace the development and significance of this cult of athleticism from its early beginnings in a handful of English schools until its maturity in the 20th century.

The term 'Public School' was not officially defined until 1942. The President of the Board of Education then ruled that membership of the Headmasters' Conference or of the Governing Bodies' Association entitled a school to call itself a Public School. One hundred and eighty-eight institutions satisfied the conditions laid down. During the preceding 800 years, from the first recorded use of the term in 1180,[3] there had never been a great measure of agreement on the meaning of the term or upon the right to use it. When, however, the British became self-conscious about their schools at the end of the 18th and beginning of the 19th century, attempts were made to reach an agreed definition. Sydney Smith in the *Edinburgh Review* in 1810 maintained that 'by a public school we mean an endowed place of education of old standing to which the sons of gentlemen resort in considerable numbers and where they continue to reside from eight or nine to eighteen years of age.[4] Even if such a definition were accepted it could still be disputed whether any particular school came within it. When the Clarendon Commission was set up in 1861 to examine the management of Public Schools, they confined their attention to nine: Eton, Winchester, Westminster, Charterhouse, St. Paul's, Merchant Taylors', Harrow, Rugby and Shrewsbury. In 1864, however, when the Taunton Commission was appointed to cover schools not examined by the Clarendon Commission, neither witnesses nor the commission itself could agree upon the meaning of the term Public School, and even within the ranks of the select nine agreement on their status was not wholehearted. When the captain of cricket at Shrewsbury School invited the captain of cricket at Westminster School to arrange a match, the latter declined, replying that Westminster played only Public Schools.[5] It was, however, indisputably in the boarding schools that the development of athleticism was most marked. As late in the 19th century as 1864, when games were a prominent feature of boarding school life, they still formed an insignificant part of the communal life of St. Paul's and Merchant Taylors'. These city schools were extremely ill-provided with fields and facilities for games.[6] Moreover, at the beginning of the century, the seven boarding schools later examined by the Clarendon Commission were the only ones that were endowed non-local schools for the upper classes. They were well developed as such by the end of the Napoleonic wars and they had no serious rivals until after 1840. Our study must therefore begin with them.

Certain differences of constitution and history must be noted among the seven schools. Winchester, the oldest of them, was founded by William of Wykeham in 1382 as a non-local boarding school for 'pauperes et indigentes'.

B

There has been some argument whether 'pauperes et indigentes' means what it appears to mean, that is 'the poor'.   A. F. Leach has maintained that the term referred to yeomen rather than the very poor.   However the argument is resolved, it is certain that William of Wykeham did not intend Winchester College for the education of the upper classes.[7]   He also founded New College, Oxford, so that scholars of Winchester were assured of proceeding to a university education.   Winchester College was to be governed by a Warden and ten Fellows appointed by the Warden and they in turn selected the Headmaster. Eton's constitution, drawn up by Henry VI in 1440 was similar, while Westminster was administered by the Dean and Chapter of Westminster. Rugby, Harrow and Charterhouse were founded by private individuals and were governed by trustees who replenished their own number as occasion demanded. Shrewsbury, almost a local school, was governed by the mayor, aldermen and burgesses of the town.   While all the schools were thus politically independent, Eton, Winchester and Westminster were more subject to ecclesiastical influence than the others, while their rigid constitution and heavy endowments fostered a conservative attitude and a distinct tendency to maintain the *status quo*. Moreover, the power of the Warden or Provost and Fellows or of the Dean and Chapter restricted the power of the Headmaster.   At the other schools with their poorer endowments and less rigid constitution it was more urgent to meet the needs of the times if they were to maintain any degree of prosperity.   Their headmasters too, although they sometimes found their governing bodies tiresome,[8] were nevertheless entrusted with more power, and their initiative had correspondingly greater rein.   It was indeed largely through the vigour of their headmasters that these schools rose from being local grammar schools to the status of Public Schools. When therefore at the beginning of the 19th century the demand for reform came, it was at Shrewsbury and Rugby rather than at Winchester or Eton that great changes were effected, just as later in the century it was the headmasters of newly risen schools, Thring of Uppingham and Sanderson of Oundle, who were the great reformers of their day. Because the reforms at Rugby under Arnold (headmaster 1828–1842) permeated the whole mass of schools in the forties and fifties, so in the world of sport the practices in vogue at Rugby tended to be copied in other schools. Its game of football spread far and wide, while the individual games at Eton and Winchester and Harrow remained peculiar to those schools.

A feature of the Public Schools which is of great importance in the development of athleticism is their upper class clientele. It has already been suggested that this feature has not always been present. Whether or not the 'pauperes et indigentes' for whom Winchester was founded were the poor or merely the relatively poor, Rugby, Harrow and Shrewsbury were certainly founded as schools for the local inhabitants and were not immediately patronised by the upper classes. Late in the 19th century, when Harrow was a national upper class school, the local inhabitants were still urging their claim to John Lyon's endowment and a free education.[9] The transformation of the schools into institutions for the education of the ruling class was gradual and did not take place simultaneously in all seven schools, but by the beginning of the 19th century it was complete. The reasons for the change are not clear. For centuries the nobility had not sent their sons to schools at all.   E. C. Mack[10] has suggested that in the 16th and 17th centuries the bourgeoisie patronised the schools in order to compensate by education for a deficiency in birth and that their example was followed later by the born gentlemen. Undoubtedly, too, the growth in importance of the House of Commons fostered the idea of a national gentry as distinct from local gentry. Such a gentry, when they made plans for the education of their sons, inclined naturally towards schools of national repute rather than towards local teachers or tutors. Moreover the improvement of transport during the 'golden age of coaching' in the late 18th century, and the building of railways in the 19th century, made it possible for the ruling classes to patronise schools far from their homes. Even at the beginning of the 18th century Defoe was criticising the idea 'that to be a good sportsman is the perfect education, and to speak good dog language and good horse language is far above Greek and Latin',[11] and by the end of the century the upper classes generally were patronising the Public Schools to the exclusion of the poor. Upper class patronage of the Public Schools is equalled in importance by the exercise of power within the institutions by the boys themselves. 'At a public school', wrote Sydney Smith, 'every boy is alternately tyrant and slave. The power which the elder part of the community exercises over the younger is exceedingly great—very difficult to be controlled—and accompanied not unfrequently with cruelty and caprice.'[12] This assumption and misuse of power by the pupil body was partly the cause of and partly the result of the failure of the masters to concern themselves seriously with life outside the classroom. For the maintenance of discipline the masters resorted to flogging, a practice that was imitated by the senior boys. From the 17th century to the 19th century the greatest masters, from Mulcaster and Busby in earlier days to Keate and Benson in the 19th century, relied upon fear of the rod. Curiously enough, while flogging was never severer than at the beginning of the 19th century—Keate's summoning of the whole school to witness the flogging of the sixth form is by no means an isolated example of severe corporal punishment—discipline and moral tone were probably never worse. Cowper's *Tirocinium*, written in 1785, must be accepted as fair comment upon at least some aspects of Public School life.

> Would you your son should be a sot or dunce,
> Lascivious, headstrong, or all these at once;
> Train him in public with a mob of boys,
> Childish in mischief only and in noise,
> Else of a mannish growth, and five in ten
> In infidelity and lewdness men.
> There shall he learn, ere sixteen winters old
> That authors are most useful pawned or sold;
> That pedantry is all that schools impart
> But Taverns teach the knowledge of the heart.

Perhaps such a hard and crude life was inevitable when boys assumed control of the institutions which their masters failed to govern effectively.

Lascivious and headstrong Public School boys may have been, but unorganised they certainly were not. One of the instruments of government which was evolved among the boys was the prefect-fagging system, by which the older and stronger enforced service from the younger and weaker. The latter were consoled by the hope that in course of time they would be in a position of strength and privilege. The organisation of a system of government by the boys and their irresponsible exercise of power were by no means approved by the masters. Indeed they were often resisted, and the rebellions which featured in the history of all seven Public Schools at the end of the 18th century and beginning of the 19th century were often caused by an attempt of the headmaster to curtail or abolish some privilege or practice that prefects had assumed. The height to which the power of the boys rose can be judged from the fact that at Harrow they considered that they should have some say in the appointment of the headmaster, and when Dr. Butler was appointed in preference to Mark Drury, the boys, led by Byron, revolted.[13] In such conditions of self-government and enmity between boys and masters, there tended to be heavy emphasis upon group loyalty, upon conformity and upon qualities of value to the herd. Swinburne was tolerated at Eton in 1849, but the Philistine view of the poet-to-be was of a 'horrid little boy, with a big red head and a pasty complexion who looked as though a course of physical exercise would have done him good'.[14] There was indeed a premium upon physical prowess which had the doubtful merit of eliminating any advantage of birth with which a boy might arrive at school. It is against this background of hostility between boys and masters, and of self-government by the boys in a large part of school life, of herd loyalty and of the association of power with physical strength and prowess, that the sports and games of Public School boys must be examined.

Games and sports occupied a large part of boys' time and energy at school at the end of the 18th century and the beginning of the 19th century. The importance of games in school life was acknowledged by those who were at school at this time and who later wrote about their schooldays. Gibbon, who was at school at Westminster, wrote in his autobiography: 'My timid reserve was astonished by the crowd and tumult of the school; the want of strength and activity disqualified me for the sports of the playfield.'[15] On the other hand, an Old Etonian in 1824 felt urged to ask, 'What Etonian was ever lukewarm in the panegyric of the scene of his boyish delights? . . . To the latest period of existence the grey headed Etonian will catch a spark of lingering fire from the subject and his eye will beam with renovated lustre in reverting to the day when he "urged the flying ball" and "cleft the glassy wave" in those favourite haunts.'[16]

As early as 1810 Sydney Smith was complaining that too much importance was being attached to games. 'Of what importance is it in after life,' he asked, 'whether a boy can play well or ill at cricket; or row a boat with the precision of a waterman?'[17] Charles Wordsworth, who was a boy at Harrow in the 1820's, spoke of the distinction which success in games among boys never failed to bring with it.[18]

Cricket and boating, together with hunting or poaching and riding, were favourite pastimes at schools by the end of the 18th century. Cricket had been adopted and developed as an aristocratic pastime in the 18th century and the earliest known code of laws dating from 1744 is thought to have been observed by players for the preceding fifty years.[19] It is not surprising therefore to find the sons of the upper classes playing the game at school. As early as 1745 Lord Chesterfield wrote to Philip Stanhope that he hoped he would 'play at cricket better than any boy at Westminster',[20] and the first school match of which the score is preserved took place in 1746. At the end of the century, in 1796, Westminster beat Eton in a match on

Hounslow Heath and it is clear that at Eton and the other five Public Schools, cricket was being played by the end of the 18th century. Cricket matches were played between Eton and Harrow in 1805 and 1818, and the long series at Lord's began in 1822. Westminster's first recorded boat race took place in 1818 and the first race against Eton was rowed in 1829, but in the middle of the previous century, Warren Hastings as a Westminster boy was described as a good boatman. At Eton traditional 4th of June ceremonies with eight- and ten-oared boats and elaborate costumes certainly took place on the King's Birthday in 1793 if not earlier. Hunting, long an aristocratic sport, was not an easy pastime to transfer from home to school and too often it became poaching, but at Shrewsbury it was adapted through the medium of the Royal Shrewsbury School Hunt.[21] The Hunt was organised with an elaborate constitution of huntsmen, whips, gentlemen and hounds. The two boys selected to carry the scent were known as foxes and the hunt was conducted in complete defiance of school bounds. Fives and tennis were played at Eton[22] and probably in some form or another they were played in the other schools. Football was played at all schools, but it had no written code of laws as cricket had. The form that it took was quite different in different schools and even in a single school the conventions of the game were not so rigid that they could not be flouted. The fact that in 1823 William Webb Ellis could 'with a fine disregard for the rules of football' pick up the ball and run with it, thus altering fundamentally the game played at Rugby, is an indication of its adaptability. It was not until 1849 that a code of laws was drawn up intended for nation-wide acceptance, and the Football Association was only founded in 1863.

Tom Brown's Schooldays contains a vivid account of a game of football as played in the early part of the century. With the younger boys crowded into the goals and doing little or nothing for two hours, the game was fought out by the teen-age toughs and heroes. The game itself was followed by celebrations, singing and beer drinking. The whole occasion suggested to one of Hughes' contemporaries an ἀγών in the Homeric style fought out in the atmosphere of Valhalla.[23]

Football was probably played with no less enthusiasm than cricket, but outside school it had not been accepted as a suitable pastime for the aristocracy as cricket certainly had been. An Etonian wrote in 1831: 'I cannot consider the game of football as being at all gentlemanly; after all, the Yorkshire common people play it.'[24]

Dr. Butler, headmaster of Shrewsbury from 1798 to 1836, was of the opinion that football was 'only fit for butcher boys', and once stated that the game was 'more fit for farm boys and labourers than for young gentlemen'.[25] His statement reveals both the upper class consciousness of Shrewsbury School and the distinction between gentlemanly sports and other sports, a distinction that had been a striking feature of English culture in the 18th century. Despite Dr. Butler's disapproval, football continued to be played.

It might be thought that although football was disapproved of, cricket and other gentlemanly pastimes would have been encouraged by headmasters who were anxious to foster the upper class affiliations of their schools. In general, however, sports did not receive active encouragement from masters at the beginning of the century. Such instances as there were of magisterial approval of games indicate an attitude of tolerance rather than of

encouragement.   At Shrewsbury, while Dr. Butler pro-
hibited football and boating and ignored the activities of
the Royal Shrewsbury School Hunt which were conducted
in defiance of school regulations about bounds, cricket was
played on part of the headmaster's farm at Cotton Hill
and must have had his acquiescence.   Dr. Goodall, headmaster of Eton from 1802 to 1809, was not antagonistic to
prowess at cricket.   When the M.C.C. were defeated in
Eton's playing fields largely through Sir Christopher
Willoughby's 'system of beautiful blocking', the match
being over, the headmaster 'greeted the modest Sir
Christopher with language savouring of the greatest
delight'.[26]   Perhaps the strongest action by the authorities at this time in favour of games was taken at Westminster.   Tuttle Fields had long been the boys' playing
fields, but at the beginning of the 19th century they were
enclosed so that they might be let for building.   However,
as the result of an appeal by the school, ten acres were
preserved as playing fields for it.

   In spite of instances of approval or toleration of games
and sports, the most common attitude of masters to athleticism was one of hostility.   Even at Westminster where
playing fields were provided by official action, the headmaster showed himself an enemy of inter-school competition.   When Westminster received a challenge from Eton
in 1818 to row a race from Westminster to Kew Bridge
against the tide, the headmaster strongly objected on the
grounds of unhealthy publicity and the beer drinking
which would follow the race.   The project was dropped.
In 1829 a fresh attempt was made to arrange a race.   Dr.
Williamson, appointed headmaster the previous year,
opposed it as his predecessor had done.   He was not so
successful.   In spite of every attempt to suppress the race

—the headmaster even went to the length of incarcerating a member of the crew in one of the boarding houses—the race was rowed.[27]   At Eton, cricket matches were played with other schools in the eighteen-twenties but Keate forbade the Eton-Harrow match in 1821 and matches were therefore played in the holidays and in London.   Boating was not officially recognised until 1840 yet it had by then been highly organised for many years and official refusal to recognise it at the annual celebrations on the 4th June was carried to absurd lengths.   This absurdity did not escape the notice of the boys, as is shown in a letter written by one of them in Keate's time.

'The scene was remarkably gay and animated.   His Highness the Duke of York was present, and Lord Chesterfield and several other persons of distinction.   The fireworks were beautiful and extremely well arranged.   Dr. Dupuis came on purpose to see the sight though it is not positively sanctioned.   Messrs. Chapman and Hawtrey were also there.   Keate was also there with his family, and yet to such a pitch of ridiculous absurdity is the affected ignorance and opposition of the masters kept up, that positively at absence, though everyone knows that we are locked up at a quarter before ten on this night, purely for the celebration of this regatta Keate thus addressed us—"Boys, it is an old custom to have you locked up later than usual on this night, that you may enjoy your game of cricket rather later than usual and that it may be harder contested."   Was there ever such nonsense?'[28]

By the eighteen-sixties this attitude by masters of hostility or, at best, tolerance had given way to a policy of active encouragement of games and sports.   The change of attitude is most clearly demonstrated by the dicta of two successive headmasters of Winchester, Dr. G. Moberly,

1838–66, and Dr. G. Ridding, 1866–84. Moberly spoke of 'the idle boys, I mean the boys who play cricket',[29] but Ridding cried: 'Give me a boy who is a cricketer, I can make something of him.'

Responsibility for effecting this change has often been attributed to Dr. Arnold, headmaster of Rugby school, but too much has probably been laid at his door. Before he came to Rugby Arnold had his own small private school at Laleham on the river Thames near Windsor, where he organised swimming, throwing the spear and gymnastics for the boys. He seems to have been particularly keen on a piece of apparatus called the 'gallows' which was probably taken from Guts Muths 'Gymnastik für die Jugend'. He joined in some of the activities with the boys.

When he was appointed headmaster of Rugby he wrote: 'The Rugby prospect I contemplate with a very strong interest: the work I am not afraid of if I can get my proper exercise: but I want absolute play like a boy, and neither riding nor walking will make up for my leaping pole and gallows and bathing, when the youths used to go with me, and I felt completely for the first time a boy as they were.'[30] He tried to introduce his favourite activities to Rugby. By 1831 he told the Archbishop of Dublin that he had a gallows and in the same year wrote, 'I spear daily as the Lydians used to play in the famine, that I may at least steal some portion of the day from thought.'[30]

Yet it was not for swimming, throwing the spear or gymnastics that Rugby school became famous but for football and cricket. These games had already been established by the boys when Arnold arrived. William Webb Ellis had performed his exploit of running with the ball five years earlier and in all probability the games would have continued to develop with or without Arnold as they were doing at other schools.

Dr. Butler had vainly tried to suppress games at Shrewsbury. His successor as headmaster in 1836, Dr. Kennedy, held altogether different views. In a letter to the Bishop of Lichfield written in 1842 he stated his belief that boys should have 'the means of innocent amusement and exercise in their leisure hours', and some twenty years later his evidence before the Royal Commission on Public Schools was in favour of organised games both for non-reading boys and for boys of high intellectual capacity. One of his first acts as headmaster had been to hire a field for cricket—although not for football—and in 1839 he officially recognised boating and made the Captain of Boats directly responsible to him.[31]

At Eton Keate, certainly no protagonist for games, made a concession to them in the eighteen-twenties by calling 'absence' on the playing fields instead of in the yard, and in 1840 boating was officially recognised. The policy of refusing to recognise this sport after failing to suppress it had led to several tragedies on the river and in 1840 Charles F. Montague was drowned close to Windsor Bridge. Two tutors, G. A. Selwyn and William Evans, conducted a campaign for the official recognition of boating together with the imposition of a rule that no boy was to set foot in a boat until he had passed a swimming test. Their campaign was successful, the bargain between boys and authority was struck and 'watermen' were engaged to teach swimming at the river bathing places. It was not long before boating changed its character. Drinking and smoking parties at the Bells of Ouseley gave way to competitive rowing.

At Harrow Charles Wordsworth recalled that in the

eighteen-twenties cricket, racquets and football were the chief sports and that masters had begun to encourage them but had not begun to place them on a par with or even above intellectual achievements. The boys had a professional down from Lord's cricket ground for the season in order to coach them for their match against Eton. This was probably the first instance of a coaching professional at a Public School and not, in Wordsworth's view, a desirable innovation.

These changes at Shrewsbury, Eton and Harrow were taking place during, and even before, Arnold's tenure of office at Rugby and it is not surprising that games were developing at his school too. Arnold himself liked cricket. He played the game with his own sons and had them coached by a professional. School cricket he referred to in a somewhat detached way, and in a letter to Coleridge confessed that he played family cricket 'on the very cricket ground of the "eleven"—that is of the best players in the school, on which, when the school is assembled, no profane person may encroach.'[32] Nevertheless when the school eleven captained by Thomas Hughes played at Lord's for the first time in 1840, this event must have had the headmaster's approval if not his direct encouragement.

Football seems also to have had the somewhat detached approval of the headmaster. When Queen Adelaide visited the school in October 1839 she expressed a desire to see a game and an impromptu match was arranged between school house boys numbering 75 and the rest of the school numbering 225. Thomas Hughes and Samuel Sandes played for school house and Sandes wrote, 'The ball came to me. I caught it up and ran for dear life to the enemy's goal where unhurt, I "touched down". I walked out, kicked up with my heel in the most approved fashion and "placed" the ball at the proper angle to Tom Hughes who kicked our second goal beautifully high.   So we won both goals that day, and I felt proud of it for Arnold and Queen Adelaide were looking on.'[33]

There is scant contemporary evidence that Arnold directly and deliberately promoted cricket and football for their educational value, but his reputation, and particularly his reputation for an interest in games has been considerably influenced by *Tom Brown's Schooldays* written by Thomas Hughes who, as a boy, was captain of cricket at Rugby and played in the football match before Queen Adelaide.   Three of the incidents which are powerfully portrayed in the book are sporting occasions, a football match, a fight between Tom and Slogger Williams and a cricket match.   The headmaster is a spectator of both football and cricket and by implication these games have his approval and encouragement.

This book, however, was written fifteen years after Arnold's death.   It was not an historical novel but a romantic novel modelled on Charles Kingsley's writings, and Thomas Hughes was at least as anxious to write a 'best seller' as he was to hand on a true portrait of Dr. Arnold.   In a letter to his publishers in 1856 he said: 'My chief reason for writing is that, as I always told you I'm going to make your fortune and you'll be happy to hear that the feat is almost or at least more than half done. I've been and gone and written or got in my head a one volume novel, a novel for boys, to wit, Rugby in Arnold's time.'[34]   A reviewer of the book writing in the *Edinburgh Review* of 1858[35] pointed out that the Arnold of Thomas Hughes is not the Arnold of Stanley's *Biography* and that one of the points of difference is Arnold's claim to be the patron saint of athleticism. Arnold, as his sermons, his letters and his biographer all showed, was obsessed by the wickedness of boys of 14, and boys' animal spirits filled him with sorrow, for 'with boys of the richer classes one sees nothing but plenty, health and youth; and these are really awful to behold when one must feel that they are unblest'. His view of chivalry as deserving the name of Anti-Christ because it fostered a sense of honour rather than a sense of duty indicates that Arnold would have looked with horror upon the path that athleticism took after his death.

One of the fundamental problems that faced Arnold was to re-establish in the school the control and moral influence of the headmaster. We have already noticed that at the end of the 18th century and beginning of the 19th century attempts by masters to curtail boys' privileges and gain power for themselves were met by defiance and even open revolt. At Winchester and Rugby school rebellions reached such proportions that the military had to be called out to quell them, and Keate at Eton, the severest master of all, had so many revolts that he became to be regarded as an authority on the subject.[36] Arnold's great achievement was to succeed where others had failed, to establish his own power and controlling influence, to infuse a new religious spirit into school life, at the same time to maintain the school as an independent boy society free from espionage by masters. This he did by legalising self-government by the boys with its prefectorial and fagging systems, and by establishing confidence between himself and his prefects or sixth form. In this way he gained a large measure of control over the whole school and gave some effect to his moral and educational ideals.

A consequence of legalising self-government by the boys

was the preparation of the ground for the growth of organised games. Poaching and the traditional country pursuits, which were by that time being carried on in defiance of law and order, had to be checked, but organised games within the school precincts could continue, and with the official recognition of fagging and even corporal punishment of boys by boys, the organisation of games and the compulsion of the young by the old to play or at least to crowd the goal was made much easier. One of the most important functions of fagging was to enable the older boys to enjoy cricket practice without the necessity of fielding the balls themselves. In the absence of netting, the only solution was human pursuit of the ball and this was achieved by the system which came to be generally known as cricket fagging and persisted until the 20th century in some schools. Arnold was not entirely happy about the effects of legalised self-government. He lamented the power of public opinion and his inability to fight it, and he lamented his inability to make the moral overcome the strong.[37] The growth of athleticism at Rugby may be regarded therefore as the price paid by Arnold for the co-operation of the boys in maintaining discipline and effecting the reforms which he desired.

Chapter 2. References

1 Duke of Wellington, Letter to *The Times*, 14 August 1951.
2 *Royal Commission on Physical Training for Scotland*, 1903, Minute 9628.
3 *Report of the Fleming Committee*, 1944, Chap. I
4 *Edinburgh Review*, August 1810, Vol. 16, p. 326, 'Remarks on the System of Education in Public Schools'.
5 *Report of the Fleming Committee*, 1944.
6 *R.P.S.C.*, 1864—written evidence in reply to questions, III, 29–42.

7   E. C. Mack, *Public Schools and British Opinion 1780–1860*, pp. 9–10.

8   W. H. D. Rouse, *A History of Rugby School*, 1898, p. 123.

9   Edward Graham, *The Harrow Life of Henry Montague Butler*, 1920, pp. 204–6.

10   E. C. Mack, *op. cit.*, p. 20.

11   Daniel Defoe, *The Compleat English Gentleman.* Ed. 1890, p. 38.

12   *Edinburgh Review*, August 1810, Vol. XVI, p. 327.

13   E. C. Mack, *op. cit.*, p. 81.

14   Edmund Gosse, *The Life of Algernon Charles Swinburne*, London, 1917, p. 14.

15   E. Gibbon, *Autobiography*, Everyman Edition, p. 26.

16   *New Monthly*, XIII, 1824, p. 497.

17   *Edinburgh Review*, August 1810, Vol. XVI, p. 328.

18   Charles Wordsworth, *Annals of My Early Life*, London, 1891, p. 9; E. C. Mack, *op. cit.*, p. 87.

19   H. S. Altham, *A History of Cricket*, 1926, Appendix A.

20   J. D. Carleton, *Westminster*, p. 108.

21   G. W. Fisher, *Annals of Shrewsbury School*, pp. 313ff.

22   H. C. Maxwell Lyte, *A History of Eton College*, 4th Edition, 1911, p. 319.

23   *Edinburgh Review*, Vol. CVII, January 1858.

24   An Etonian, *Reminiscences of Eton*, Chichester, 1831, p. 47: E. C. Mack, *op. cit.*, p. 85.

25   G. W. Fisher, *Annals of Shrewsbury School*, pp. 313ff.

26   H. J. Blake, *Reminiscences of an Etonian*, pp. 50–2.

27   J. D. Carleton, *Westminster*, London, 1938, pp. 108ff.

28   H. C. Maxwell Lyte, *op. cit.*, p. 419.

29   J. D'E. E. Firth, *Winchester College*, 1949, p. 174.

30   W. H. G. Armytage, 'Thomas Arnold's Views on Physical Education', *Physical Education*, Vol. 47, p. 28. 1955.

31   G. W. Fisher, *Annals of Shrewsbury School*, p. 313.

32   N. Wymer, *Dr. Arnold of Rugby*, London, 1953, p. 142.

33   N. Wymer, *op. cit.*, p. 182.

34   C. Morgan, *The House of Macmillan*, 1943.

35   *Edinburgh Review*, Vol. CVIII, January 1858.

36   Samuel Butler, *The Life and Letters of Dr. Samuel Butler*, London, 1896, Vol. I, p. 158.

37   James Martineau, *Essays, Reviews and Addresses*, London, 1890, Vol. I, p. 68.

CHAPTER 3

Barbarians and Philistines at Play

IT was in the eighteen-fifties and -sixties that games at Public Schools were organised and won recognition as a medium of education. The movement in this direction was common to a large number of schools, but the lead was taken, not by the older schools, but by such newly established schools as Marlborough and Uppingham.[1]

The foundation of new schools to rival the old ones was a remarkable feature of the rise of a new middle class to privilege and power. In the 18th century the schools had been safely in the hands of the upper classes, whether Tory squirearchy or Whig oligarchy, and they, while regarding discipline imposed by masters and instruction in religion as necessary, regarded character traits as more important than Latin and Greek, and the influence of boys upon each other as more valuable than instruction and discipline imposed by masters. Little notice was at first taken by these classes of the industrial revolution, of the rise of a new middle class and of the growth of nonconformity. After the French Revolution the upper classes resisted both political and educational reform more fiercely than before, but in 1810 Sydney Smith's article in the *Edinburgh Review*, which has already been quoted, started an agitation for reform which had eventually to be satisfied. Arnold's reforms at Rugby and their influence in other schools satisfied to some extent complaints about the

Public Schools and attracted a clientele which would not have patronised Public Schools in their unreformed state, but the existing schools still did not and could not provide adequate educational facilities for the new middle class. Their curriculum was too restricted and there were not enough of them.   On the other hand, the middle class was unwilling to send its children to schools provided for the poor by the National Society of the Church of England founded in 1811 and by the British and Foreign School Society founded in 1814.   Nonconformists were the first to provide middle class education, at Kingswood founded in 1793 and at Mill Hill founded in 1807 as a Grammar School for the Sons of Protestant Dissenters.   It was, however, from 1829 onwards that the great mass of new schools came into being.   They were for a long time called 'proprietary schools', and the Taunton Commission, which examined many of them, described how they developed as capitalist ventures.   'By the command of large capital beyond the reach of private individuals, arrangements can be made for the comfort and reception of scholars. They have influential names at their head.   Each of the shareholders—a numerous body—is directly interested in filling the school and acts as an advertisement for it; he most legitimately takes his own custom there and induces others to do the same.'[2]   Some of these ventures failed but many prospered and became famous.

The earliest middle class schools, King's College School (1829), University College School (1830), Blackheath (1830) and Liverpool College (1840), catered for their immediate neighbourhood, but Cheltenham (1841), Marlborough (1843), Rossall (1844), Brighton (1845) and Radley (1847) were intended from the first to draw boys from a distance, and were, in this respect, rivals to Harrow,

Rugby and the older schools. Some existing grammar schools like Uppingham and Oundle, under forceful headmasters, developed along similar lines. In 1848 Nathaniel Woodard published his *Plea for the Middle Classes*. He had already started in 1847 the school which became Lancing College, the first of the seventeen Woodard Schools, and his avowed intention was to provide 'a good and complete education for the middle classes at such a charge as will make it available to most of them'.[3]

The wealthier sections of the middle class found their way into existing Public Schools. Their invasion was naturally resented by some. The Rev. William Pound, an Old Etonian, complained that 'the wealthy from the middle classes sought in these schools [the schools examined by the Clarendon Commission] for their children, that education which, together with their wealth, should give them a standing among the upper class, and increase the intellect as well as the wealth of the nation. . . . The contact which had taken place between the wealth of the middle class and the educational tone of the upper, brought an exchange unfavourable to the latter.'[4] Nevertheless the middle class influenced developments within the schools whether for good or ill, and pressure from it was responsible for the setting up of the Clarendon Commission in 1861.

By the eighteen-sixties the middle classes had forced their way into the educational preserves of the Public Schools and Matthew Arnold was able to distinguish two groups within the upper reaches of society: 'I often, therefore, when I want to distinguish clearly the aristocratic class from the Philistines proper, or middle class, name the former in my own mind, the Barbarians.'[5]

It was in two Philistine schools, Marlborough and Uppingham, that athleticism made its most significant advances in the eighteen-fifties. Marlborough was founded in 1843 but had an inauspicious start and after a school rebellion along traditional lines the headmaster resigned and G. E. L. Cotton was appointed to the post. Cotton had been a master at Rugby under Arnold and is referred to as the young master in the discussion on the merits of cricket at the end of *Tom Brown's Schooldays*. In a speech to the school he showed himself a disciple of Arnold in his determination to rule through his prefects. 'The Council informed me on my appointment that the school was in a bad state of discipline, and they hoped I would allow no boys to go out except in pairs with a master. I told them that I could not accept office on such terms, that the school I hoped to govern was a public school, not a private one, and I would try and make it govern itself by means of prefects. The school now knows how matters stand. They must either submit to the prefects or be reduced to the level of a private school and have their freedom ignominiously curtailed.'[6] But he went further than his master in thinking that he saw in organised games a means of effecting Arnold's moral purposes. They would surely teach loyalty, self-sacrifice and co-operation, but their immediate benefit would be to provide socially harmless outlets for the exuberance of youth. He therefore sent a circular to parents in which he stated that 'the mass of the school are not trained up to cricket and football at all, which, as healthy and manly games, are certainly deserving of general encouragement. Instead of this, the money [from boys' subscriptions] which should be devoted to the legitimate games of the school, is spent on other amusements, often of a questionable character in themselves, or at least liable to considerable abuse, and which have no effect in providing constant and wholesome recreation for the boys. Many do not spend their half holidays in the playground, but in wandering about the country, some in bird's nesting, or in damaging property of the neighbours, or other undesirable occupations.'[7] Cotton encouraged the form of football which was played at Rugby and this became the official pastime for boys during the winter. By this move, not only were games adopted as an instrument of policy at Marlborough but football was recognised as a pastime fit for gentlemen rather than for 'butcher boys'. The first inter-school Rugby football match was not played by Marlborough until 1864, against Clifton, but differences of rules militated against football matches. Cricket matches were started with Rugby in 1855 and Cheltenham in 1856.[8]

Not only Marlborough but other new schools for the middle classes accepted Arnoldianism and with it the cult of athleticism and the game of Rugby football. During the fifties and sixties Clifton, Haileybury, Wellington and King Edward VI School, Birmingham, all had headmasters who had been pupils or masters under Arnold and they all adopted the Rugby game, as did many other schools. The six original Public Schools other than Rugby, namely Shrewsbury, Eton, Winchester, Harrow, Westminster and Charterhouse, felt Arnold's influence later and all continued with their own games of football from which later emerged the Association game. Even today the hard core of that small group of Public Schools which still play Association football is drawn from these schools together with Lancing, Bradfield, Malvern which was founded as a copy of Winchester, and Repton which felt Arnold's influence indirectly from Harrow, a school which did not adopt Rugby football until the nineteen-thirties. They were nevertheless strongly affected or infected by the cult of athleticism. Uppingham rose from being an obscure grammar school to be a famous Public School under its forceful headmaster, Edward Thring. From the start Thring encouraged the playing of games and disapproved of what he called slackness and shirking. The first entry in his diary is significant, 'On the 10th September 1853 I entered on my headmastership with the very appropriate initiation of a whole holiday and a cricket match, in which I recollect I got 15 by some good swinging hits to the great delight of my few pupils.'[9]   Such encouragement of games by the headmaster of a Public School was unusual, to say the least, but Thring went further than this by playing both fives and football with the boys.   In 1862 he recorded in his diary that he was asked to play football although he had long ago given up playing; he went on, 'I could not help thinking with some pride what headmaster of a great school had ever played a match at football before.   Would either dignity or skin suffer it?   I think not.'[10]   He continued to play fives until 1870.   To enable games to occupy their rightful place in school life, school began at an early hour and the main heavy work was finished by twelve o'clock and this was 'a great boon to masters and boys'.[11]   Another contribution made by Thring to physical education at Uppingham was the gymnasium.   It was opened in 1859 and was the first gymnasium to be built at any Public School.   The gymnastic master who was put in charge of it also taught music, and his appointment was the first of its kind.[12]

Thring's influence outside his school was very great. When he first went to Uppingham in 1853 there were but twenty-eight boarders; by 1868 there were 268 boys, and the school had a national reputation.   In the following year Thring founded the Headmasters' Conference[13]—a Philistine protest against preferential treatment of seven Barbarian schools under the Public Schools Act of 1867. His enthusiasm for games and his personal participation in them were important factors in the conscious development of games for training character and manly qualities.

Whatever the encouragement for games from masters and headmasters, the compulsion upon all boys to play came not from masters but from boys themselves.   It was a consequence of the retention and recognition of boy government by Arnold and his disciples, and its development was clearly described to the Clarendon Commission by the Rev. H. M. Butler, headmaster of Harrow.   'I ought perhaps to conclude what has been said on this subject by explaining that fagging and compulsory attendance at football are parts of the internal government which was, so far as we know, originally established by the boys themselves, and is now certainly administered by them alone.

'The existing system is conducted with the full knowledge and sanction of the masters and would of course be modified to any extent if the headmaster saw reason to desire it.   But it was not created by any master, nor does any master, except on rare occasions, interfere with its administration.   Its value consists in its being in the main independent of masters, though subject to their general control.'[14]

In some schools even the financial administration was done by boys.   At Rugby the 'big side levée' managed the school close and games, and levied taxes on all boys for the support of games with the proviso imposed from above that the tax paid by the levée should be twice that paid by the middle and lower school, and at Eton it was estimated that a sum of £1,300 annually was spent through the clubs including the athletic clubs. In view of such heavy emphasis on self-government in games it is not surprising that domination of a game by the coach, which has become such a notable feature of American college sport, has been conspicuous by its absence in British schools and colleges.

The cult of athleticism first received public expression in Thomas Hughes' novel, *Tom Brown's Schooldays*, published in April 1857. As evidence of upper middle class views on the Public School system in general and athleticism in particular it is most significant. Already Public School education was being consciously related to success on the battlefields and in the garrisons of the Empire. Tom Brown in speaking to a master about his friend East is asked,

' "By the by, have you heard from him?"

' "Yes, I had a letter in February, just before he started to join his regiment."

' "He'll make a capital officer."

' "Ay, won't he," said Tom, brightening. "No fellow could handle boys better and I suppose soldiers are very like boys." '

It was later in the century that the battlefield and the playing field became closely associated, but this forthcoming development had already cast its shadow before it in Hughes' novel.

The value of games, particularly team games, in training character and developing qualities of value to a ruling class was already appreciated and received ample and even extravagant praise in a conversation about cricket between Tom Brown and one of his masters.

' "Come, none of your irony, Brown," answers the master. "I'm beginning to understand the game scientifically. What a noble game it is, too!"

' "Isn't it? But it's more than a game. It's an institution," said Tom.

' "Yes," said Arthur, "the birthright of British boys old and young, as habeas corpus and trial by jury are of British men."

' "The discipline and reliance on one another which it teaches is so valuable, I think," went on the master, "it ought to be such an unselfish game. It merges the individual in the eleven; he doesn't play that he may win, but that his side may."

' "That's very true," said Tom, "and that's why football and cricket, now one comes to think of it, are such much better games than fives or hare and hounds, or any others where the object is to come in first or to win for oneself, and not that one's side may win."

' "And then the captain of the eleven!" said the master, "what a post is his in our school-world! almost as hard as the Doctor's, requiring skill and gentleness and firmness, and I know not what other rare qualities." '

Tom Brown's Schooldays was a best seller; 11,000 copies were sold during 1857, bringing £1,250 to Hughes by November. Many editions were brought out during the rest of the century and the influence of this novel on educational thought and practice has been incalculable.

Hughes' eulogy of games was generally approved and the only notable public expression of doubt was made by Fitzjames Stephen in the *Edinburgh Review* of January 1858. To him *Tom Brown's Schooldays* suggested 'the conclusion that the author's personal relations with his master when at school were comparatively slight, that he afterwards learnt to admire and understand him; and that he now looks back upon him and his system through a sort of halo shed upon them by the light of Mr. Kingsley's writings'. Charles Kingsley's *Westward Ho* had been published in 1855. Both *Westward Ho* and *Tom Brown's Schooldays* were novels whose heroes were drawn in glowing colours and were intended to display the excellence of simple understanding and unconscious instinct to do good. They were moreover adorned with every sort of athletic accomplishment. These books were thus representative of the school of 'Muscular Christianity' of which Kingsley was the chief apostle. Stephen recognised two dangers in this type of book. In the first place simplicity and vigour might easily be replaced by mere artistic admiration for simplicity and vigour. Secondly the authors were not content with asserting the value of bodily strength but they threw by implication a certain slur on intellectual ability, and while they themselves might believe in the dependence of muscle on mind, this impression was not conveyed to the ordinary reader. However, in his general criticism, Stephen was reactionary. He criticised games because when organised, they ceased to be mere amusements, and became 'something between a battle and a sacrifice'. He would return to a system wherein 'self-government and the elimination of all direct supervision except during the few hours actually spent at lessons are the true education for life'. 'Hedge a boy around with routine discipline, turn his physical education into a task and his education becomes unreal.' Stephen's 'routine discipline' was of course imposed by boys, not by masters.

Stephen's public criticism of Hughes' book was an isolated phenomenon in the fifties. *Tom Brown's Schooldays* was well received, perhaps too well received, for the ironic fate of its author was that he came to regret the cult of athleticism whose early growth he himself had fostered.[15]

Within the schools themselves some attempts were made to check the growth of athleticism and the most interesting was that of Dr. Moberly at Winchester. In 1854 he, together with the headmasters of Harrow and Eton, terminated the annual cricket matches held between the three schools at Lord's. There were undoubtedly abuses attendant upon the teams residing in London for a week or more without supervision. Moberly was quite willing for the match with Eton to be played on the playing fields of either school and so it was for the next four years. In 1858 the match between Eton and Harrow was resumed at Lord's but Moberly refused to allow Winchester to play there with them. This action aroused great opposition from Old Wykehamists, who started a campaign for the resumption of the Lord's matches. In this they were supported by the Press. To conduct the campaign more effectively, a committee was formed under the chairmanship of Sir Claude de Crespigny with Frederick Gale as secretary. Lord Eversley was to act as ambassador at the court of the headmaster. The approach of the Old Wykehamists was emotional rather than rational, and the memorandum which they submitted to the headmaster is significant of contemporary feeling on games. They argued that games were a preparation for the battle of life, that they trained moral qualities, namely respect for others, patient endurance, unflagging courage, self-reliance and self-control, vigour and decision of character 'to which England owes so much of her greatness'. They argued further that the Lord's matches were an advertisement for the school and that its prestige depended upon success at games, and they expressed alarm at competition from the new foundations which were growing apace. They argued finally that the contact between boys and old boys was a pleasant occasion. The London venue for the matches was essential to achieve these objects.[16]

Dr. Moberly's reply was essentially rational and unemotional and effectively answered the specific points pressed by the memorandum. He went on to add that the dangers to boys' morals in going to town were considerable and that the hospitality of Old Wykehamists had not been found to lessen them. He pointed out that the Lord's matches had exacerbated relations between the schools, but when the matches had been played on home grounds they had made for better understanding and had enabled all the boys to see the match. His chief argument was that schoolwork was interfered with by preparation for the match and the ambition of getting into the eleven. 'What was in theory *play*, and as play most useful and excellent, became the first and most enthralling *business*.'[16]

After further negotiation a compromise was effected whereby Moberly agreed to a match at Lord's against Harrow only, provided it was played during term time. This match never materialised because the headmaster of Harrow refused to allow a match at Lord's in addition to the one already played against Eton. Moberly may be said to have won his battle, but he lost the war. The cult of athleticism grew even at his own school. He was not wholeheartedly supported by Charles Wordsworth, his second master. Wordsworth combined a deeply religious outlook with brilliant ability in games. He was the joint founder of the University Cricket Match and the Boat Race. At Winchester he had the Meads laid out as a cricket ground and he reformed Winchester football. The *Winchester Register of Cricketing and Athletic Sports* published by the college bookseller in 1858 at sixpence is an indication of the growing interest among the boys in school games.

Similarly at Eton in the fifties the spirit of athleticism was growing in strength. Freedom and individualism which had characterised games at Eton in the thirties and forties were giving way to organised sport. Boating became competitive rowing and by 1860 there were house cups and house colours.[17] Intensive competition was rearing its ugly head. It is clear that while schools like Marlborough and Uppingham took the lead in developing games, the older schools were not far behind. To some extent the pace in the latter schools was forced. The alarm expressed by the Old Wykehamists at rivalry from new foundations and their argument that the prestige of Winchester depended upon success at games supports this view. At schools old and new, athleticism, with or without the support of the headmaster, continued to gain ground.

Chapter 3.   References

1   T. C. Worsley, *Barbarians and Philistines, passim.*
2   *R.S.I.C.*, Vol. VII, pp. 60–1.
3   K. E. Kirk, *The Story of the Woodard Schools*, London, 1937, p. 28.
4   Rev. William Pound, *Remarks upon English Education in the Nineteenth Century*, London, 1866.
5   Matthew Arnold, *Culture and Anarchy*, London, 1889, p. 65 (first published 1869).
6   A. G. Bradley, *A History of Marlborough College*, p. 138.
7   G. E. L. Cotton, unpublished circular letter, June 1853.
8   L. Warwick James, unpublished memorandum.
9   William S. Patterson, *Sixty Years of Uppingham Cricket*, London, 1909, p. 48.

10 G. R. Parkin, *Edward Thring's Life, Diary and Letters*, London, 1898, p. 223.

11 *R.S.I.C.* 1868, 'Minutes of Evidence', Vol. 5, p. 97.

12 G. R. Parkin, *op. cit.*, p. 76.

13 *Report of the Fleming Committee*, 1944, p. 28.

14 *R.P.S.C.*, 'Minutes of Evidence'. Written reply from Harrow III, §29.

15 Thomas Hughes, *The Manliness of Christ*, New York, 1880, p. 583.

16 Unpublished memorandum. See also J. D'E. E. Firth, *Winchester College*, 1949, pp. 140f.

17 E. C. Mack, *Public Schools and British Opinion 1780–1860*, p. 369.

CHAPTER 4

The Royal Commissions and the Arrival of the Games Master

PRESSURE within and without Parliament forced the State to intervene in Public School education in 1861. In that year the Clarendon Commission was set up 'to inquire into the revenues and management of certain colleges and schools and the studies pursued and instruction given there'. Its report on nine schools: Eton, Winchester, Westminster, Charterhouse, St. Paul's, Merchant Taylors', Harrow, Rugby and Shrewsbury, was published in 1864. The report stated clearly a number of facts about these schools and not the least important was that Public School education was an instrument for training character. 'It is not easy to estimate,' the report stated, 'the degree in which the English people are indebted to these schools for the qualities on which they pique themselves most—their capacity to govern others and control themselves, their aptitude for combining freedom with order, their public spirit, their vigour and manliness of character, their strong but not slavish respect for public opinion, their love of healthy sports and exercise.'[1] The Commission recognised the value of organised games in training character, but one result of the emphasis on this aspect of games was a lack of emphasis on the desirability of skilled performance. In football it was more important to show courage and stamina and an ability to withstand knocks without flinching than to exhibit ball control, and at cricket the qualities praised were not so much skill in wielding the bat as traits of character revealed in facing up to a fast bowler in bad conditions of pitch and light.   There were, of course, advances in skill and professional coaches were employed, but these moves were accepted with reluctance by many people, including the Commissioners. 'Those who regret—not perhaps without reason—that cricket has become so elaborate an art as to need professional instruction would be not the less sorry that the interest of their boys in it should flag; and those who are most anxious that their pupils should work diligently are desirous also that they should play heartily and with spirit.'[2]

A second consequence of playing up the moral value of games was the decrying of those sports which did not appear to produce the qualities desired.   This led Tom Brown and the master with whom he was talking to rate hare and hounds and fives less highly than team games, on the ground that the latter fostered group loyalty while the former did not.   For similar reasons the Clarendon Commissioners thought gymnastics of little value.   They gave their blessing to gymnastic exercises but dubbed them as a continental practice of limited value compared with games played at English schools.   They stated that cricket and football fields were not merely places of exercise and amusement; they helped to form some of the most valuable social qualities and manly virtues and they held, like the classroom and the boarding house, a distinct and important place in Public School education.   A similarly inferior position was given by the Commissioners to drill.[3]   This attitude to drill and gymnastics was partly the cause of and partly the result of handing over the teaching of it to sergeant instructors.[4] Thereby it immediately had a social status inferior to the better established upper class game of cricket and even football. From this lowly status gymnastics and drill have never raised themselves in Public Schools. In direct contrast, physical education in elementary schools has had gymnastics and drill as its bedrock. Especially is this true of the Swedish system. The distinction between major and minor sports likewise stemmed from assumptions about the social significance of different sports. The distinction was not based upon the number involved nor the skill required, but upon whether any particular game promoted team spirit and group loyalty. By this yardstick swimming, athletics, fives and many other games fall short of football and cricket, and have hardly yet established themselves in Public Schools as sports demanding equal attention with any others.

The exact place of games in the life of the nine schools can be gauged from material supplied to the Clarendon Commission. A written questionnaire was sent to all schools and eight of the questions which it contained were directly concerned with games.[5] They concerned matters of compulsion, the acreage and nature of playing fields, common games, the amount of instruction given, and the relationship of intellectual to athletic distinction. Verbal questions were also asked about the amount of time spent upon games. The answers to these questions were most revealing. It was admitted that at Eton, in order to obtain a place in the cricket eleven, a boy needed to spend five hours three times a week and two hours three times a week at the game.[6] The captain would spend five hours every day and so would boys of 13 and 14 who were ambitious. At Winchester the corresponding figures were three hours every day for cricketers and at Rugby three hours for three days a week and two hours for three days. At Eton, too, a boy who hoped to obtain a place in the eight would spend four hours a day on the river.[7] Dr. Moberly, however, who has already been noted as a level-headed opponent of the cult of athleticism, also had positive views on the development of physical education. He told the Commission that he employed a visiting sergeant to give corrective exercises and that if he saw a boy with round shoulders he sent him to join a special class. Moreover in early days at Winchester there was but one cricket game and one football game, and the only form of participation by the younger boys was to 'fag out' for the seniors. By 1862 Moberly could claim with pleasure that there were separate games of cricket and football for the little boys.[8] From the other schools the Royal Commission elicited evidence of increasing and unchecked interest in games, although the poor facilities available to the city day schools of Charterhouse, St. Paul's and Merchant Taylors' limited very severely the growth of organised games in them.

The report of the Clarendon Commission revealed that Fitzjames Stephen and Moberly had had good grounds for their fears that intellectual interests would suffer as a result of the growth of athleticism. Games were already becoming the focus of boys' minds. The laws of cricket and the conventions of the playing field were beginning to occupy that pride of place in boys' attentions which Arnold had designed for religious activity and moral ideals.

The glorification of physical prowess and the worship of boy heroes gradually obscured the moral purposes for which Cotton and the Arnoldians had originally supported organised games. Masters, however, were caught up as well as boys and the intellectual side of school life was in danger of lack of interest on all sides.   Finally, as the century wore on, boys and masters combined to preach conformity and group loyalty and to kill such individualism as the old Barbarian way of life had encouraged.   'In its final form the religion of athletics seems the perfect expression of the Philistine age.'[9]   Yet in 1864 the Clarendon Commission hardly saw the red light and stated that 'the importance which boys themselves attach to games is somewhat greater, perhaps, than might reasonably be desired, but within moderate limits it is highly useful'.[10]

The Taunton Commission was appointed in 1864 under the title of the Schools Inquiry Commission to examine those schools which had not come within the scope of the Clarendon Commission or the Newcastle Commission on Popular Education of 1858.   It considered grammar schools, proprietary schools and private schools as well as the education of girls.   The report, published in twenty-one volumes in 1868, gave information on a vast number of schools; 782 grammar schools were examined as well as the proprietary and private schools.   As might be expected, the facilities for and the time devoted to physical education varied very much from school to school. Apart from some of the proprietary and private schools, facilities for games were not good nor were games at all highly organised.   Eight schools, Christ's Hospital, St. Olave's in Southwark, Dulwich College, King Edward's School in Birmingham, Manchester, Bedford, Tonbridge and Monmouth, received a questionnaire which included twelve questions on physical education.[11]   The answers revealed that all except Christ's Hospital had playing fields, although at Birmingham the field was three miles off and the majority of boys made no use of it.[12]   None

had a covered gymnasium.[13]   There was no supervision
of games, although masters occasionally took part in them,
and at some schools drill was taught by sergeant instructors.   There can have been few schools worse off for
games than Christ's Hospital, then situated in Newgate
Street.   The Commission reported that there was no
organisation of games of any kind and that the Blue Coat
boys did not know how to play except with peg tops, whip
tops and marbles.[14]

Apart from these few schools selected from many parts
of England and Wales, the schools were examined by
individual commissioners each covering an allotted area.
This meant that there was no collective body of opinion
on the value of games but a series of individual opinions.
Commissioner Fearon, who visited schools in the Metropolitan Area, was very much in favour of games, but
Commissioner Hammond after reporting that no boarding
school in Norfolk was without a playing field complained:
'For my part I consider that too much importance is
already attached to mere games and athletics. . . .   The
endowed classical schools especially appear to have
adopted the muscular theories of the day, and may be
trusted to prepare boys for University distinction in
athletic, if not in academic exercises.'[15]   It seems that
although many schools were ill provided with facilities for
games, those with greater financial backing were already
elevating games to a lofty position.   Even Commissioner
Fearon, after reporting that in eight out of nine Scottish
burgh schools inspected by him there was no provision for
physical education, tempered his regret with the consola-
tion that boys in Scotland were at least prevented from
transferring to their games that allegiance which was due
to their studies.[16]   In many schools the time and facilities

for games fell little short of those enjoyed by the Clarendon seven.

The Clarendon Commission's view of gymnastics was echoed by Matthew Arnold, who reported to the Taunton Commission on Education in Germany. 'The Germans, as is well known, now cultivate gymnastics in their schools with great care. Since 1842 gymnastics have been made a regular part of the public school course; there is a Central-Turnanstalt at Berlin, with 18 civilian pupils who are being trained expressly to supply model teachers for the public schools. The teachers profess to have adapted their exercises with precision to every age, and to all the stages of a boy's growth and muscular develop-ment. . . . Nothing however will make an ex-schoolboy of one of the great English schools regard the gymnastics of a foreign school without a slight feeling of wonder and compassion, so much more animating and interesting do the games of his remembrance seem to him.'

In the decades following the reports of the Clarendon and Taunton Commissions athleticism grew apace. Some headmasters such as Temple at Rugby[17] and Montague Butler at Harrow opposed it with but moderate success, others, the majority, swam with the tide. Ridding at Winchester himself provided a playing field and at Eton Oscar Browning was dismissed by Dr. Hornsby for his opposition to athleticism.[18] The growth of the games cult between 1850 and 1880 can be appreciated from the fact that in 1850 during the Eton and Harrow match there were scarcely enough spectators to make a continu-ous line round Lord's, and ropes were not needed until 1864. By 1880 the match was so important that it affected the duration of the London Season.[19] Both with-out and within the schools there were some remarkable manifestations of romantic attachment to school games. Harrow became famous for its songs. Forty-two were written and published between 1860 and 1900 and there is scarcely one that does not contain a reference to prowess on the playing field; some contain little else. One song even suggested playfully that it was by decree of Queen Elizabeth that 'hits to the rail shall count for three, and six when fairly over'. 'Forty Years On', the song for which Harrovians past and present show invariably their respect by standing, reveals better than any the semi-religious nature of the cult of athleticism at Harrow in the 19th century.

Verse 2.   Routs and discomfitures, rushes and rallies,
Bases attempted, and rescued, and won,
Strife without anger, and art without malice,
How will it seem to you, forty years on?
Then, you will say, not a feverish minute
Strained the weak heart and the wavering knee,
Never the battle raged hottest, but in it,
Neither the last nor the faintest, were we
    Follow up!   Follow up!   Follow up!
    Follow up!   Follow up!   Follow up!
    Till the field ring again and again,
    With the tramp of the twenty-two men.
    Follow up!   Follow up!

Verse 4.   Forty years on, growing older and older,
Shorter in wind, as in memory long,
Feeble of foot, and rheumatic of shoulder,
What will it help you that once you were strong?
God give us bases to guard or beleaguer,
Games to play out, whether earnest or fun;
Fights for the fearless, and goals for the eager,
Twenty, and thirty, and forty years on!
    Follow up! etc.

As the playing field was idealised, so old boys of the various schools helped forward the cause of games both by their interest and by their financial support of the provision of playing fields. By 1900 Old Harrovians had been instrumental in providing some twenty acres for cricket and fifty acres for football.[20] Other schools benefited similarly from the generosity of their former pupils.

The precise form that athleticism took varied from school to school, but certain features of internal organisation were sufficiently general to merit remark. Firstly self-government in games usually took the form of a games committee or similar body with general control, while the administration of individual sports was in the hands of the captains and other officers of those sports. At Harrow the Philathletic Club founded in 1852 by the most prominent athletes became the organising body. Composed entirely of boys, it had complete control over the organisation of games and appointment of captains and 'keepers', subject only to the veto of the headmaster. In some schools a games committee of boys and masters was set up, but often masters had no voting rights. With such power devolving upon athletes it was only natural that prefects and monitors should be appointed from their ranks, and prowess on the playing field came to be the most important qualification for any position of authority. At Eton, 'Pop' or the Eton Society underwent a change from a literary association to a social club 'which rarely opened its doors to anyone who had not distinguished himself at cricket, at football, or on the river'.[21]

The distinction between major and minor games persisted, as did the lowly place accorded to gymnastics. One writer in the *Journal of Education* considered the methodical use of exercises to be the 'mere Greek Iambics of physical training'. He went on 'it has its elements of truth as all pedantry has, and has in its physical results a certain poor degree, as all pedantry has, of success. But what a substitute for football, and what a reflection for us, that men who know and have tasted the powers and pleasures of play should yet in cold blood drive children into this dead and barren routine.'[22] The emphasis on character training obscured the possible physiological effects of games and exercise.

At some time during the century games became a recognised means of preventing certain forms of immorality, masturbation and the physical manifestations of homosexual relationships. It is difficult to decide when these became features of boarding school life because writers hesitated to refer to them in any but the vaguest terms. For detailed evidence, recourse must be had to Havelock Ellis and the post-Victorian novelists. Nevertheless games and the physical fatigue resulting were considered, somewhat naïvely, to be the best antidote to 'impurity'.[23]

A third characteristic of organised games was the house system and the competitive element. There were house cups and house colours at Eton by 1860.[24] The school officials for games had their counterparts in the boarding houses and routine games were organised largely on a house basis. The difficulty of finding in a population of sixty with an age range of 13 to 18, fifteen boys of approximately equal age, ability and size was usually insuperable. As, however, the game was primarily an opportunity for the display of keenness and 'guts' rather than of skill, this difficulty was not recognised as a very serious one. Competition, however, ran riot. Every activity came to have a cup for which houses competed, and masters identified themselves with their houses to such an extent that they suffered or rejoiced at defeat or victory as keenly as their boys.

Other features of Public School athleticism which became widespread were professional coaches and games masters. Professionals for teaching purposes appeared at Eton in 1840 when 'watermen' were engaged to teach boys swimming at the river bathing places, but it was in cricket that the professional established himself in Public School life. The growth of inter-school rivalry and the need for a school to maintain its prestige on the playing field made it desirable for boys to practise batting against really good bowling. At Harrow visiting professionals were engaged in the eighteen-twenties and Rugby engaged John Lillywhite in a full time capacity in 1850. James Lillywhite went to Winchester in a similar capacity in 1851 and moved to Marlborough in 1853 and then to Charterhouse in 1855. By 1863 all these schools together with Eton, Westminster, Brighton, Tonbridge, Sherborne, Shrewsbury and Repton had engaged cricket professionals.[25] Later on professionals were engaged in order to provide good class opposition at rackets. Their primary function in games was not to coach but to provide opposition which would extend the young gentlemen's skill up to and beyond its limits. In the winter game of football the possibilities for teaching were as great as they were for cricket, but the techniques of the various games of football which were in vogue in mid-century had not been sufficiently worked out for professional coaching to seem necessary.

Coaching in games was done for the most part by masters. When masters first took an interest in boys' games they probably did little except take part in an occasional game. Thring certainly played cricket with boys in 1853, and his chief assistant, W. J. Earle, had played with them before Thring was appointed headmaster. Both Thring and Earle played in the school eleven for several years. This practice of including masters in the school team was not unusual in small schools, and was not finally stopped at Marlborough until 1872.[26]   It was but a small step from playing with boys to coaching them and when W. J. Earle retired from Uppingham in 1878 tribute was paid to his services to the school's cricket.[27] At Eton Edmund Warre, appointed to the staff in 1860, almost at once began to act as adviser to the Captain of Boats and to coach the college eight. He continued to do this until 1884 when he became headmaster of the college.[28]   He was then succeeded as rowing coach by Mr. S. A. Donaldson.

It is difficult to state exactly when masters were appointed to schools for the primary purpose of coaching games, because few headmasters would have admitted making such an appointment. However, R. A. H. Mitchell, who joined the staff at Eton in 1866, not only took an interest in cricket, but took an absorbing interest in it. By 1870, according to Patterson, at Eton 'not only were there two permanent professionals, but two masters, G. R. Dupuis and R. A. H. Mitchell, were capable of taking upon themselves, and did actually take upon themselves, the constant task of teaching the Eleven'.[29]   The particular feature of 'forward play' which characterised cricket at Eton at this time was identified with Mitchell's influence.   Percy Lubbock, who was a boy at Eton when Mitchell was a master, has recorded that although Mitchell had a 'division' and a 'house' he was not an ordinary master, but 'he held a position that was other and peculiar; he guarded and guided the cricket of the school, at least on its more exalted levels, and of the eleven he was known to be the genius, the friend and critic ever at their right hands'.[30]

In other schools too games masters were appointed, not so much upon any known ability to teach either in the classroom or on the playing field, as upon their personal prowess at one or more of the major sports.   By the end of the century a writer in the *Contemporary Review* recorded the legend of a 'blue' who on completing his century in a university cricket match received five telegrams from as many headmasters, offering him posts at their schools.[31] The writer does not suggest that the legend is true, but makes clear that by 1900 the games master was a regular feature of Public Schools.   Another writer in the *Edinburgh Review* stated: 'to be a "blue" now counts for much in the qualifications of a candidate for a mastership at a public school.'[32]

Athleticism which grew and flourished in Public Schools did not confine itself within their walls.   Its extension to the country at large became most noticeable in the eighteen-sixties and eighteen seventies, although in some quarters it was seen earlier.   The Universities of Oxford and Cambridge were the first places to develop organised games along similar lines to those in Public Schools.   At the beginning of the 19th century country pursuits together with cricket were the recreations of undergraduates.   Boxing was considered suitable for gentlemen in Cardinal Manning's Balliol days, but Dr. Jenkyns, who became Master of Balliol in 1819, thought rowing for exercise was not gentlemanly.[33]   However, the first recorded boat race at Oxford took place between Brasenose College and Jesus College in 1815.   The year 1826 saw a meeting of college 'strokes' to draw up rules for the Head of the

River races. The first boat race between Oxford and Cambridge took place in 1829 on the initiative of Charles Wordsworth, who became a master at Winchester, and from 1856 it became an annual event. The first cricket match between the two universities was played in 1827 also largely on the initiative of Wordsworth, and this match became an annual event from 1838 onwards. Football was not played at an inter-university level until 1873, but athletics, racquets and tennis all featured in inter-university contests before 1860.

There was one important difference between games at universities and Public Schools. At the universities there was no compulsion or even undue pressure put upon students by their fellows to play games. An increasing number of undergraduates did take part in major games and in rowing, but others like William Morris and his friends resorted to MacLaren's gymnasium in Oriel Street for fencing, boxing, singlestick and gymnastics.[34] Others took their exercise in country walks and still others, according to MacLaren, made neither physical nor mental exertion of any kind.[35]

The Football Association was founded in 1863 on the initiative of former Public School boys and so was the Rugby Union in 1871. Through Sunday schools and school missions, started in the poorer districts of large towns, Public School men spread the theory and practice of muscular Christianity. This only became possible as Saturday afternoon became a holiday. As early as 1847 the building trades had secured a 'four o'clock Saturday' in some towns.[36] By 1874 it was possible for young men connected with Aston Villa Wesleyan chapel at Lozells, Birmingham, to form a club to play football on Saturday afternoons. In the same way and in the same year a

club was formed at Bolton.[37]   It was not long before
Aston Villa and Bolton Wanderers Football Clubs out-
grew and abandoned the Sunday schools which had been
their midwives if not their parents.   In 1871 the F.A.
Challenge Cup Competition had been started on the
initiative of an Old Harrovian, C. W. Alcock.   It was in
effect 'an adaptation on a national scale of what Alcock
and his fellows had known at school'.[38]   So successful
were the Public Schools in spreading football that in 1883
the Old Etonians were beaten in the final of the cup
competition by Blackburn Olympic, and no team of
former Public School boys ever reached the final again.

About 1870 criticism of the growth of athleticism was
heard both inside and outside the Public Schools.   Dr.
Weymouth at Mill Hill, in his inaugural address as headmaster, admitted the importance of outdoor exercise and
manly sports as an essential element in a complete and
generous education but uttered a word of warning on the
difficulty of keeping a sense of proportion about games.[39]
More significant were the misgivings of Edward Thring,
who had strongly supported games some fifteen years
earlier.   His sermon in 1868, on the text 'For He hath no
pleasure in the strength of a horse, neither delighteth He
in any man's legs', was a warning against hero-worship of
the athlete.   In 1870 he wrote in his diary, 'While I am
going to give way to the demand for a resident professional, I must show that both the school honour and the
school government are above cricket.'   He did so only
because he believed it better to make and control a movement than be dragged by it.   Perhaps he was dragged
further than he realised, for at the end of his life he wrote:
'Mark me, cricket is the greatest bond of the English
speaking race, and is no mere game.'[40]

Outside the schools a real counterblast to muscular Christianity was delivered by Wilkie Collins. Just as Hughes and Kingsley chose the novel to develop their theme, so Collins wrote a novel to deliver his counter-attack. In 1870 *Man and Wife* appeared. It purported to deal with two social questions, 'the present scandalous condition of the Marriage Laws of the United Kingdom' and 'the influence of the present rage for muscular exercises on the health and morals of the rising generation of Englishmen'. The villain of the novel, Geoffrey Dela-mayn, a nobleman's son, was associated with the Christ-ian-Pugilistic-Association. He rowed stroke oar in the university boat race and shortly after the novel opened he went into strenuous training for a footrace to represent the South against the North. The moral argument against this type of athleticism was put by Sir Patrick Lundie, a lawyer.

'The essential principle of his rowing and racing (a harmless principle enough, if you can be sure of applying it to rowing and racing only), has taught him to take every advantage of another man that his superior strength and superior cunning can suggest. There has been noth-ing in his training to soften the barbarous hardness of his heart, and to enlighten the barbarous darkness of his mind. Temptation finds this man defenceless when temptation passes his way . . .' 'I show, to the best of my ability how completely the moral and mental neglect of himself, which the present material tone of public feel-ing in England has tacitly encouraged, leaves him at the mercy of all the worst instincts of his nature; and how surely, under those conditions, he *must* go down (gentleman as he is) step by step . . . from the beginning in ignorance to the end in crime.'[41]

The physical dangers were put by a surgeon: 'From my own experience I can tell you, as a medical man, that a proportion and by not any means a small one, of the young men who are now putting themselves to violent athletic tests of their strength and endurance, are taking that course to the serious and permanent injury of their own health.' Others besides Wilkie Collins had misgivings about the physical effects of training and in 1869 John Morgan conducted an elaborate 'Enquiry into the After Health of the Men Who Rowed in the Oxford and Cambridge Boat Race'. His findings were negative.

Needless to say Geoffrey Delamayn came to a bad end both physically and morally. However, while the novels of Hughes and Kingsley continued to be popular, *Man and Wife* does not appear to have made a great mark on public opinion. Athleticism went from strength to strength.

Chapter 4. References

1   *R.P.S.C.*, I, p. 56.
2   *R.P.S.C.*, I, p. 41.
3   *R.P.S.C.*, I, p. 40.
4   *R.P.S.C.*, answers to written questions supplied by Harrow, Shrewsbury, Charterhouse and Rugby.
5   *R.P.S.C.*, section III, questions 29–30 and 36–42.
6   *R.P.S.C.*, I, p. 97.
7   *R.P.S.C.*, Minutes of Evidence, 7885ff.
8   *R.P.S.C.*, Minutes of Evidence, 806.
9   E. C. Mack, *op. cit.*, p. 338.
10 *R.P.S.C.*, I, p. 40.
11 *R.P.S.C.*, II, p. 136.
12 *R.S.I.C.*, VIII, p. 142.
13 *R.S.I.C.*, VII, p. 499. The gymnasium here referred to is obviously a piece of open ground, with some apparatus erected on it. Any building used for gymnastics appears to be referred to throughout the report as a 'covered gymnasium'.

14 *R.S.I.C.*, VII, p. 499.
15 *R.S.I.C.*, VIII, p. 352.
16 *R.S.I.C.*, VI, p. 41.
17 E. C. Mack, *Public Schools and British Opinion since 1860*, p. 97.
18 E. C. Mack, *op. cit.*, p. 99.
19 Edward Lyttelton, 'Athletics in Public Schools', *Nineteenth Century*, January 1880.
20 E. D. Laborde, *Harrow School Yesterday and Today, 1948, passim.*
21 H. C. Maxwell Lyte, *A History of Eton College*, 4th Edition 1911, p. 547.
22 *Journal of Education*, February 1884, 'Games'.
23 E. C. Mack, *Public Schools and British Opinion since 1860*, p. 242.
24 A. C. Ainger, *Memories of Eton Sixty Years Ago*, London, 1917, p. 125.
25 W. S. Patterson, *Sixty Years of Uppingham Cricket*, London, 1909, pp. 54–5.
26 L. Warwick James, private communication.
27 W. S. Patterson, *op. cit.*, p. 116.
28 H. C. Maxwell Lyte, *A History of Eton College*, London, 1911, p. 563.
29 W. S. Patterson, *op. cit.*, pp. 54–5.
30 Percy Lubbock, *Shades of Eton*, London, 1932, Chap. XIII, p. 161.
31 H. J. Spenser, 'The Athletic Master in Public Schools', *Contemporary Review*, July 1900.
32 *Edinburgh Review*, April 1897, 'Old Eton and Modern Public Schools'.
33 C. E. Mallett, *A History of the University of Oxford*, pp. 193–4.
34 J. W. Mackail, *The Life of William Morris*, London, 1922, Vol. I, p. 67.
35 Archibald MacLaren, *Physical Education*, Ed. W. MacLaren, 1895 (first published 1869), pp. xlviff.
36 G. Green, *The Official History of the F.A. Cup*, London, 1949, pp. 97–8.
37 'Tityrus', *The Rise of the Leaguers*, London, 1897.
38 G. Green, *op. cit.*, Chap. 1.
39 R. F. Weymouth, D.Litt., *Inaugural Address*, London, 1870.
40 W. S. Patterson, *op. cit.*, p. 51 and p. 137.
41 Wilkie Collins, *Man and Wife*. Ed. 1902, pp. 178ff.

CHAPTER 5

Athleticism and Warre

IN 1880 Edward Lyttelton wrote an article in the *Nineteenth Century* magazine[1] pointing out the lengths to which athleticism, encouraged by the national Press, had already gone. Apropos the boat race he complained that 'the minutest facts connected with the play of each oarsman's muscles are anxiously picked up on the spot, form a paragraph in the daily papers, and are telegraphed to the Antipodes'. The fame of Public School athleticism had already spread to the Continent. French and German admiration for Public Schools, according to Lyttelton, was not for their intellectual attainments nor for their apparent liberty, but for their cult of athletics. Some years later Pierre de Coubertin, founder of the Olympic Games of the modern era, described how in France Public School athleticism had been introduced into 200 Lycées and colleges. Other features of the Public Schools, such as the house system, were not introduced.[2]

Athleticism probably reached its peak at Eton during the headmastership of Edmund Warre. When this post became vacant in 1884 and it was known that Warre was a strong candidate, a letter appeared in *The Times* over the signature Academicus saying that Warre had made no mark as a scholar, preacher or man of letters and that his claim to fame was 'as the best rowing coach in England and as an able field officer of Volunteers'.[3]

Four days later, on 29 July, Warre was elected head-master. One of his policies was to make sure that all boys' leisure was taken up with organised games and in 1888 he wrote a letter to his colleagues expressing con-siderable anxiety that there might be as many as 300 boys not occupied in games or rowing. It became steadily more difficult for any boy to slip through the meshes of organised games. Percy Lubbock, who was a boy at Eton under Warre and had no taste for games, managed to escape occasionally, but only 'by artfulness, by some judicious deceit, above all by patient unwearying obsti-nacy'. Organised games seemed to Lubbock an instru-ment to enforce conformity.

'This huge unpausing roundabout of pastime doesn't maintain its pace without infinite care and forethought, as we know; there is nothing unpremeditated in these revels. Do you suppose that the boys come tumbling out of school, rejoicing in their release, to disperse to their games on the inclination of the moment—to fly to the field or the river, the court or the wicket, as fancy dictates? No such freedom is theirs. The great machine is pre-pared for the ordering of their sports, as of their lessons in school; it catches and despatches them to their pleasure prescribed. Do they make their own compulsion, do they themselves invent that immense particularity in the scheming and ordaining of their delights? They simply don't know; so it is and so they accept it. Certainly they are firm in enforcing it, as utterly as they may, on any young rebel or fugitive in their midst; they aren't tender to eccentricity, they hold the rods of discipline and they do not neglect them.'[4]

The tyranny of organised games was the subject of a lengthy correspondence in *The Times*. It was started in

September 1889 by Etonensis,[5] who complained of the compulsion on small boys exercised by big boys to play cricket fourteen times a week and football five times a week. Although his precise figures for cricket were denied by later correspondents, no one denied that the general picture was true. An interesting feature of the correspondence was the distinction which was drawn between the organised games of the Philistines and the old Barbarian country pursuits. Senex noticed a possible connection between this change in physical recreation and a change in the clientele of Eton. In his day (1828–36) Eton boys were mainly the sons of country gentlemen who spent most of their time in open-air pursuits without any need of compulsion. Harroviensis, too, pined for a return to Barbarian country pursuits of hunting, shooting, stalking, fishing, yachting, travelling or any pursuit that developed the power of dealing with unexpected turns of events. Manliness of this kind, he said, 'cannot possibly be developed by cricket or football, tennis or fives, or any other game that merely involves the propulsion of a ball from one point to another according to fixed rules'.

In spite of these Barbarian attacks the Philistine lines were hardly even dented. Success in school continued to be won on the playing field and the river rather than in the class-room and there were many like the writer in the *Edinburgh Review*[6] who hoped that the day was far distant when cricketers and sportsmen would cease to be influential in English society, in Parliament and in all departments of government. Organised games were indeed an intrinsic part of the education of the ruling classes.

Towards the end of the century and in the first few

years of the succeeding one, the playing field not only made a valuable general contribution to government, it also performed the specific function of training an officer class for the army. The doctrine that Public Schools trained good army officers was voiced by Thomas Hughes in a passage quoted earlier. By the end of the century it was not the Public School system in general, but the playing fields that were associated with the imperial battlefields. There was no secrecy about this. J. G. C. Minchin wrote in 1901: 'If asked what our muscular Christianity has done, we point to the British Empire. Our Empire would never have been built up by a nation of idealists and logicians.'[7] More than anyone else, Henry Newbolt glorified the battle training that took place on the playing field, particularly in his poem 'Vitaï Lampada'.

> There's a breathless hush in the Close tonight
> Ten to make and the match to win—
> A bumping pitch and a blinding light,
> An hour to play and the last man in.
> And it's not for the sake of a ribboned coat,
> Or the selfish hope of a season's fame
> But his captain's hand on his shoulder smote—
> Play up! Play up! and play the game.
>
> The sand of the desert is sodden and red—
> Red with the wreck of a square that broke—
> The Gatling's jammed and the Colonel dead,
> And the regiment blind with dust and smoke.
> The river of death has brimmed his banks
> And England's far and Honour a name,
> But the voice of a schoolboy rallies the ranks;
> Play up! Play up! and play the game.

This is the word that year by year,
While in her place the School is set,
Everyone of her sons must hear,
And none that hears it dare forget
This they all with a joyful mind
Bear through life like a torch in flame,
And falling, fling to the host behind—
Play up!   Play up! and play the game.

This insistence that military training took place upon the playing field is the more interesting because since 1860 there had been steadily growing a 'volunteer' movement for specifically military training in Public Schools. Furthermore one of the protagonists of it was also a champion of organised games, Edmund Warre.   It is sometimes stated that the Victorian era was one of peace, but from the accession of Queen Victoria until 1860 there were eleven wars fought by the British Army in various parts of the world.[9]   The last two of these, the Crimean War, 1854–6, and the Indian Mutiny, 1857–9, were the longest and the most arduous of these campaigns. Moreover, the Crimean War in particular revealed very serious defects in the British Army.   Anxiety was widespread.

In 1860 a meeting was held in the Thatched House Tavern under the chairmanship of Lord Elcho 'for the purpose of establishing military drill in public schools'.[10] A number of august persons were invited.   Even those who, like Viscount Palmerston and the Bishop of London, could not come expressed their approval of the object of the meeting.   Dr. Hawtrey, the Chaplain to the Forces, and other gentlemen did attend.   A committee was formed to give effect to the meeting's resolution but only needed to meet two or three times.   Within a few weeks military drill had been established at Rugby, Harrow, Eton, Westminster and other schools. It had also been introduced into many proprietary schools. By the end of the century the headmaster of Eton was able to secure a unanimous vote by a committee of the Headmasters' Conference in favour of a resolution that 'all persons in statu pupillari at the universities or Public Schools above 15 years of age, able ('and willing'—these words were a later insertion) to bear arms, should be enrolled for the purpose of drill and manœuvre and the use of arms'.[11]   Yet in spite of the flourishing volunteer corps in Public Schools, it was still the playing field that held pride of place in the training of officers for the battlefields.

This conception of the value of games in warfare had its critics, among whom was Kipling—Kipling was certainly not opposed to militarism as such. At the end of *Stalky and Co.* Dick Fane, and of course the reader, was urged to 'imagine Stalky let loose on the South side of Europe with a sufficiency of Sikhs and a reasonable prospect of loot. Consider it quietly.' It was not British hegemony and the acquisition of the British Empire by military and other methods that Kipling objected to, but the theory that games, house spirit, conformity and the prefect system were the only means of achieving such an object. Kipling's Stalky, M'Turk and Beetle were all school rebels. They sneered at their fellows for being boys who 'play cricket and say "Yes, sir" and "No, sir" '. They themselves shirked cricket and joined the natural history society in order to escape from school. Their exploits nearly always ended with a thrashing. The qualities they extolled were courage and cunning and individual ingenuity. In *Stalky and Co.* Kipling was extolling the old Barbarian country pursuits which had gradually been supplanted in the Public Schools by the Philistine tyranny of organised games.

Kipling criticised the means rather than the ends of physical education. Other criticisms were more fundamental and at the turn of the century two Eton masters, Lionel Ford[12] and A. C. Benson,[13] started a wave of criticism which grew in magnitude in the 20th century and played an important part in the subsequent modification of the pattern of physical education in public schools.

Owing to the excessive development of the cult of athleticism in the late Victorian school and the intense public criticism which it aroused, it is only too easy to overlook the value of the contribution which Public Schools made through organised games to the national life and to the larger world of sport. If games were instrumental in producing a recognised type of self-confident and loyal but uncritical and unimaginative rulers and administrators, they also helped to make the schools more humane and better disciplined, and they enabled boys and masters to meet on a basis of amity and even technical equality unknown in countries on the other side of the English Channel. To the 'spirit of the game' the schools also made a contribution which is not without merit. While games were played to the very limit of human endurance and the element of competition was often overdone, yet 'victory at any price' was not an idea that ever found favour. Even defeat could bring satisfaction and was not dishonourable provided that the game was played hard and keenly contested. At their best, games were played for fun as much as for victory. At their best, too, Public School games demonstrated that 'art without malice and strife without anger' was a worthy, and an attainable, ideal.

The technical developments in games and sports which are now world-wide were achieved primarily through the initiative of boys and old boys from the Public Schools, and by the end of the 19th century the old boys were even being surpassed in technical proficiency by those whom they had taught.   This trend has already been noticed in Chapter 4 in connection with the development of Association football.

Towards the end of the century two events took place within the Public School world itself which were significant of a new educational movement within the upper classes.   The founding of Abbotsholme School in 1889, and of Bedales in 1893, offered to the upper classes an alternative education to that provided by their established institutions.   These two schools were not the first of their kind, but unlike their predecessors they flourished and became the parents of the 'new school movement' in England.

Dr. Reddie, first headmaster of Abbotsholme, was strongly opposed to the traditional Public School system of games in which 'the cricket ground is kept by servants, and even the tennis nets are put up by servants, and the young aristocrat has only to saunter down for his hour or two of play having done nothing useful to maintain even his own amusements'.[14]   At Abbotsholme boys were to build their own cricket pavilion, repair their boats and lay their turf.   They also spent considerable time on the manual jobs involved in gardening and estate management.   Less time was therefore spent on games than was spent in traditional Public Schools, and the intensive competition of games was counteracted by the performance of physical tasks which were essentially exercises in co-operation.   Bedales also departed radically from the traditional Public School pattern of games. As at Abbots-holme, there was a broad programme of physical activities including gardening and other outdoor work as well as games. Cricket was compulsory and so was football for the boys, and lacrosse for the girls, but seniors who showed neither interest nor aptitude were enabled to contract out. The most radical departure from tradition was in the inclusion in the curriculum of a daily period of gymnastics in the winter and swimming in the summer.[15] The Swedish system of exercises was adopted, first for the girls and later for the boys. The boys were not taught by a sergeant-instructor or a retired officer, as they might have been at most orthodox Public Schools, but by a member of the teaching staff, the equal of his colleagues both in education and in social status. All boys and girls thus received skilled attention and gymnastic training. One of the defects of Public School games had been the neglect of the poor performer and the concentration of coaching upon the boys with proved ability. Bedales set little store by a victorious football or cricket team and all boys whether with good or with bad physique received their share of attention in a planned programme of physical education. The stage was thus set for new developments in physical education which were to take place at Public Schools in the 20th century.

Chapter 5. References

1 Edward Lyttelton, 'Athletics in Public Schools', *Nineteenth Century*, January 1880.
2 Pierre de Coubertin, 'Are the Public Schools a Failure?', *Fortnightly Review*, December 1902.
3 *The Times*, 25 July 1884, quoted by C. R. L. Fletcher, *Edmund Warre*, London, 1922, pp. 106–7.

4 Percy Lubbock, *Shades of Eton*, London, 1932, pp. 118–19.
5 *The Times*, September 1889, 'A New Tyranny at Eton'. See also succeeding issues.
6 *Edinburgh Review*, April 1897, 'Old Eton and Modern'.
7 J. G. C. Minchin, *Our Public Schools*, London, 1901, p. 113.
8 Henry Newbolt, *Poems Old and New*, pp. 78–9.
9 G. M. Young, *Early Victorian England*, London, 1934, Vol I, p. 369.
10 *Hansard*, 8 July 1862, 3rd Series, Vol. 168, Col. 27.
11 C. R. L. Fletcher, *Edmund Warre*, London, 1922, p. 267.
12 Rev. Lionel Ford, 'Public School Athletics', in *Essays on Secondary Education*. Ed. C. Cookson, Oxford, 1898.
13 A. C. Benson, *The Schoolmaster*, 1903, Chap. X, and *The Upton Letters*, 1905, pp. 42–3.
14 B. M. Ward, *Reddie of Abbotsholme*, p. 153.
15 J. H. Badley, *Bedales*, 1923, pp. 89–90.

CHAPTER 6

Gymnastics and Drill before 1870

WHILE organised games were developing in the Public Schools, a different approach to physical education was being made elsewhere. Originating in Germany, the gymnastic approach derived primarily from the educational theories of Rousseau and his disciples. On the practical side it was at Basedow's Philanthropinum founded at Dessau in 1774[1] that a gymnastic system suitable for schoolchildren was first devised. When the school was opened, the physical education there consisted of instruction in the four 'knightly exercises' of dancing, fencing, riding and vaulting the live horse. Johann Friedrich Simon, who was in charge of physical education at Basedow's Philanthropinum from 1776 to 1777, realised the unsuitability of these exercises for younger children and therefore devised a simple system of 'Greek Gymnastics' consisting of organised exercises in running, jumping, throwing and wrestling, balancing exercises and ball games such as tennis, fives and skittles. The youngest children had hoops and see-saw. Simon's successor, J. J. du Toit, added skating and swimming, climbing and hanging exercises on an inclined ladder, and walking expeditions in the surrounding country.

The breadth of the programme at Dessau shows that the first gymnastic approach to physical education in modern times was neither narrow in scope nor formal in treatment. Both of these characteristics appeared later.

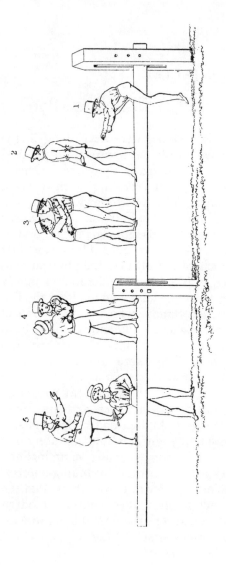

Balancing.

A balancing exercise from *Walker's Manly Exercises*, 1834

FIGURE I

Basedow's Philanthropinum was imitated and his work was developed by C. G. Salzmann, who opened his own school at Schnepfenthal in 1784. Here in 1786 the physical education of the pupils was handed over to J. C. F. Guts Muths. He not only developed and systematised the work of his predecessors but he was also the first practising teacher to publish manuals of physical education. *Gymnastik für die Jugend* appeared in 1793 and *Spiele zur Uebung und Erholung des Körpers und Geistes, für die Jugend, ihre Erzieher und alle Freunde unschuldiger Jugendfreuden* was published in 1796. These books, as well as later works, appeared at a time when the Napoleonic wars were directing attention as never before towards the need for physical fitness among the masses, and within a few years versions of Guts Muths' *Gymnastik für die Jugend* appeared in Denmark (1799), Bavaria (1800), U.S.A. (1802), France (1803), Austria (1805), Holland (1806) and Sweden (1813). The first English edition was published in 1800 and was wrongly attributed to Salzmann, whose name appeared as the author on the title page.[2] *Gymnastik für die Jugend* was originally published in two volumes, the first of which was a plea for gymnastics, the second and longer volume being a practical manual describing the open air gymnasium and classifying the exercises. Like his immediate predecessors, Guts Muths included a very wide range of activities: jumping, running, throwing, wrestling, climbing, balancing, lifting, carrying, pulling, dancing, walking, military exercises and swimming. He also considered that gymnastics included such activities as behaviour in case of fire, keeping watch at night, and declaiming, and fasting.

The influence of Guts Muths' work in England is not easy to assess but he must have made a favourable impression on the military authorities for in 1822 P. H. Clias, an officer of the Swiss Army and one of Guts Muths' disciples, was appointed to organise courses of gymnastics at military and naval establishments. The Royal Military College, Sandhurst, the Royal Military Academy, Woolwich, the Royal Military Asylum, Chelsea, and the Royal Naval Asylum, Greenwich, came under his direction. He also claimed to be superintendent of gymnastics at 'the Public School of the Charter House'.[3]   Unfortunately there is no record at the school of his appointment, and it is not possible to say exactly what his functions there were. If his claim is to be believed, this was certainly the earliest adoption of educational gymnastics by any Public School. At the time of his assignments in England Clias had already published his own version of Guts Muths' work in German (1816) and French (1819). In 1823 he produced an English version entitled *An Elementary Course of Gymnastic Exercises*. The book was written in four chapters. Chapter I was concerned with 'exercises of the lower extremities', walking, running, jumping, and balancing exercises which included an introduction to dancing. Chapter II dealt with 'exercises of the superior extremities' and contained thirteen arm exercises as well as 'complicated movements of the arms and feet'. Chapter III described 'complicated exercises', wrestling, jumping, running and skipping with hoops and cord, skating, elementary vaulting exercises (which were in fact mostly hanging and arm travelling exercises (fig. 3), more advanced vaulting exercises and exercises on the parallel bars. Chapter IV was devoted to 'Art of Swimming' (fig. 4). Clias had considerably restricted the scope of Guts Muths' gymnastics and laid his emphasis upon the artificial exercises rather than the more natural activities.

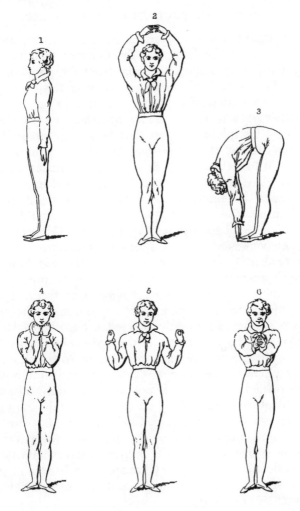

Extension Motions.

Extension motions from *Walker's Manly Exercises*, 1834
FIGURE 2

F

Furthermore, Clias was himself an army officer, and his assignment in England was for military training. He approached his subject therefore from the point of view of military drill. He made no secret of this, but specifically stated that when many boys had to be instructed together it was indispensably necessary to establish a military discipline in order that they might execute the greater part of the elementary exercises together.[4]   Not only did his scheme include such commands as 'Fall-in', 'Dress', 'Attention', but even the standing long jump was performed to numbers. A desire for the precision and formality of the barrack square may also have influenced Clias' views on good style in movement. Certainly some of these views are peculiar if judged by modern standards. We read that 'To run fast and gracefully, one should, as it were, graze the ground with the feet, by keeping the legs as straight as possible whilst moving them forward, raise onself from one foot upon the other, and make the movements of the feet rapidly succeed each other. During the course, the upper part of the body is inclined a little forward, the arms are, as it were, glued to the sides, and turned in at the height of the hips, the hands shut and the nails turned inwards.'[5]   If this style was really adopted it is difficult to credit Clias' claim that several boys at the Royal Military Academy, Chelsea, ran 580 yards in 68 seconds, the equivalent of 51·6 seconds for 440 yards! However that may be, the military flavour imparted to educational gymnastics by Clias appeared later in physical drill in elementary schools and thereafter persisted throughout the century.

From a technical point of view the most interesting chapter is the last one. The new style of swimming, which Clias described and which he claimed to have tried for the first time in 1809 on the sons of Marshal Blücher, was the breast stroke. Already this stroke had been introduced by Colonel Pfull into the Prussian Army and was practised in many European cities. It was, of course, to have a great future in England too.

An attempt to adapt the gymnastics of Guts Muths and Clias to suit the needs and inclinations of the British people was made by Donald Walker in *Manly Exercises*—a book which was first published in 1834 and which had run into ten editions by 1860 (figs. 1 and 2). Further evidence of the popularity of Guts Muths' gymnastics in England is found in the opening of a public 'Government Gymnasium' on Primrose Hill on Good Friday, 1848 (Plate IV). This gymnasium was an open-air enclosure with climbing and swinging apparatus which was erected 'by desire of Viscount Morpeth, the Chief Commissioner of Her Majesty's Woods and Forests.'[6]

The first part of Walker's book dealt with the familiar activities of walking, running, leaping, vaulting, pole leaping, balancing, skating, carrying, climbing and swimming; the second half was devoted to rowing, sailing, riding, and driving, which the author thought would be very improperly omitted from a course of British exercises.[7] The writer nowhere acknowledged his debt to Clias, but his treatment of the activities and particularly breast stroke swimming clearly owed much to Clias' work. Some of the line drawings of swimming and life saving even appear to have been directly pirated and used with hardly any alteration. The latter part of the book owed little to foreign sources, neither did that part which dealt with running training. In this sphere the author could secure a wealth of information from famous 'pedestrians' of the day, particularly 'Captain Barclay', whose feat of walking 1,000 miles in 1,000 hours was widely known.

Walker's Exercises for Ladies was a parallel volume and paid special attention to the treatment of postural defects by means of exercises with dumbbells, wands and the Indian sceptre. The book's full title describes its scope. It was 'calculated to preserve and improve beauty and to prevent and correct personal defects, inseparable from constrained or careless habits on physiological principles'.[8]

Both of Walker's books were written primarily for adults. Children also felt the influence of Guts Muths and Clias. Their books provided the inspiration and the basis for those physical exercises that were done in some elementary schools in the early part of the century. By 1839 it was common for pupil teachers to conduct classes of children in exercise, either 'elementary movements' or 'more complex combinations', according to their ability.[9]

There was no national system of elementary education in England before 1870. In the early part of the century elementary education was in the main provided by the British and Foreign School Society, a dissenting body, and by The National Society for the Education of the Poor according to the Principles of the Church of England. Until 1833 the work of both societies depended on voluntary subscriptions and the meagre fees of pupils, but in that year Parliament made a first grant of £20,000 in aid of elementary education, the payments to be made only through one or other of the two societies. This necessitated administrative machinery and in 1839 a committee of the Privy Council was appointed 'to superintend the application of any sums voted by Parliament for the purpose of promoting Public Education'.[10] The committee was given a permanent secretary, and following the example of the Factory Act of 1833 which set up Factory

Inspectors, its first minute provided for the appointment of two inspectors of aided schools. To ensure their independence of judgement, the inspectors received their appointment from the Queen, and have ever since been known as Her (or His) Majesty's Inspectors of Schools, or H.M.I. for short, a status much prized by those who have enjoyed it. From the beginning the Education Department, as it came to be called, took an interest in physical education. Inspectors were instructed to encourage the provision on the sites of schools to be erected of the means of recreation and exercise. In existing schools which they visited they were to inspect the state of the exercise ground and report on the competence of pupil teachers to take classes in physical exercises.[11] The committee itself passed a minute for the benefit of would-be promoters of elementary schools, and therein made the first statement of government policy on physical education. 'In selecting the site, it is very important to provide a closed exercise ground for the children. In the absence of a school playground the street becomes the resort of the children after school hours; there they are remote from the influence and superintendence of the master; they meet with vicious men and women, and with children of their own age, who have been corrupted by vicious parents, or other bad example, or even children trained to desperate courses by thieves. In a rural parish there is little chance of their meeting with children expert in vice and knavery; but if the master be unprovided with an exercise ground, he is without the most effectual means of ascertaining, by being a spectator, or joining in their sports, the characters of the children under his care, and of training their habits. At the best the teacher of a day school cannot hope altogether to correct the effects of evil example at the child's home;

Exercises on the Mast.
from *Gymnastic Exercises* by P. H. Clias, 1825
FIGURE 3

and therefore to increase the beneficial influence of his own more elevated mind on the thoughts and habits of his scholars he should possess the means of attracting them to spend a large portion of the time devoted to exercise in the neighbourhood of the school-house, where the development of character may proceed under his better than paternal care.

'The physical training of the children may therefore be usefully provided for on other grounds than its tendency to develop the muscular powers, and to render the scholars robust and vigorous. The physical exercises of the playground extend the moral influence of the teacher, by encouraging the children to remain under his care during the hours of recreation'.[12]

The following year Her Majesty's Inspectors were instructed to put special questions to infant schools on the amusements of the children, what games were encouraged, what gymnastic apparatus, if any, was provided, whether the children were trained methodically in walking, marching and physical exercises, what was the result, and how often the intervals for recreation occurred.

As the reports of the inspectors came in, the hopes and intentions of the Education Department were seen to be unduly optimistic. At a few schools, like the Abbey Street School, Bethnal Green, a new school opened in 1839, the schoolmaster took children in gymnastic movements in the playground after school hours,[13] but at most schools the master could not have done this even if he had wished to do so. Of thirty-five schools of the British Society in the Metropolitan District inspected by H.M.I. Tremenheere only three had playgrounds of any kind.[14] Similar conditions were found by Her Majesty's Inspectors in other parts of the country. Physical education did not receive much further attention from the Education Department for many years. The appalling physical conditions of the schoolrooms, the lack of books and equipment, the poor quality of the teachers, and the abysmal ignorance of many of the children at the schools presented problems more pressing than the lack of physical education.

In 1861 the government set up a Commission to inquire into the state of popular education in England. A number of assistant commissioners were appointed to visit and report on every part of the country. The instructions which they received made no reference to physical education or to playgrounds. Most commissioners therefore ignored this aspect of education but the Rev. James Frazer who was appointed to report on schools in Worcester, Hereford, Somerset, Dorset and Devon wrote:

'The playgrounds attached to the schools are of very slight utility for any purpose of recreation beyond affording a place where the children can be turned out between lessons to get a mouthful of fresh air. A solitary pole for a giant's stride (at the time of my visit, which was in the winter, with the ropes generally missing) is the only feature to indicate that the ground before you is for purposes of play. In one or two places there is a covered shed, nominally for use in wet weather. The games played seemed generally aimless, as though there were no one taking any interest in them or directing them—for good games need to be taught as well as lessons—and I do not think that the encouragement of healthy athletic sports such as cricket, football, etc., has yet found the legitimate place in the education of boys of this class which Public School men would desire, who vividly remember how much it contributed to their own.

FIGURE 4. Swimming instructions

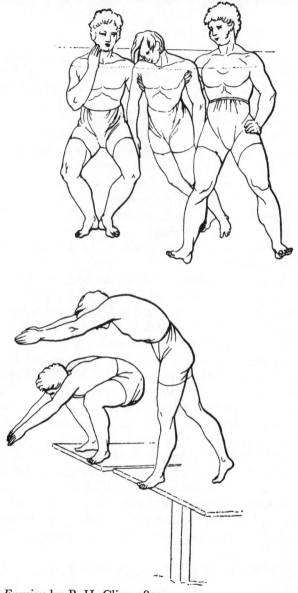

astic Exercises by P. H. Clias, 1825

'As games of this kind are unsuitable for girls, they, or at any rate the elder ones, might find a little wholesome physical exercise, meanwhile, in cleaning out the school . . .'[15]

Between 1839 and 1870 the development of educational gymnastics took place away from the schools and was achieved by two groups of people working independently of each other. On the one hand Archibald MacLaren at Oxford, supported by the military authorities, developed the earlier work of Guts Muths and Clias. On the other hand, the disciples or missionaries of P. H. Ling in Stockholm imported into England and developed here that form of gymnastics which came to be known as the Swedish system.

Archibald MacLaren was born in 1819 or 1820 at Alloa in Scotland. After studying fencing, gymnastics and medicine in Paris, he settled in Oxford and opened a fencing school and gymnasium in Oriel Lane. There in 1855 'William Morris and several others of his set used to go pretty regularly to fence, box and play singlestick . . . Between them and MacLaren himself, a man in the prime of life, cultivated and full of enthusiasm, a mutual intimacy and liking sprang up and grew into a warm friendship. Three or four times in a term they would go and dine with him in Summertown, where they saw their own enthusiasms combined with the charm of a simple family life.'[16] MacLaren's connections with the university and his own intellectual calibre made his contributions to physical education very valuable. In 1858 he had built his own gymnasium at the corner of Alfred Street and Bear Lane and there set to work on a scientific study of physical education.

MacLaren's first publication appeared as an article in

MacMillan's Magazine in February 1863 entitled 'National Systems of Bodily Exercise',[17] in which he compared the merits and demerits of ancient and modern systems of gymnastics.   Neither the ancient Greek, nor the modern Swedish, Prussian or French systems satisfied him; although his own view of the fundamental aim of gymnastics was not very different from those whose methods he criticised, he believed that by exercises suitably devised and arranged the body could be prepared for any task. In the early stages of training, therefore, gymnastics should aim at increasing the body's strength and stamina and stimulating its organs to healthful activity.   If this were done, dexterity would be achieved easily later.

MacLaren's viewpoint was not merely that of an instructor, but rather that of a far-seeing teacher.   He set forth his views on the place of physical education in general education in the preface to his book entitled *A System of Physical Education, Theoretical and Practical*.   'The Battle of Life requires for combatant the *whole* man, not a part; and the whole too in as good condition as can be brought into the conflict.'[18]   'Yes, it is *health* rather than *strength* that is the great requirement of modern men at modern occupations; it is not the power to travel great distances, carry great burdens, lift great weights, or overcome great material obstructions; it is simply that condition of the body, and that amount of vital capacity, which shall enable each man in his place to pursue his calling, and work on in his working life with the greatest amount of comfort to himself and usefulness to his fellow men.'[19]   He went so far as to prescribe mental occupations for those of his pupils who were misguided enough to desire nothing but bodily health and strength.   Moreover the artificial gymnastics which he devised were not in his view a complete and sufficient means to health; they should be combined with swimming, country pursuits, riding, walking and other 'agents of health'. The particular merit of gymnastics was that it was more practicable and more easily indulged in than these other activities, by schoolchildren, men in the forces and men in offices, warehouses and shops. It was, moreover, an essential if the forms of malgrowth and underdevelopment which he noticed in undergraduates were to be counteracted. Underdevelopment worried him more than malformation, and it was because he found that in almost every youth passing from school to university there was a considerable amount of attainable power and material capacity undeveloped that he strongly advocated the adoption of a clearly defined system of bodily training at large schools.

The same methodical approach was made to games and sports, and MacLaren's book on rowing, with a preliminary essay on training methods, was a masterly analysis of the physical requirements of the oarsman.[20]   He was quick to see that muscular strength was best developed by exercises against resistance and in a crude form he enunciated the modern principle of 'overload'. He saw too that while rowing made great calls upon the respiratory system, the restricted position of the chest in rowing militated against adequate development of that system. It must therefore be developed by activities other than rowing, such as running.

MacLaren did not allow his interest in the methodical study of games and sports to run away with him. He recognised the limitations of games and the games system which was already gaining so much approbation in Public Schools. He did not fail to give credit where credit was due, and admitted that the influence of national games upon the national character was 'valuable beyond computation'. The defect of games, however, was that not one of them had the development of the body or bodily health and strength as its primary object. Inevitably games produced one-sided development. 'Use gives facility of execution, and facility of execution causes frequency of practice, because we all like to do that which we can do well: and thus inevitably, because based on the organic law of development being in relation to activity or employment, certain parts of the body will be cultivated and become developed to the exclusion of the others.'

MacLaren took it for granted that such development was undesirable and he advanced systematised exercise as the antidote. The same assumption led him to make a fundamental distinction between recreation and education. 'All exercise,' he said, 'may be classed under two distinct heads, Recreative and Educational.'[21] The recreative class embraced all school games, sports and pastimes, the educational class consisted of systematised exercise. This dichotomy within physical education between recreation and education, or games and physical training, has been fundamental in its development in England, and made its appearance later in many official government statements. The distinction had a social as well as a technical significance in that it corresponded with the difference between the two systems of physical education that grew up in the independent Public Schools on the one hand and the state-aided elementary schools on the other.

MacLaren's greatest contributions to the practice of physical education were in the spheres of military training and anthropometry. In 1860, at about the same time as

Lord Elcho held his meeting at the Thatched House Tavern to launch military drill in Public Schools,[22] Mac-Laren was invited to reorganise physical training in the Army. In 1861 two detachments of non-commissioned officers under the command of Major Hammersley were sent to the Oxford gymnasium on a six months' course to qualify as instructors and form the nucleus of an extensive group of instructors who would develop a military gymnastic system. Their ultimate base was to be Aldershot, and a gymnasium, built on the plan of the Oxford gymnasium, was organised there in 1861.[23] In the same year H.R.H. the Duke of Cambridge, General Officer Commanding in Chief, 'having decided that the whole of the troops shall be regularly instructed in gymnastic exercises as part of their military education' and that a normal school should be set up at Aldershot with this object in view, requested all commanding officers to consider whether there were any existing buildings that could be used for the purpose. Gymnasia were accordingly established at Chatham, Portsmouth, Woolwich and Skegness.[24] MacLaren's course of training for these instructors included simple movements and positions, dumbbell and barbell exercises, but consisted mainly of exercises with apparatus. Ropes, poles, masts, horizontal bars, parallel bars, vaulting horses, trapeze, rings and ladders were all used for strengthening exercises and exercises in dexterity. From this beginning gymnastics spread throughout the British Army, and through gymnastic societies which sprang up in large cities, to the civilian population as well.[25] Gymnasia with similar equipment appeared even in Public Schools such as Harrow, Wellington and Winchester, without, however, dislodging the playing fields from their pride of place.

MacLaren was a pioneer in the use of anthropometry, both to secure information about average development and also to secure a measure of the effect of his own exercises upon the physique of the soldiers and civilians who came under his care. He even went so far as to use photography, then in its very early stages, to compare the bodies of his military pupils at the beginning and at the end of his course. In the appendices to his *System of Physical Education* MacLaren gave the results of his anthropometric activity. He illustrated certain forms of regular and irregular growth (A), gave tables to show the growth of children between the ages of 8 and 18 (B), and of university students (C). Appendix (D) showed the effects of systematised exercise on different individuals and Appendix (E) gave the measurements of his military trainees before and after training. These appendices raise the book from being a useful practical manual of instruction to the status of a work of methodical research, while the introduction outlined an approach to physical education which was unique in England both for its breadth and for its thoughtfulness.

One curious feature of MacLaren's work was his condemnation of Ling's Swedish gymnastics. He gives Ling credit for 'the first attempt to bring a knowledge of the structure and functions of the human body to bear upon its culture',[26] but free exercises without apparatus were not, he thought, adequate for ordinary healthy men and women. Ling had let his enthusiasm for physiological knowledge carry him away. 'It must have been the strong conviction of the value of this knowledge—so strong that it seared and scorched where it should have radiated genial light and warmth—that warped the judgement and overheated the imagination of Ling, the enthusiast

Swede, when he gave the free will offering of a laborious life to the preparation of a system of bodily exercise in its main characteristics suitable to the invalid only. . . .' 'Chicken broth may yield ample nutriment to the invalid, but the soldier would make but a poor day's march on it; you must give *him* the chicken too.'[27]

This condemnation was based upon a misunderstanding of the content and purpose of Ling's work in Sweden. When we see, however, the form in which the Swedish system first came to England, MacLaren's misinterpretation is understandable. P. H. Ling opened his Central Institute of Gymnastics in Stockholm in 1814. There he attempted to give gymnastics a scientific basis and classified it into educational, medical, military and aesthetic gymnastics. It was to medical and military gymnastics that he devoted most attention. Swedish educational gymnastics were developed later by his successors at the institute, in particular by his son Hjalmar Ling who took a teaching post at the institute in 1843. Much later, in 1864, the course was reorganised and Hjalmar Ling was placed at the head of the section of school gymnastics. Ling's system was first brought to England by John Govart In De Betou in 1838. In De Betou started work as a practitioner of medical gymnastics in London and in 1842 published *Therapeutic Manipulation*. In the early forties Lieutenant C. Ehrenhoff settled in London for the same purpose, and in 1850 Carl August Georgii opened a private institute in London and published a pamphlet entitled *Kinesipathy*.[28]   These three pioneers all set themselves up as practitioners of medical gymnastics and it was as such that they made their living in London. It was moreover among doctors that such followers as they had in England were to be found. J. W. F. Blundell,[29] M. J.

Chapman,[30] and Mathias D. Roth,[31] who wrote books upon the Ling system and published them in the fifties, were all doctors and their approach was that of the physician to the invalid. MacLaren may therefore be forgiven if he could see little in Ling's work that was appropriate for healthy and robust soldiers and civilians.

Georgii continued to practise in London until 1877, but it was the indefatigable efforts of Mathias Roth in making propaganda and in bringing pressure to bear in Parliament and elsewhere that finally resulted in the introduction of the Swedish system into the elementary schools of England. At the time of his original publication[32] Roth was physician to the Hahneman Hospital. The next year he produced an abbreviated version of the original book entitled *Movements or Exercises according to Ling's System for the Development and Strengthening of the Human Body in Childhood and Youth*. The year 1853 saw new developments in Roth's thought and practice. He set up his own institution at 16a, Old Cavendish Street, for the treatment of disease by movements, and he published a book on *The Gymnastic Free Exercises of P. H. Ling* in an effort to capture the attention of the healthy as well as the ailing.[33] In this book too he launched his campaign for the development of educational gymnastics based on a knowledge of anatomy and physiology. 'Many parents, tutors and principals of educational institutions think it enough to engage a drill sergeant, or a teacher of callisthenic movements . . .' 'It is very singular, observes Rothstein, that we would not confine the care of a horse to a man who had not a knowledge of the animal's anatomy and physiology; while the man who is intrusted with the development and strengthening of the human body is not expected to possess so much science as is deemed absolutely necessary in the trainer of our horses.'[34]

Roth continued to quote this analogy throughout his campaign during the following thirty years. He claimed for rational gymnastics not only a contribution to health but a capacity to prevent vicious practices, to promote feelings of fellowship through concerted exercise, and to produce habits of obedience and precision. Roth continued his medical practice against considerable opposition. In 1855 he was at first refused permission to read a paper before the physiological section of the British Association, then, when permission was granted, the secretary refused to insert the paper or the abstract in the *Transactions*.

In the sphere of education also Roth at first had little success. In 1854 he wrote and published *A Letter to the Rt. Hon. the Earl of Granville, Lord President of the Council of Education etc. etc. on the Importance of Rational Gymnastics as a Branch of National Education and as a means of Elementary Instruction; on the advantages arising therefrom to the Industrious Classes, the effect upon the Public Health, the Fine Arts, Military Affairs, and the Diminution of the Poors' Rates*. He was moved to do this after an interview with His Excellency Chevalier Bunsen, the Prussian ambassador in London. The Prussian cabinet had given its blessing to educational gymnastics in 1842 and in the following year a beginning had been made with the organisation of physical education throughout the state. Roth emphasised the medical and military importance of 'rational gymnastics', and he advanced a great variety of other arguments in favour of its adoption on a nation-wide scale. He suggested that his system would lead to a decrease of the mortality rate and would teach people the means of preserving health.

It would keep the working classes out of gin palaces (he complained with some force that the literary and mechanics' institutes which were being established made no provision for physical education). It would counter-act the occupational injuries of workers and women, particularly those of middle age. Roth addressed his arguments to the Army, the Board of Health, the Poor Law Board, and above all to the Education Department. 'The Council of Education might very soon show some practical results of Rational Gymnastics, by introducing into all schools connected with them that part of Ling's system which comes under the title of Free Exercises, a name derived from their being executed without the help of technical apparatus.'

In this open letter Roth showed himself as contemptuous of MacLaren's methods as MacLaren was of Ling's gym-nastics, and complained that MacLaren and his like seemed to think that climbing poles, ascending ropes, leaping, flinging the body round a bar and other *tours de force* constituted gymnastics. The consequence was that drill sergeants, teachers of callisthenics, dancing and fencing masters were entrusted with the management of what was called physical education.

As a result of this letter Roth was granted an interview with the First Clerk in the Education Department and the Rev. Mr. Temple, then Head of Kneller Hall Training College. He was told bluntly that future schoolmasters already had too much to do and had no time for training in 'rational gymnastics'.

Roth was not the only one to approach the Government on Physical education. The movement for army reform which had led to the introduction of military drill into the Public Schools and had induced the Commander-in-Chief to set up army gymnasia and a Normal School of Gymnastic Training at Aldershot also produced a debate in Parliament on the desirability of physical training in elementary schools. On 8 July 1862 Lord Elcho, who had been largely responsible for initiating the volunteer movement in Public Schools, moved:

'That the physical, moral and economic advantages arising from a system of physical training have been largely shown in evidence before the Education Commission:

'That it is expedient for the increase of bodily as well as mental aptitudes of children for civil, industrial, as well as for possible Military Service that encouragement and aid should be given for the extension of the practice of systemised gymnastic training, and for teaching Military and Naval Drill as now practised in the district half time Schools for Orphans and Destitute Children, and in other Schools for Pauper Children.'[35]   In his supporting speech Lord Elcho said that the schools where military training had been tried catered for 'children of the very lowest and most criminal class, many of them stunted in growth and naturally scrofulous' and that 'it was really astonishing to see what tidy, obedient and respectable boys the military training to which they were subjected made them'.   The same results could be achieved elsewhere for only a penny per head per week.

Robert Lowe, Vice-President of the Committee of the Privy Council for Education, replied and turned down the proposal on the ground of expense.   The cost of education was a serious worry to the Government.   The Parliamentary grant had risen from £20,000 in 1833 to £813,441 in 1861, yet the educational level of the people did not appear to have risen in proportion.   A desire to see value for money led the Education Department to introduce in

1862 the system of 'payment by results', whereby the grant paid to any school would depend upon the result of an annual examination carried out by the inspector. The time was not propitious for any suggestion of additional expenditure and Robert Lowe pointed out that Lord Elcho's figure of a penny per week per child amounted to 3s. 8d. per year. The maximum grant paid by the State for instruction in the three Rs was 12s. per child and an increase of 25 per cent for the provision of physical education was unjustifiable. Mr. Lowe went further and showed how restricted was the official view of the State's interest in the education of her citizens. He said that Lord Elcho's proposal 'embodied an idea—the idea that it was the duty of the Privy Council to devise means in addition to the existing grant to promote the teaching of anything because it might be deemed useful—which he must altogether repudiate'.[35]

Little was done for physical education in elementary schools during the fifties and sixties, but public concern was growing. The influence of doctors like Mathias Roth, and the reports of H.M. Inspectors, who often complained of the lack of playgrounds and the absence of physical exercises, may have had few readers, but the Muscular Christians like Kingsley and Hughes had a considerable following, and when men with a national reputation like Herbert Spencer, John Ruskin and Matthew Arnold pleaded for physical education, the country was bound to listen. Herbert Spencer's four essays on education were published in 1859 and one was devoted entirely to physical education. He was chiefly concerned with the omission of physical education from the bringing up of girls, but he applied many of his remarks to boys' education and quoted the timetable of a men's training college to show that between rising at 6 a.m. and going to bed at 10 p.m. there was no provision at all for any exercises except a walk which was often not taken.   Spencer maintained that the physical education of children was seriously faulty and that the preservation of health was a duty. 'The fact is,' he said, 'that all breaches of the laws of health are physical sins.'[36]

Ruskin too in *Unto This Last*, published in 1862, demanded the teaching of 'The Laws of Health and the exercises enjoined by them', and reiterated his plea in *Time and Tide*.[37]   Matthew Arnold was more specific, and recommended gymnastics as the form that physical education should take, simply because, if boys had to work long hours, or if they worked hard, gymnastics would do more for their physical health in the comparatively short time allotted to recreation than anything else could do. Again, for little boys, carefully taught gymnastics would be better than games which were adult pastimes and inappropriate for the very young.[38]

Edwin Chadwick was yet another writer and worker outside the world of school who prepared the ground for developments in physical education later in the century. Although primarily concerned with sanitation, mortality and ill health in towns he pointed out to the Newcastle Commission in 1859 that a child could not stand more than three hours teaching a day without some exercise or manual work. He pressed for physical exercises in schools through the Royal Society of Arts and the National Association for the Promotion of Social Science, and led a number of deputations to the government.[39]

The fifties and sixties were a period in which, while the government did little or nothing for physical education, private individuals did much to arouse and to shape public opinion, and those who were not primarily educationists did as much as, if not more than, those who were.

Chapter 6.   References

1   F. E. Leonard and G. B. Affleck, *A Guide to the History of Physical Education*, London Ed., 1947, Chap. X.

2   *Gymnastics for Youth: or a Practical Guide to Healthful and Amusing Exercises for the use of Schools. An essay towards the necessary improvement of Education chiefly as it relates to the body; freely translated from the German of C. G. Salzmann, Master of the Academy at Schnepfenthal and author of Elements of Morality.* Printed for J. Johnson, London, 1800.

3   P. H. Clias, *An Elementary Course of Gymnastic Exercises*, Fourth Ed., London, 1825, title page.

4   *Op. cit.*, p. 28.

5   *Op. cit.*, p. 47.

6   *Illustrated London News*, April 1848.

7   'Craven', *Walker's Manly Exercises*, London, 1860, Tenth Ed., p. 1.

8   Donald Walker, *Exercises for Ladies*, London, 1835.

9   *Minutes of the Committee of Council on Education*, 1839–40, p. 19.

10 *Op. cit.*, p. vii.

11 *Op. cit.*, pp. 19–20.

12 *Op. cit.*, p. 71.

13 *Minutes of the Committee of Council on Education*.

14 *Op. cit.*, p. 464.

15 *Reports of the Assistant Commissioners appointed to inquire into the State of Popular Education in England*, Education Department, London, 1861, Vol. II, p. 98.

16 J. W. Mackail, *The Life of William Morris*, London, Edn. 1922, p. 67.

17 *MacMillan's Magazine*, VII, pp. 277–86.

18 A. MacLaren, *A System of Physical Education, Theoretical and Practical*, Oxford, 1869, revised and enlarged by Wallace MacLaren, Oxford, 1895.

19 *Op. cit.*, pp. xxviii and xxxvi.

20 A. MacLaren, *Training in Theory and Practice*, London, 1866.

21   A. MacLaren, *A System of Physical Education*, Ed. 1895, p. xlvi.

22   See Chapter 5.

23   A. MacLaren, *A System of Physical Education*, Ed. 1895, p. xcv.

24   *The Times*, 23 July 1861.

25   A. MacLaren, *op. cit.*, Preface, 1895.

26   A. MacLaren, *op. cit.*, Introduction, 1895.

27   *MacMillan's Magazine*, February 1863, VII, pp. 277–86.

28   Tidskrift, *Gymnastik*, I, 989–99: II, 225–35: and IX 293–7.   Also
     F. E. Leonard and G. B. Affleck, *A Guide to the History of Physical
     Education*, London, 1947, pp. 160, 210.

29   J. W. F. Blundell, *Medicina Mechanica, or the Theory and Practice of
     Active and Passive Exercises and Manipulations considered as a branch of
     Therapeutics and as adapted both to the treatment and cure of many forms
     of chronic diseases*, London, 1852.

30   M. J. Chapman, *Ling's Educational and Curative Exercises*, London,
     1856. The fourth edition was edited by C. A. Georgii.

31   M. D. Roth, *The Prevention and Cure of Many Chronic Diseases by
     Movements*, London, 1851.

32   M. D. Roth, *op. cit.*

33   M. D. Roth, *The Gymnastic Free Exercises of P. H. Ling*, London,
     1853, Preface.

34   M. D. Roth, *op. cit.*, p. iv.

35   *Hansard*, 8 July 1862, Vol. 168, Col. 22.

36   Herbert Spencer, *Education Intellectual, Moral and Physical*,
     London, Ed. 1891, p. 170.

37   John Ruskin, *Time and Tide*, London, 1868, Chap. XVI, pp. 95f.

38   *R.S.I.C.* 1868, Vol. VI, pp. 589–90.

39   S. E. Finer, *The Life and Times of Edwin Chadwick*, London, 1952.

CHAPTER 7

Between the Acts

IN 1870 the introduction of the Education Bill into the House of Commons provided a fresh opportunity for pressing the claims of physical education. The indefatigable Mathias Roth at once addressed a pamphlet[1] to W. E. Forster, Quaker, Radical, Yorkshireman, and Vice-President of the Committee of Council on Education, whose task it was to pilot the Bill through Parliament. Roth wanted the Education Department to refuse to consider a school 'efficient' for purposes of grant unless regular daily physical education took place, for he considered that the subject should be on a par with the three Rs. He managed to produce some startling evidence of national debility in figures for the rejection of recruits for the Army and Navy. In 1866 the Army had rejected recruits at the rate of 380 per 1,000 on physical grounds, while the figures for the period of years 1864–7 were even higher, 408 per 1,000. The Navy had had to reject no less than 4,410 out of 5,567 boys who applied for naval service in 1869. Similar figures for physical defects were available for railway employees and children in workhouses. Many of the specific defects which were noted were remediable or could have been prevented by physical education. Roth argued that games and sports, even had they been practicable for elementary school children, were quite inadequate as physical education. Rational gymnastics on the other hand would increase work and military power—

Roth quoted a Prussian general as saying, 'We have not vanquished the Austrians, we have outmarched them'— they would also save money by the diminution of the Poor Rates, the Police Rates, and the expenses of criminal machinery; lastly it would increase the number of healthy, strong and beautiful mothers.   Roth's suggestions for implementing his ideas were essentially practical; they included the introduction of physical education and health education into training colleges with an examination in theory and practice at the end of the course (1908), vacation courses for practising teachers (1907), unattached teachers to visit schools and give theoretical and practical instruction to teachers (1917), the inclusion of physical education in the payments by results scheme (1895), and the approval of manuals of health education and physical education (1902).   The dates in brackets show the year in which the Government first gave effect to each idea either by financial aid or by administrative action. Mathias Roth received no credit for them; indeed, as he himself said, there was no evidence that Mr. Forster ever read the *Plea* that was dedicated to him.[2]   Certainly no comprehensive system of physical education was incorporated or even mentioned in the Act.   It could hardly have been otherwise, since the Act was not intended to create a new national system of education, nor a compulsory system nor a free system, but merely in Forster's own words, 'to fill up gaps'.[3]

The Education Department made one small concession on physical education but not along the lines of free gymnastics suggested by Roth.   The revised code of regulations which followed the passing of the Forster Education Act stated that 'attendance at drill under a competent instructor for not more than two hours per week and twenty weeks in the year may be counted as school attendance'—for purposes of financial grant from the Government.

Four features of this administrative measure are noteworthy. First it was permissive legislation, and no obligation was put upon any school to provide physical education. Secondly, physical education was permitted for boys only. It took further reports and recommendations by H.M.I.s to secure permission for girls to receive any physical education. Thirdly, the permitted physical education took the form of military drill. The Education Department made arrangements with the War Office for instruction by drill sergeants at the rate of sixpence a day and a penny a mile marching money, and the exercises were to be taken from the War Office's *Field Exercise Book*. Fourthly, the main purpose of this drill was disciplinary. The exercises, in the words of the Committee's *Report*, 'would be sufficient to teach the boys habits of sharp obedience, smartness, order and cleanliness'. The fact that the Franco-Prussian war had broken out in the year preceding the issue of the new code may have been partly responsible for the strong military flavour of the regulations.

What this drill meant in terms of human experience is seen from the account written by E. G. Holland, who was at school in 1877. 'My first experience carries me back seventy-two years, when as a boy in my ninth year, I marched with the boys of my own class to a small village drill hall, about a furlong from the old "British School" building in Highgate, once a week, for a half hour's drill under the direction of an ex-military sergeant. You will note that, although the old British School was a co-educational school, it never entered the heads of the powers that then were, that girls required any sort of physical culture. The instructions consisted in "standing to attention", "standing at ease", "standing easy", "falling in", "falling out", "dressing in line", "eyes right", "eyes left", "eyes front", "left turning", "right turning", "about turning", "slow marching", "quick marching", "double marching", "halting", "right wheeling", "left wheeling", "about wheeling", "breaking off", "numbering", etc. You can easily imagine that to boys such as we were, novel as this seemed in the first few lessons, it soon became unbearably boring, and we had to relieve the monotony by naughtiness. This usually consisted in purposely doing a movement wrongly—nudging or colliding with one another, getting out of step and so on. But the one "high light" in such proceedings was this. One of us, having fitted a miniature catapult of string-like elastic to his thumb and first finger, and having stored, in his pocket, some small pieces of orange peel, would fire an occasional shot at a line of military drums stored on the top of a cupboard down the longer side of the hall. We made it a point of honour never to be in possession of any knowledge as to who the offender was. The "ping" or "pong" according to the size of the drum that was hit, fully compensated for the half hour's dreariness of the lesson.'[4] Mr. Holland was not correct in his assertion about the neglect of physical education for girls. In 1872 the School Board for London had recommended to the Education Department that the next year's Code should provide for the attendance of girls at drill under a competent instructor to count as school attendance. The Department replied that the drill referred to was systematic military drill and therefore unsuitable for girls. Nevertheless the Board's Drill Instructor reported in November 1873 that 4,922 girls had been drilled, that the girls highly appreciated the drill and that the mistresses considered the introduction of drill into their schools a great boon to the children. Thirty of the mistresses had attended a class for teachers. In 1876 the School Board for London resolved that physical exercises must be given in every girls' department and that the Board's Drill Instructor should inspect the physical exercises of girls as well as the drill of boys.[5]

During the years immediately following the Forster Education Act, the number of schools which included military drill in their curriculum steadily increased. In 1872 there were 926 such schools and by 1880 the number had risen to 1,277. As the total number of schools inspected also rose from 8,919 in 1870 to 17,325 in 1880 the increase of military drill was more apparent than real and was not as great as many hoped. Her Majesty's Inspectors in their annual reports commended the introduction of military drill and in Lancaster H.M.I. Mr. Brodie reported its introduction into mixed schools, 'the girls even partaking (and why should they not?) in its advantages'.[6] That official recognition of physical education should be restricted to military drill was a great disappointment to Mathias Roth, but he continued to campaign for a higher conception of the aims of physical education than 'habits of sharp obedience, smartness, order and cleanliness' and for a more scientific approach to the subject. Nor was he alone in his work. Even his professional opponent MacLaren at Oxford had objected to military drill for boys under the age of 13 or 14, and in 1876 H.M.I. Mr. Jolly read a paper on 'Physical Education and Hygiene in Schools' to the Economic Section of the British Association which led to a minute recommending the General Committee 'to press on the government the view of fostering physical education by giving grants for its teaching and of making physical training and hygiene necessary elements in the professional training of teachers'.[7] Similar views were pressed on the Government in Parliament. In March 1875 Mr. P. A. Taylor suggested in the House of Commons that gymnastic exercises be made a branch of the nation's education system, and in July of the same year Mr. Butler-Johnstone called the attention of the House to the desirability of introducing physical education in the public elementary schools of the country.[8] No one, he maintained, had a greater respect for the drill sergeant than he, but it was defeating the very object of military training to call in the drill sergeant too early. 'You must work your cotton into yarn before it can be woven into cloth', and gymnastic exercises should come before drill. Butler-Johnstone saw too that Disraeli's *Two Nations* had their own peculiar forms of physical education or lack of it. In 1875 England was a nation of contrasts. Side by side with vast accumulations of wealth were ugly patches of misery and wretchedness. Side by side with athleticism and good physical development were disease, deformity and a lack of physical education. Moreover the Government were complacent. Viscount Sandon, as Vice-President of the Committee of Council on Education, replied to Mr. Butler-Johnstone that he had every reason to believe that the introduction of military drill into schools would be attended with very advantageous results and he could not promise that any further steps would be taken.[8]

By a curious twist of the British Constitution, the Vice-President of the Committee of Council on Education was responsible not only for the Education Department, but also for the registration and importation of all foreign cattle, and for the removal of English cattle to prevent cattle disease. This combination of functions in one dignitary may have benefited the cattle of the country but it is difficult to believe that it contributed to the status or vision of the Education Department.

The first big step towards systematic physical education in elementary schools was taken not by Parliament nor by the Education Department but by the School Board for London. In 1878, on the initiative of Mrs. Westlake, member of the School Board for Marylebone and a friend of Mathias Roth, Miss Concordia Löfving was invited by the Board from Sweden to take up an appointment as 'Lady Superintendent of Physical Education'.[9]

From its very inception after the passing of the Education Act in 1870 the School Board for London had decided to promote physical education. In 1871 it resolved that means should be provided for physical training, exercise and drill in every elementary school under its authority.[10] The Huxley Committee set up to advise upon the curriculum had recommended that music and drill should be among the essential subjects rather than the discretionary subjects for infants, juniors and seniors.

The concept of physical training and exercise, however, was a narrow one; in fact it was military drill in spite of attempts by a few members of the Board to broaden the programme. In 1872 Regimental Major William Sheffield was appointed Drill Master at a salary of £2 10s. a week. He instituted a Drill Certificate for teachers who proved competent in preliminary drill in turnings, left, right, left about and right about, in marching, slow and quick, and in company drill.

Opposition to military drill was voiced in the School Board Meetings as it was in Parliament. In 1875, on the

H

motion for a drill inspection two members proposed this amendment: 'that in the opinion of the Board reviews or inspections of boys in military fashion tend to create a passion for what is called "glory", pernicious in its consequences to thousands by diverting their thoughts and aspirations from honourable and useful labour to a life of idleness and all its terrible concomitants, dreaded as a plague by their parents'.   The amendment was lost by 3 votes to 12.   Again in the next year the School Board received petitions from the Workmen's Peace Association, the Pancras Working Men's Club, the Women's Peace and Arbitration Auxiliary and the Ratepayers to exclude the military element from drill, but the Board took no action.

While military drill continued to be done other forms of exercise of a gymnastic nature were introduced and in 1877 the Board resolved to equip the playgrounds of eighteen schools with gymnastic apparatus, but the appointment of Miss Löfving to introduce Swedish Gymnastics was for six months only in the first instance. Her reappointment was opposed in 1880 and in 1881. That her work was well supported in the schools there was no doubt.   Within a year of her appointment there had been applications from 600 schoolmistresses for her courses.

Miss Löfving resigned in 1881 and Miss Martina Bergman was appointed in her place in spite of opposition in the School Board.   Even when it became clear that the Swedish system had a great deal to recommend it for boys as well as for girls the Board would only agree to its adoption for boys in 1883, 'care being taken that the Military Drill required by the New Code of the Education Department in the case of boys be not interfered with'.

Swedish gymnastics had wealthy and powerful friends.

Lord Brabazon offered to pay for the equipping of a school with Swedish apparatus with a view to the establishment of school gymnasia throughout the metropolis. He also offered to pay the cost of appointing a male instructor from Sweden. In April 1884 therefore Captain Haasum, a Swedish army officer was engaged for six months to give instruction in Swedish exercises and the use of apparatus.

For a time Swedish gymnastics for boys and for girls developed in parallel and Miss Bergman and Captain Haasum of course co-operated. Miss Bergman started her own college for training teachers in 1885 but continued to work for the London School Board until 1888 by which year she had fully or partially trained 1,312 teachers and had introduced her system into 276 schools.[11] By that year she had become Madame Bergman Österberg, and in spite of the demands of her own college she would have been prepared to continue as an assessor of teachers in London had the Board been willing to accept her professional standards and the level of fees which she demanded. After Madame's departure the Swedish system continued in use for girls.

Physical education for boys took a rather different course. The death of Regimental Major Sheffield, the Drill Instructor, in 1888 provided an occasion for reorganisation, and two appointments were made. Dr. Allan Broman, who had come to England from Sweden and had already given gratuitous courses for teachers in the Swedish system, was appointed Organising Master of Physical Exercises in Boys' Departments at a salary of £250 per annum. Thomas Chesterton was appointed Physical Instructor in an assigned district in London to superintend what came to be called an English system of physical education at a salary of £150 per annum.

After two years, the original term of Dr. Broman's appointment, his engagement was terminated and the post was abolished on the grounds, according to Chesterton, that only thirty-one teachers had chosen the Swedish system in the previous year while 134 teachers had chosen the English system.[12]   Chesterton claimed that his system was eclectic from various continental systems and there may not have been a vast difference between the two. Certainly Chesterton asserted that his system, although combined with drill, was not preparatory military training, but was primarily designed to counteract the effects of school life.   A manual on the system was published but no tables of exercises were included.   Chesterton was adamant that no table of exercises, however scientifically arranged, should be countenanced because of the danger of the physical training lesson becoming a monotonous task to be repeated day after day until both teachers and pupils were thoroughly bored.

The substitution of some system of physical exercises for military drill was not confined to London.   As early as 1876 the Chairman of the Birmingham School Board had said publicly, 'we have a double duty to perform—we have the care over the physical health of the children who are entrusted in part to our charge, as well as over their mental education and we believe that the exercise of the body is, in fact, a part of the education and general instruction of the children'.   In 1880 a system of 'physical exercises' was introduced and staves, dumbbells, horizontal and parallel bars were supplied to any school whose headmaster asked for them.   Four years later a thousand children were receiving instruction in gymnastics on apparatus.   The Board was pleased with the results and in 1885 resolved that 'physical exercises should form part of the training given in all public elementary schools'.[13]

The training of teachers to conduct these programmes called for special measures and in 1886 the Board appointed one of its teachers, Samuel Bott, to be Superintendent Teacher of Physical Exercises, and at the same time laid down that twenty minutes daily should be devoted to physical exercises.[14] The Education Department's code of regulations did not allow for this to count as school 'attendance' and school hours had to be extended in order to accommodate the new subject. Classes were limited to sixty children per teacher and the exercises were to consist largely of formation, marching, running, the maze, free, dumbbell, and stave exercises. Manchester, Liverpool, Bristol and other of the larger school boards followed the example of London and Birmingham and appointed supervising instructors, who often came from the Army.[15] In Leeds, however, Swedish drill was introduced in 1883.[16]

An impetus was given to physical education by the Cross Commission which was appointed in 1886 to review the state of elementary education since 1870 and reported two years later. The commission was impressed by the evidence which was brought before it on the subject of physical training. Both teachers and the military authorities pressed for the inclusion of some system of physical exercises in elementary education, and in its report the commission made a recommendation to the same effect suggesting that the systems already put into operation by the War Office, by the Birmingham School Board and by the London School Board through Mrs. Bergman Österberg, might be more widely adopted.[17] In 1890 therefore the Education Department 'recognised' physical exercises as well as 'drill',[18] but the work continued to be based largely upon military handbooks together with MacLaren's *System of Physical Education*, which was republished in 1895.

In 1895 the Education Department at last made physical education eligible for grant as a subject of instruction. The system of payment by results was still in operation and it was obviously difficult to examine the results of physical education in the same way that the results of instruction in the three Rs were examined. To obviate the difficulty the Education Department issued a statement that 'after 31st August 1895 the higher grant for Discipline and Organisation will not be paid to any school in which provision is not made for instruction in Swedish or other drill or suitable physical exercises'.[19] Swedish drill and physical exercises were during this period confined to free standing exercises without the use of climbing or other fixed apparatus. The government's 'Rules to be Observed in Planning and Fitting up Schools', which were published from time to time from 1871 onwards, did specify in later editions that playgrounds and halls of certain dimensions must be provided but as late as 1902 the 'Rules' stated, 'since fixed gymnastic apparatus is unsuitable for children under 14 years of age, a separate gymnasium is not required and cannot be approved'.[20]

By making *per capita* grants for discipline, a higher one of one and sixpence and a lower one of a shilling, and by making schools which did not include physical exercises in their curricula ineligible for the higher grant, the Education Department gave an inducement to schools to provide physical education. At the same time the official attitude to the subject was revealed; physical education was primarily for discipline.

It was the need for better discipline in the Public

Schools which had first led Cotton and other Arnoldian headmasters earlier in the century to sanction and encourage organised games. It was the same need that encouraged the introduction of drill and physical exercises into public elementary schools and there is no doubt that the problem of indiscipline and unruliness among children in urban areas was a major one. The difference between the two methods of tackling the same problem in different types of school is remarkable. Many inspectors and others interested in physical education would have liked to have used games in elementary schools as they had been used in Public Schools. Chesterton, in reporting on his own system of physical exercises, said that games were the best form of physical training, but were quite impracticable in the Metropolitan area.[21] In London schools as in other large cities, with their huge classes of children drawn from homes where dirt, disorder and illiteracy were common, the problem was not so much at first to give instruction as to establish conditions in which instruction could be given. Drill was used to this end, nor is it easy to see how any other form of physical activity could have been provided with the facilities that then existed. In 1895 Her Majesty's Inspector for the Metropolitan Division estimated that there were 25,000 scholars within one mile of Charing Cross with no playground at all, and in most parts of London very few playgrounds worth the name were to be found.[22] In such circumstances it required great ingenuity to provide any physical exercise at all and often the class would be divided into five squads, four squads standing at ease or marching round while one squad performed exercises in the middle. Buildings and facilities and the background of the children therefore encouraged, if they did not actually dictate, Government policy of 'sharp obedience, smartness, order and cleanliness' through the medium of the Swedish and other systems.[22]

The Swedish system, which has been so closely linked with the name of Ling, and the 'harmonious development of the whole body', first commended itself to the Education Department and the school boards as much for its disciplinary value as for the scientific principles upon which it was based.

By 1895, therefore, social and economic conditions had produced in England two distinct systems of physical Education, one for the privileged rich and the other for the under-privileged poor. Contemporary writers did not shut their eyes to this situation. On the contrary, Wallace MacLaren, in a preface to a new edition of his father's book, described the existing state of affairs clearly and concisely.

'In dealing practically with such a question [gymnastics in the education of all classes] a broad distinction must at once be drawn. On the one side we have to deal with the upper and middle classes, in fact with all that large class who are sent to private and Public Schools or training colleges for their education, and proceed to the army, to the Universities or to business life. On the other side is the still larger class of those whom the nation educates, a class which the subject of gymnastics may be thought to touch more nearly, in as much as, after an early age, they have little or no time for recreation like those socially above them, and the gymnasium is therefore to them a vital source of health.

'The requirements of these two classes physically are in themselves distinct, and must be dealt with from an altogether different standpoint.'[23]

Either in spite of or because of the appalling facilities for physical education in State-aided elementary schools, many inspectors looked ahead and made recommendations which were only implemented long afterwards. Medical examination of schoolchildren,[24] the provision of gymnastic apparatus[25] and the inclusion of organised games in the curriculum because, as one inspector put it, military drill and callisthenic exercises with clubs and dumbbells were not enough,[26] were all put forward as recommendations by different inspectors. Within the schools teachers were not content with mere recommendations. They were struck by the contrast between the bored faces of children at drill and the 'happy joyous delight' that they showed when at play in the yard. Their own interest in team games led them to help and encourage the playing of such games by their children. They arranged games against neighbouring schools in parks or on the nearest available ground and they organised school clubs for football, cricket and other sports. From this enthusiastic and devoted work by teachers outside school hours, sprang in 1885 the South London Schools' Football Association.[27] A number of School Boards responded to the enthusiasm of teachers. In London, for instance, it was resolved in 1888 that 'the playgrounds attached to schools be used for the formation of clubs for hardy sports, gymnastic exercises and drill, and that the school organisations be used for the establishment of field clubs and swimming classes'. The Chairman of the Board was also asked to convene a meeting to consider organised physical education out of school hours.[28]

Soon the organisation of school games by teachers became a national movement. The South London Schools' F.A. became the Elementary Schools' Football

Association, and by 1895 teachers in Birmingham,
Brighton, Cardiff, Huddersfield, Liverpool, Manchester,
Nottingham, Sunderland and many other large towns
were organising inter-school competitions in football,
cricket, athletics or swimming. Swimming was actually
included in the school curriculum in London and 12,000
children were taught to swim between 1894 and 1896,[27]
but, by and large, swimming, together with other sports
and games, depended upon the initiative and enthusiasm
of pupils and teachers working together without financial
assistance from local or central government.

Nowhere was the out-of-school organisation of games
more highly developed than in Birmingham, where
teachers received much help from the Birmingham
Athletic Institute. Founded in 1866 by a few enthusiasts
who wished to practise gymnastics, the Birmingham
Athletic Club, as it was then called, quickly turned to
other activities and to a wider public. In 1868 three
bicycles were provided and at the annual display in 1868
Professor Hubbard appeared on the floor of the hall on a
bicycle 'and the ease with which he controlled the instrument was the theme of universal approbation'.[29] Later,
about 1880, at the invitation of the School Board for
Birmingham, the members devoted themselves to school
activities and the training of teachers for the board schools.
Under the auspices of the institute cricket, football, swimming, running and gymnastics were systematically
organised and financed. Competitions were organised
and the finals were played on well-known grounds, the
football final at Villa Park and the cricket final on the
county ground. Swimming too was organised with the
help of the City Baths Committee, who granted free passes
to the baths to children who learned to swim.[30]

The work of the B.A.I. and of many teachers in other cities did not fail to win the approval of Her Majesty's Inspectors,[31] and the *Annual Report* of the Education Department in 1897–8 welcomed the efforts of teachers 'to secure for the scholars in elementary schools some of the advantages of that side of school discipline and comradeship which has become a characteristic feature of higher grades of English education'.[31] Nevertheless games were not eligible for financial grant as were Swedish drill and physical exercises, nor was there at this time any official encouragement to school boards to provide facilities and equipment for games.

It was in 1900 that the newly constituted Board of Education first instructed inspectors that games were a suitable alternative to Swedish drill or physical exercises as far as the conditions of the code were concerned. Games were to be supervised by some member of staff 'who should teach the most skilful method of play, and should encourage orderly behaviour and stop quarrelling.'[32] However, the hard realities of the situation were inescapable. Games were still impracticable in many city schools and some form of drill or gymnastics seemed the only possible alternative. But recognition of games had been won even if facilities had not been provided.

Two other sectors of the educational system where physical education was developed in the latter part of the century were those for the education of juvenile delinquents and waifs and strays in so-called Industrial Schools and for further education in Day Continuation Schools.

Industrial Schools had been first established between 1835 and 1855 as remedial measures for the prevention of juvenile crime. The Act of 1870 required School Boards to provide such schools for a population which was described in a report to the Board for London in these words: 'The streets swarmed with waifs and strays who had never attended school, a number of whom habitually frequented the riverside, the London railway termini, the purlieus of Drury Lane and Seven Dials, and courts of Holborn and the Strand . . . and many similar parts of the metropolis. These children slept together in gangs in such places as the Adelphi arches, on barges, on the steps of London Bridge, in empty boxes and boilers at Bankside, in empty packing cases down the "Shades" covered over with tarpaulins and old sacks.' Healthy food was the first need of these children but by the end of the century the Industrial Schools tried to provide gymnastics drill and swimming, organised for them cricket, football and boxing and ran summer camps.[33]

Day Continuation Schools for boys and girls in factories included in their programme various forms of drill and dancing, but although the government requested Her Majesty's Inspectors to report on experiments to make evening classes more attractive by means of gymnastics or recreative activities, Sir John Gorst for the government roundly condemned dancing as a suitable form of physical exercise for grant earning purposes.[34]

The turn of the century was indeed the start of a new era for physical education. The Board of Education had been set up in 1899, a comprehensive organisation of elementary and secondary education could not long be delayed, and the Boer War was already drawing attention to the shocking physical condition of recruits for the army. In the development of physical education military needs were proving a more powerful persuasive force than educational theory had been.

Chapter 7.   References

1 M. D. Roth, *A Plea for the Compulsory Teaching of the Elements of Physical Education in our National Elementary Schools, or the claims of physical education to rank with reading writing and arithmetic*. London, 1870.

2 M. D. Roth, *On the Neglect of Physical Education and Hygiene by Parliament and the Education Department, etc.*, London, 1879.

3 *Hansard*, 17 February 1870, Vol. 199, Col. 444.

4 E. G. Holland, formerly headmaster of Highgate Elementary School, personal communication.

5 *Minutes of the School Board for London*, 31 July 1872, 30 April 1873, 5 November 1873, 2 August 1876.

6 *R.E.D.*, 1872–3, p. 52.

7 M. D. Roth, *On the Neglect of Physical Education and Hygiene by Parliament and the Education Department*, London, 1879.

8 *Hansard*, 1 July 1875, Vol. 222, Col. 1409: Vol. 225, Col. 794.

9 *Minutes of the School Board for London*, 18 December 1878.

10 For the development of physical education in London schools 1871–92 see the *Minutes of the School Board for London*, 25 January 1871, 1 February 1871, 19 June 1872, 15 January 1873, 14 July 1875, March 1876, 21 November 1876, 18 December 1878, 8 December 1881, 8 November 1883, 3 April 1884, 19 February 1885, 6 August 1885, 14 February 1889, 7 March 1889, 6 October 1892.

11 Jonathan May, *The Contribution of Madame Bergman Österberg to the Development of British Education*. M. Ed. thesis, University of Leicester, 1967, p. 28.

12 *E. D., Special Inquiries and Reports*, 1898, Vol. 2, pp. 186ff. T. Chesterton, *Physical Education under the School Board for London*.

13 D. D. Molyneux, *The Development of Physical Recreation in the Birmingham District from 1871–1892*, M.A. thesis, University of Birmingham, 1957, p. 217.

14 *Birmingham School Board Report*, 1886, pp. 45–6.

15 E. Major in *Textbook of Gymnastics* by L. E. Christensen and P. M. Trap, London, 1938, pp. 19–20.

16 *E.D., Special Inquiries and Reports* 1898, R. E. Thomas, *Physical Training under the Leeds School Board*.

17 *Final Report of the Cross Commission*, 1888, p. 145.

18 *R.E.D.*, 1889–90, p. 118.
19 *R.E.D.*, 1893–4, p. 333.
20 *E.D.*, Rules to be Observed in Planning and Fitting up Schools, 1871, 1885, 1891 and 1899, and *Board of Education*, Rules to be Observed in Planning and Fitting up Public Elementary Schools, 1902.
21 *E.D.*, Special Inquiries and Reports, 1898, Vol. 2, p. 188.
22 *R.E.D.*, 1895–6, p. 134.
23 A. MacLaren, *Physical Education*, Oxford, 1895. Preface by Wallace MacLaren, p. vi.
24 H.M.I. W. Scott Coward, *R.E.D.*, 1889–90, p. 303.
25 H.M.I. Rev. T. W. Sharp, *R.E.D.*, 1894–5, p. 134.
26 H.M.I. Danby, *R.E.D.*, 1889–90, p. 362.
27 *E.D.*, *Special Inquiries and Reports*, 1898, Vol. 2, p. 159 and p. 194.
28 *Final Report of the School Board for London 1870–1904*, p. 97.
29 E. L. Levy, *History of the Birmingham Athletic Club 1866–1898*, Birmingham, 1898.
30 *R.B.E.*, 1899–1900, p. 173.
31 *R.E.D.*, 1897–8, p. xx and p. 173.
32 *R.B.E.*, 1899–1900, p. 633.
33 *Final Report of the School Board for London 1870–1904*, p. 298.
34 *Hansard* 7 May 1901, Col. 984–5.

CHAPTER 8

The Education of Girls and the Training of Teachers

IN the early part of the nineteenth century girls from the middle classes who were not educated at home went to private schools where a very low level of intellectual attainment was reached and where social accomplishments such as needlework, music and deportment were allowed a considerable amount of time but were badly taught. The Taunton Commission set up in 1868 to examine girls' as well as boys' schools inveighed heavily against the state of middle class female education.[1] Herbert Spencer in his Essay on Physical Education had already condemned with particular emphasis the lack of physical education in the general education of girls.

'We have a vague suspicion that to produce a robust physique is thought undesirable; that rude health and abundant vigour are considered somewhat plebeian; that a certain delicacy of strength not competent to sustain more than a mile or two's walk, an appetite fastidious and easily satisfied joined with that timidity which commonly accompanies feebleness, are held more ladylike. We do not expect that any would distinctly avow this; but we fancy the governess mind is haunted by an ideal young lady bearing not a little resemblance to this type. If so, it must be admitted that the established system is admirably calculated to realise this ideal.'[2]

Mr. Fearon, appointed by the Taunton Commission to report on the Metropolitan area, confirmed Herbert Spencer's impression. An analysis of his returns from 100 private schools for girls shows that sixty provided no form of exercise other than 'walking abroad, croquet, and dancing', while thirty-two provided nothing but a form of callisthenics.[3] Even where callisthenics was provided the commissioner noted that upper middle class parents failed to appreciate their value, and as they were expensive, parents refused to pay the extra fee. Mr. Fearon commented on the prevalence of failures in health and attributed them in large part to the neglect of physical training.[4]

However, even at the time when the Taunton Commission was sitting, two pioneers of girls' education were already at work. Frances Mary Buss and Dorothea Beale had both been pupils at Queen's College, which had been founded in 1848 on the initiative of F. D. Maurice and Charles Kingsley, both protagonists of 'muscular Christianity'. Miss Buss later started her own school, which developed into the North London Collegiate School. Miss Beale was appointed headmistress of Cheltenham Ladies' College in 1858. Both believed that girls were capable of as great intellectual achievement as boys and to a great extent their schools were counterparts of boys' schools. The problem of providing a counterpart in physical education was of great concern to them. They were in agreement with Herbert Spencer on the unsatisfactory nature of current practices, but the rough sports of contemporary boys' Public Schools were unsuitable for girls.

Miss Buss solved the problem by making callisthenics compulsory four times a week while the younger girls were encouraged to take exercise in the playground.[5] Miss Beale also introduced callisthenics but when she gave evidence before the Taunton Commission she was far from content with the physical education at her school. 'The vigorous exercise which boys get from cricket etc., must be supplied in the case of girls by walking and callisthenic exercises, skipping etc. We have a room specially fitted up with swings etc.: It is to be wished that croquet could be abolished, it gives no proper exercise, induces colds, and places the body in a crooked posture; besides, as it does not fatigue, girls are able to go on for five or six hours and induced to be idle. It would seem worthwhile to inquire what is done in America respecting exercise. I believe they pay more attention to this subject than we.'[6]

Miss Beale was obviously not aware that the influence of America was already making itself felt in England. The musical gymnastics of Dio Lewis had been imported by Mr. Moses Coit Taylor some three years previously, and had found its way into twenty girls' schools in London where it so favourably impressed Mr. Fearon that he wrote a detailed account of it (fig. 5). This account was published as an appendix to the *Report* of the Taunton Commission.[7] Wherever there was spare ground available Mr. Fearon could not too strongly impress upon the proprietors of schools 'that they ought to provide their pupils with games which shall be sufficiently difficult to thoroughly divert their minds'. But for schools without much spare room either outside or inside, Mr. Dio Lewis's musical gymnastics provided a better solution to the problem of providing physical education than any of the current practices. Neither the commissioners nor witnesses mentioned Ling's gymnastics which Mathias Roth

I

Dumbbell exercises for women devised by Dio Lewis from
The New Gymnastics, 1866.

FIGURE 5.

had been trying to popularise in England since the early eighteen-fifties. Roth's gratuitous training of teachers sent by the Educational Union[8] can have had little effect upon the general educational system.

Following the report of the Taunton Commission, Parliament passed the Endowed Schools Act in 1869 which laid it down that 'in framing schemes under the Act, provision shall be made, as far as conveniently may be, for extending to girls the benefits of endowments'.[9] In many towns sister schools to existing boys' schools were founded. Other schools were started as commercial ventures on the lines of boys' proprietary schools. These banded together to form the Girls' Public Day School Trust. Other schools again were founded as boarding schools and were closely modelled on boys' Public Schools. One of the earliest was St. Leonard's, founded at St. Andrews in Scotland in 1877. From the beginning St. Leonard's contained many features taken directly from boys' Public Schools, including a house system, a prefect system, and organised outdoor games. Soon other schools on similar lines were founded in England and so something of the Public School cult of games found its way into girls' Schools.

It was between about 1885 and the end of the century that the great development of physical education in girls' schools took place. At first some surprise and even opposition was aroused by the novel practices of the pioneer schools. Roedean, which was founded in 1885, insisted on two hours' exercise in winter and three hours' in summer. Not only did the school encourage running, swimming, gymnastics, fencing and dancing, but also hockey, tennis, and cricket. The headmistress of Roedean was convinced that the moral value of games which was accepted as a truism in boys' schools must have similar respect in girls' schools. 'Considered merely as exercise and recreation' she wrote, 'other agencies might replace them, but considered as a means of training character they stand alone and they provide precisely that element in girls' education which has hitherto been lacking.' Such a programme was unheard of for girls in England,[10] and special precautions had to be taken so that the dress worn for playing games did not 'excite attention by any eccentricity'. A similarly wide programme was to be found later at Wycombe Abbey School, whose head-mistress, Miss J. F. Dove, had come from St. Leonard's. Miss Dove's recommended syllabus included lawn tennis, fives, bowls, croquet, quoits, golf, swimming, skating, archery, tobogganing, basketball, rounders and hailes as well as lacrosse, hockey and cricket.[11] National prestige and the expansion of the empire, which at the end of the century were so closely associated in men's minds with the playing fields of boys' Public Schools, were also used by Miss Dove to justify games in her own school. 'Most of the qualities,' she said, 'if not all, that conduce to the supremacy of our country in so many quarters of the globe, are fostered, if not solely developed, by means of games.' Thus girls, as well as boys, were to be educated to shoulder the responsibilities of empire.

There was one significant difference between physical education at boys' Public Schools and girls' secondary schools. While boys' schools tended to regard games as the be-all and end-all of physical education, girls' schools did not. Many schoolmistresses realised that games ought to be supplemented by careful observation of children's development, and by systematic physical training. At Roedean the training must have been tough.

The headmistress reported in 1898 that some years previously not one girl could show her head above the horizontal bar from the hanging position, whereas at the time of writing, half the upper school and many in the lower school could do this, and nearly every girl could go hand over hand up a sixteen foot rope. At Wycombe Abbey Miss Dove did not consider that it was safe to allow girls to indulge in outdoor games without restriction or unless they were receiving systematic muscular training in the gymnasium. Two gymnastic lessons per week were the rule and the gymnastics mistress carefully noted the girls' physical development and gave corrective exercises when they were needed. She also used measurements of height and weight as aids in assessing the health of her pupils. Similar organisation of physical education was to be found by the end of the century in day schools as well as boarding schools, and at Sheffield High School girls entering the school with incipient postural defects were even placed in a lower form than they would otherwise have been, so that adequate attention might be paid to remedial treatment.[12]

The execution of a system of physical education and therapy as elaborate as those at Wycombe Abbey and Sheffield called for teachers with high specialist qualification. The headmistresses of both schools had appointed as their gymnastics mistresses former students of the Central Institute of Gymnastics in Stockholm, but as the merits of their comprehensive scheme of physical education were more widely recognised, a local supply of specialist teachers was needed. It was to meet just such a need that Miss Bergman founded her physical training college in 1885.

The introduction of military drill into elementary

schools had presented few problems in supplying instructors. Apart from the instructors whom the War Office
made available to the Education Department in 1871 at
sixpence a day,[13] many men's training colleges had, since
1860, enrolled their students into a volunteer corps and a
modicum of military training was thus acquired. Moreover the *Field Exercise Book*, which was recommended for
use in schools, was probably adequate even for those who
had not themselves experienced the drilling of a sergeant
instructor. Apart from military drill the training colleges
made little or no provision for the physical education of
their students, a defect which deeply impressed Matthew
Arnold who had visited training colleges in Germany and
Switzerland and seen the provision for gymnastics at
Küssnacht in Canton Zurich.[13] Life at English training
colleges was spartan indeed. If students found time for
games, they had to secure the use of a ground and pay for
it out of their own slender funds; a trapeze or horizontal
bar might be erected in the college grounds so that those
who cared to might amuse themselves at gymnastic feats;
the only regular exercise was the weekly drill session under
a sergeant of volunteers. Women fared no better than
men. At the London College for Women, the only
exercise taken was a 'daily walk two by two along the
same road preceded by two or three governesses all primly
dressed'. 'The only time when students were permitted
to go out unaccompanied was on Saturday afternoons
when freedom was enjoyed until roll call at 5 or 7 p.m. . . .
Then one recalls the physical education of those days,
before drill costumes were thought of, when, in thick
boots and long frocks, the students were drilled by a
military sergeant once a week.'[14] The Cross Commission
reporting in 1888 had knowledge of only two colleges, at

Edge Hill, Liverpool, and Whitelands Training College, where teachers in training had any kind of course in physical exercises. Students from Edge Hill College went to the Liverpool gymnasium once a week and received instruction in simple gymnastic exercises from the Director, Mr. Alexander.[15] At Whitelands, Madame Österberg had introduced Ling's gymnastics.

A large number of teachers never went to training colleges but entered the profession as pupil teachers. Their physical welfare was a matter of concern to many inspectors. Girls or 'young female teachers', as they were referred to, would spend five to six hours a day with large classes and receive one hour of instruction from the head teacher. Above this they had private preparation and no opportunity to indulge in 'rougher exercises by which their colleagues of the other sex were wont to counteract the sedentariness of their pursuit'. H.M.I. Rev. C. H. Parez was concerned about the prevalence of stooping backs and round shoulders and wished to see more callisthenics and an official inquiry into the means provided by school managers for the preservation of health of young teachers.[16] Pupil teachers were as ill catered for as students in training colleges, and the Education Department, when approached by Matthias Roth on the introduction of gymnastics, refused to take any action on the grounds of 'lack of time'.[17]

The arrival of Swedish drill and the general adoption of 'physical exercises' as well as, or instead of, military drill raised new problems. Sergeant instructors were not ideally suited to the new approach to drill, but except in very few areas neither teachers in schools nor teachers in training were being qualified to take classes of children in the new systems. The employment of military instructors was perforce continued in many districts; gradually, however, the superintendent teachers, which some school boards appointed from 1878 onwards, together with a number of voluntary institutions, succeeded in training a large number of teachers in various systems of exercises.

Matthias Roth had in the early seventies trained a number of teachers in Ling's gymnastics gratuitously.[18] The appointment of Miss Löfving to train London school teachers was the first attempt by a school board to meet the growing need among teachers for guidance in conducting physical exercises. Miss Löfving thought that once children knew the movements 500 could be made to perform them with great accuracy under one teacher. The demand, however, was too great to be met by courses run by the few school boards that were capable of holding them, and both local organisations, like the Birmingham Athletic Institute, and national organisations, like the Amateur Gymnastic Association and the British College of Physical Education, took up the task of training teachers in physical exercises. The latter body was set up in 1891 for the express purposes of training teachers and protecting the good name of instructors who were already in practice.[19] Before 1891 an instructor could produce no guarantee of competence. The British College of Physical Education, therefore, made provision for members, licentiates and associates. Members could only be elected after passing an examination in both German and Swedish systems of gymnastics. Licentiates held a preliminary qualification and were only licensed to serve under fully qualified instructors. Associate membership was open to anyone interested in physical education and carried with it no certificate of competence. With such stringent conditions for membership the college naturally did not have a very large membership. By 1903 there were 114 members, of whom 71 were women. Nevertheless the college did valuable work in teaching teachers and in 1900 it was recognised by the Board of Education as a suitable body to issue certificates of competence. The other bodies recognised at the same time were the military authorities at Aldershot, the Amateur Gymnastic Association, and the Birmingham Athletic Institute.[20] Physical education for elementary schoolchildren had been almost forced upon the Government by the enthusiasm and far-sightedness of private individuals, and however anxious individual inspectors were to foster the growth of physical education, the Government was quite content that the training of teachers, who alone could make that possible, should remain in the hands of private individuals and voluntary organisations.

Perhaps the most enterprising and far-reaching experiment in training teachers was made by Miss Bergman. She had succeeded Miss Löfving as Superintendent Teacher to the London School Board in 1881 and in 1885, while continuing to work for the London School Board, she set up her own training college in Hampstead. Later, in 1895, the college moved to Dartford and there the Bergman Österberg Physical Training College became the first residential college for training specialist teachers in physical education. There was a strong feminist motive in her pioneer work. To the International Council of Women she said: 'I will not labour, but let us once for all discard man as a physical trainer of women; let us send the drill sergeant right about face to his awkward squad. This work we women do better, as our very success in training depends upon our having felt like women, able to calculate the possibilities of our sex, knowing our weakness and our strength.'[21] So it was that the men whom she at first engaged on her staff to teach cricket, lawn tennis and vaulting were replaced as soon as possible by her own former students.

Towards the end of the century and at the beginning of the next, other colleges for training women specialists were founded.   One of these, Miss Rhoda Anstey's college which was started near Birmingham in 1899, adopted the Swedish system from the start.   Other colleges began on other lines and only took over Swedish gymnastics later. Chelsea College was started in 1898 in connection with the Polytechnic and used the German system of exercises. The work of the college did not become entirely Swedish until 1905.   Battersea College, which, like Chelsea, was first run in connection with a Polytechnic, was not reorganised on Swedish lines until 1913.   In Southport, near Liverpool, Mr. and Mrs. Alexander opened their training college and gymnasium in 1891 and offered training in many systems of gymnastics, games, swimming and fencing to enable students to become teachers.   They did not, however, offer Swedish gymnastics until 1906 and six years later they found it necessary to engage a woman teacher from the Central Gymnastic Institute in Stockholm.

Irene Marsh was a pupil of the Alexanders in 1893 and in 1904 advertised the Liverpool Gymnasium and Training College for Gymnastics and Sports Mistresses. Although she employed a Swedish teacher to teach gymnastics her system was not entirely Swedish.   She used musical drill and refused to give it up in spite of pressure from teachers of Swedish gymnastics.   Similar resistance to the overriding demands of the 'Swedish' champions was offered by Beatrice and Evelyn Bear who started a gymnasium for intending women teachers at Queen Alexandra's House in 1898. Only after the 1914–18 war did this college drop the mention of British Gymnastics from prospectus and testimonials. This action was taken after students had petitioned the Misses Bear because they were finding it difficult to obtain posts in competition with applicants who had had a purer and more intensive training in Swedish gymnastics.[22]

Miss Anstey's action in opening the first college for Swedish gymnastics after the Bergman Österberg college was at first regarded by the Swedish gymnastic world of Britain as an act of disloyalty and effrontery rather than an expansion and development of the gospel of hygiene and physical education which it really was.[23] In 1903 physical training colleges for women were opened at Bedford, Bournemouth and Manchester, and their students studied Swedish gymnastics. All these colleges were private institutions for fee-paying students and, for forty years or more, none had any financial assistance from the State. They therefore tended to draw their students from middle class families who could afford the fees for board and tuition which they demanded. In opening the way for a respectable career the colleges fitted in well with the movement of women's emancipation.

Halévy has pointed out in his *History of the English People* that although an Act of Parliament had in 1875 permitted universities to confer degrees on women and another had forbidden the Royal College of Surgeons to exclude them, it was still difficult, in the years before 1914, for women to enter many professions. Women medical students were rarely admitted to study in hospitals and many went abroad for their training. Even then the hospitals would not accept them as doctors. The Universities of Oxford and Cambridge continued to refuse to admit women to examinations in medicine, theology and law. The one career which had been open to women all through the 19th century was teaching, and, during the second half of the century, after the foundation of Queen's College, Harley Street, in 1848, the number of Girls' High Schools and Public Schools grew steadily. It was to these schools, for the upper and middle classes, that women specialists in physical education found their way.

The pioneers of the Bergman-Österberg College made a great impact on the country in many respects. Two achievements of the early years of the college were the devising of the game of netball from the American game of basketball and the designing of the gym tunic which became almost universally adopted for physical education and many games by girls and women.

A third achievement, however, was only made in the teeth of opposition from Madame. Many of her former students by the turn of the century felt the need for a professional organisation. 'On Monday, January 9th 1899, an informal meeting was held at the Hampstead Gymnasium by thirty-one old students of Madame Österberg's Physical Training College, with the object of forming what is now called the "Ling Association." '[24]

It was decided to admit as members all women trained at Madame Österberg's or the Central Institute, Stockholm. The association was established for the purpose of banding together the graduates of these institutions, with the intention of placing physical education on a higher basis than before; of ultimately obtaining a registered list of those duly qualified to teach Swedish gymnastics and to give massage in a thoroughly trained manner; and of arranging meetings and holiday courses at different times.[24]   It was announced that Madame had agreed to be president, but Madame was on holiday at the time and on her return she wrote to all her former students saying that the name of the new association, the Swedish Physical Educationalists, was impossible and absurd and that she had no connection with the association.   In the next year she founded her own rival organisation of Dartford students and refused to co-operate with the Ling Association in any way for the rest of her life.[25]   Nevertheless the foundation of the Ling Physical Education Association gave a firm foundation for the build-up of therapeutic gymnastics in the 20th century.   It was from the start determined to promote the Swedish system exclusively and rejected the application of Irene Marsh's college for affiliation because the principal refused to abandon other systems of exercise when she introduced the Swedish system.

The 19th century had witnessed three major developments in physical education, each largely independent of the others.   In the boys' Public Schools organised games and athleticism developed into a cult of overriding importance in the education which was provided by those schools.   In the elementary schools drill and drill-like exercises were evolved to meet the exigencies of appalling facilities and huge classes of unruly children.   In girls' secondary schools therapeutic gymnastics were imported to meet the needs of health as well as beauty.   Although by the end of the century the Government had recognised the value of organised games for elementary school-children, it was only in some of the girls' secondary schools that games, gymnastics and drill had begun to be welded into a comprehensive scheme of physical education.

Chapter 8.   References

1   *R.S.I.C.*, Vol. I, pp. 548–9.
2   Herbert Spencer, *Education: Intellectual, Moral and Physical*, London, 1859. Ed. 1891, pp. 152–3.
3   *R.S.I.C.*, Vol. VII, pp. 556, 562, 566.
4   *Op. cit.*, p. 388.
5   *R.S.I.C.*, Vol. V, p. 265.
6   *Op. cit.*, p. 740.
7   *R.S.I.C.*, Vol. VII, Appendix XII, pp. 587ff.
8   *Hansard*, 1 July 1875, Vol. 225, Col. 794.
9   Endowed Schools Act 1869, Par. 12.
10 *E.D.*, *Special Inquiries and Reports*, Vol. II, p. 145.   Miss P. Lawrence, 'Games and Athletics in Secondary Schools for Girls'.
11 Dorothea Beale, Lucy H. M. Soulsby and Jane Frances Dove, *Work and Play in Girls' Schools*, London, 1901, Chap. III.
12 *E.D.*, *Special Inquiries and Reports*, Vol. II, p. 133. Mrs. Woodhouse, 'Physical Education at Sheffield High School for Girls'.
13 See Chapter 7.
14 *R.B.E.*, 1912–13. 'History of the Training of Teachers', pp. 57, 66.
15 *Report of the Cross Commission*, Vol. II, p. 497, Minutes 29483 and 52174.
16 *R.E.D.*, 1872–3, p. 112.
17 See Chapter 6.
18 *Hansard*, 1 July 1875, Vol. 225, Col. 794.
19 *Annual Report of British College of Physical Education*, 1912.
20 *R.B.E.*, 1900–1, p. 633.
21 J. May, *The Contribution of Madame Bergman Österberg to British Education*, M. Ed. thesis, University of Leicester, 1967, p. 78.
22 I. Webb, *Women's Physical Education in Great Britain 1800–1966*, M. Ed. thesis University of Leicester, 1966.
23 Barbara Whitelaw, *E. Adair Impey. Letters of Remembrance by some of her family and friends*, Guernsey Press, 1965.
24 *Annual Report of Ling Association*, 1899, quoted in *Journal of P.E.*, March 1949, p. 31.
25 Barbara Whitelaw, *op. cit.*

CHAPTER 9

New Ideas and the Shocks of the Boer War

ON 24 March 1902 the Balfour Education Bill was introduced into the House of Commons. It was discussed in committee on the same day that the end of the Boer War was announced. The awakening of public opinion upon education and the subsequent passage of educational legislation were features of each major war in which Britain was involved during the first half of the 20th century. The Balfour Act of 1902, the Fisher Act of 1918 and the Butler Act of 1944 were all prompted by a concern for future generations which was sharpened by the insecurity of the immediate present. The Balfour Act itself did not specifically reform physical education, but the same ideas which prompted the act also profoundly influenced the theory and practice of physical education, and the Act itself did provide the administrative framework without which the subsequent rapid development of physical education would hardly have been possible.

In 1894 a Department of Special Inquiries on Educational Subjects was set up under Mr. (afterwards Sir) Michael Sadler to investigate and report on systems and methods of education at home and abroad. The contrast between the logical and centralised schemes abroad and the chaos which had developed in Britain since W. E.

Forster's Act 'to fill up gaps' in 1870, was at once evident.

In 1899 the Board of Education was established by Act of Parliament to unify in one department the educational functions previously exercised by the Education Department of the Privy Council, the Department of Science and Art in South Kensington and the educational functions of the Charity Commissioners. The way for the passage of Mr. Balfour's Bill through Parliament was now clear.

It is interesting to note here that in the period 1901–14 with its great developments in public health and national insurance as well as in education, the leading ideas in nearly all social policies were imported from abroad. So it was with physical education. Scandinavia was visited by officers of the armed services as well as by representatives of the Board of Education, and many Danish and Swedish practices were copied in our schools, drill halls and gymnasia.

Michael Sadler appointed as his assistant in the Office of Special Inquiries Robert Morant, a man of ambition who was determined to introduce order into the organisation of English education and who became the real architect of the bill presented to Parliament by Mr. Balfour. When this bill was finally enacted the school boards were swept away and replaced by local education authorities which were the county and county borough councils, now made responsible for both secondary and elementary education, and by certain 'Part III' authorities responsible only for elementary education, so called because they were dealt with in Part III of the Act. Education was reorganised on a municipal basis and thus brought into the main stream of local finance. However, the so-called 'dual system' was retained. Some schools were 'provided' by the L.E.A., others, 'non-provided' denominational schools, were eligible to receive aid from the rates, but the cost of capital expenditure on buildings, as well as of structural repairs and alterations, was thrown on the religious body to which each school belonged. This sometimes worked to the disadvantage of physical education. One of the great needs was space and facilities for games and physical activities. However well intentioned in this matter religious bodies might be, they often could not find the money to provide the facilities which the Government and public opinion began to demand. Representatives of the Church, therefore, were found in strong opposition to measures for the compulsory improvement of buildings and playgrounds. When, for instance, in 1912 a Departmental Committee on Playgrounds recommended legislation to ensure adequate playgrounds or playing fields for new schools, and conformity of existing schools to fixed standards,[1] it was hotly opposed by the 'Church Schools Emergency League' on the ground that the great majority of existing church schools (i.e. non-provided schools) would have to be closed. The league admitted that in Birmingham all church schools had less playground space than the fifteen square feet per child recommended by the committee, yet these were the conditions which the league wished and strove to perpetuate[2].

Fortunately for physical education Robert Morant, an ardent Old Wykehamist, who became Permanent Secretary of the Board of Education, was as keen on the physical welfare and physical development of children as he was upon administrative tidiness. His preface to the New Code of Regulations for Elementary Schools in 1904 reveals a new and refreshing official attitude to education. 'The purpose of the Public Elementary School is to form and strengthen the character and to develop the

K

intelligence of the children entrusted to it, and to make the best use of the school years available, in assisting both girls and boys according to their different needs, to fit themselves, practically as well as intellectually, for the work of life. . . . The school must afford them [the children] every opportunity for the development of their bodies, not only by training them in appropriate physical exercises and in encouraging them in organised games, but also by instructing them in the working of some of the simpler laws of health. . . . The corporate life of the school, especially in the playground, should develop that instinct for fair play and for loyalty to one another which is the germ of a wider sense of honour in later life.'[3] Gone was the notion of education being a condescending charity to the poor. The idea that no more was required of physical education than the inculcation of habits of sharp obedience, cleanliness and smartness was markedly absent. Rather physical education was now to play its part in the development of character and social living. Gone was the day when in 1901 grant could be withdrawn from evening continuation schools because some had included dancing in their physical education, and when swimming instruction was only permitted on dry land.[4] A broader conception of physical education was at hand and Morant was preparing the way for some infusion of the Public School 'spirit of the game' into elementary schools. Already in 1900 the Board of Education had envisaged the development of physical education to include games wherever circumstances permitted, but no provision for games had been included in the elementary school code of regulations. The man who took the initiative in securing an alteration in the code was one of His Majesty's Inspectors, Mr. A. P. Graves. In 1904, he found that the Marchioness of Londonderry, wife of the President of the Board of Education, was interested, like himself, in physical education, and at her suggestion he wrote an article on physical education in primary schools for the *Contemporary Review*.[5]   In this article he deplored the way in which school playgrounds were so little used for organised games, whether during school hours, or on Saturdays, and he urged the introduction of games into the elementary school curriculum.   He was told, 'You must first alter the Education Code so as to allow that reasonable time for playing organised games should be provided under it.'[6]   The Board of Education did not amend the code.   However, Mr. Augustine Birrell, on succeeding to Lord Londonderry, accepted an invitation to meet His Majesty's Inspectors at a dinner party.   On this occasion Mr. Graves, who was seated next to Mr. Birrell, interested him in his concern for games in elementary schools.   Within a few days Mr. Birrell asked the Chief Inspector, Mr. E. G. A. Holmes, to consult with Mr. Graves about introducing an article into the new code. Together they drafted an article of a permissive, not compulsory character, providing for properly organised games under competent supervision and instruction.   This article was accepted by Mr. Birrell and in 1906 organised games, cricket, hockey and football for boys and similar suitable games for girls were officially allowed in school hours.[7]   This policy, however, seems to have met with criticism.   Three arguments were put forward by the Board in its favour.

First, games had played a great part in building up the physique and moulding the characters of children in secondary schools, that is, in Public Schools, and grammar schools modelled on Public Schools.   Secondly, both the health and the *esprit de corps* of scholars had improved in certain elementary schools where organised games were played outside school hours. It was further argued that the spirit of discipline, of corporate life, and of fair play was acquired largely through games.[8] Already a new conception of the function of public elementary education was becoming accepted and was affecting official policy towards physical as well as general education.

The Boer War, quite apart from its influence on the general educational trend, made a direct impact upon physical education. The initial defeats on the field and the rejection of large numbers of recruits at home focused attention upon the physical state of the population of Britain. In Manchester in 1899 out of 11,000 volunteering for enlistment 8,000 were rejected outright and only 1,200 were accepted as fit in all respects.[9] The publication of figures such as these and the appearance in 1901 of B. Seebohm Rowntree's book, *Poverty; A Study of Town Life*, caused widespread alarm and calls for action.

To meet the demand for greater physical fitness the Board of Education in 1902, in consultation with the War Office, drew up and issued a *Model Course of Physical Training for use in the upper departments of Public Elementary Schools*. This was framed on the army methods of training, and consisted chiefly of military drill, together with dumbbell and barbell exercises. Schools were directly encouraged to employ instructors 'who should, if possible, have been trained in the Army Gymnastic Course', and those schools requiring further physical training, and desiring to proceed to military drill, were referred to *Infantry Training 1902*, a handbook published by the War Office. Thus physical training in public elementary schools was given a distinctly military bias.

To implement this policy Colonel G. Malcolm Fox, formerly Inspector of Army Gymnasia, was appointed Inspector of Physical Training and his main task was to introduce a system of drill by peripatetic instructors. They visited schools and gave the classes 'drill' as frequently or as seldom as the number of schools which they had to visit allowed. The effect of the army influence on school work was unfortunate in several respects. In the first place the training of instructors in the Army was entirely restricted to N.C.O.s. Officers never actually took a class, nor did they even lecture until many years later. N.C.O.s in those days were ill-educated and when they were projected into schools 'drill' came to be regarded as well beneath the dignity of the trained school teacher, and the whole crusade to convince people that the education of a child's body needed a scientific basis, which should be applied by educated and trained teachers, suffered unnecessarily. In the Navy, the system was quite different from that of the Army. After 1902, it was the staff officers who gave the instruction in physical exercises and they gave all the lectures. Had it happened that the Navy was invited to assist in schools in 1902, the whole set-up might have been different and much future frustration might have been prevented. Colonel Fox's instructors, once appointed, persisted in their work, even into the nineteen-twenties. Very few were subsequently recognised by the Board of Education as 'organisers' and the development of physical education was severely handicapped in some areas by their existence. They were faithful servants to their authorities but were so lacking in intelligence that not even further courses could equip them adequately for physical education in schools.

Another unfortunate result of army influence in schools

was in the nature of the drill imposed.   While the London
School Board and other authorities had fostered and
developed the Swedish system, the Army was still using
barrack square drill and a haphazard collection of exercises without order or system which had originally been
introduced into the Army by Archibald MacLaren in
1861.   The introduction, therefore, of the model course
in 1902 was for many schools a retrograde step.   Copies
of the model course issued by the Board contained a letter
from the War Office urging school managers to compel
their teachers, men and women, to attend at drill sheds
and other places for drill.   *The Times* also supported compulsory military training 'in order to lay the foundations
of a military spirit in the nation'.[10]   A great outcry was
raised, Dr. Macnamara, M.P., claiming that the model
course was part of a systematised endeavour to take advantage of the current cry for physical training by making the elementary schools and the Board of Education
a sort of antechamber to the War Office.[11]   The National
Union of Teachers also strongly protested at the retrogres-
sion of physical education and at the pitiful spectacle in
fields near big towns of schoolmistresses of 50 and 60 years
of age, being compelled to undergo drill by a sergeant
instructor.   The Ling Physical Education Association
drew up a Memorial to the Board of Education attacking
the model course, and collected 1,408 signatures from
teachers, doctors, professors and other interested people.[12]

The protests were not without effect and an interdepartmental committee was set up to examine the Model
Course of Physical Exercises.   It reported in 1904 that
the course was unsatisfactory because there were no underlying 'general principles educed from a consideration of
the function of physical exercise in a well ordered course

of general education for children'.[13]   The report included
a syllabus of exercises and an introduction in which a
distinction was drawn between the physical effect and the
educational effect of exercises.   The use of dumbbells and
weights was ruled out and so was the use of music during
the initial learning of exercises.   The new syllabus was
certainly regarded as an improvement on the model
course, but was still largely based upon army recruit
training.

Two other reports which were published at this time
affected the development of physical education, the *Report
of the Royal Commission on Physical Training (Scotland)*, 1903,
and the *Report of the Interdepartmental Committee on Physical
Deterioration*, 1904.   The Royal Commission appointed on
31 March 1902 was primarily concerned with Scotland, a
country which is outside the scope of this study, but it
held its early sittings in London and made visits to schools
in and around London to gain familiarity with existing
systems of physical training.   For this reason and because
its report had many repercussions in England, its work
cannot be ignored.

The commission was greatly influenced by practices in
foreign countries and took evidence about systems of
training in France, Germany, Switzerland, America and
Sweden.   This was indeed the age of 'systems'.   Every
champion of physical training professed to practise one or
other of the national systems.   The Royal Commission
reported on these and even followed the fashion to the
extent of reporting that in France, where no system had
existed, there had been frequent changes of system.   A
witness explained that in France military drill had to be
abandoned by schools because the children not only
learned drill but also habits of spitting and swearing in

true barrack-square manner. The Royal Commission found some good in most of the other systems, but regarded none of them as wholly satisfactory. Finally, it recommended a committee to devise a national system of physical training for Britain. It further stated that the national system should be based on three principles: (1) that physical training should be regarded as of equal importance with mental training, (2) that during school life physical training is quite as important for girls as for boys, (3) that systematic physical training is necessary both for country and town children. These recommendations undoubtedly influenced the committee on physical exercises, whose findings have already been noticed.

The commission considered games and sports to be as important as systematic physical drill but sadly lacking in the education of the bulk of the school population. It did not really face up to the appalling difficulties presented by urban concentration and lack of facilities and contented itself with recommending that schools should co-operate with clubs and voluntary organisations to secure coaching and facilities for games. Such co-operation, useful though it might be, could hardly affect more than a small fraction of elementary school children.

In general, the commission saw that the need for physical training was but a part of the physical needs of children. Concern was expressed about the lack of medical inspection and treatment and about malnutrition. One of the difficulties in the way of providing what was needed for the physical welfare of children was the Victorian fear of 'pauperising' the poor. The commission hesitated to recommend comprehensive free meals because, it said, 'it is a matter for grave consideration whether the valuable asset to the nation in the improved moral and physical state of a large number of future citizens counterbalances the evils of impaired parental responsibility'.[14]

The same fear of pauperisation influenced the Inter-departmental Committee on Physical Deterioration. This committee had been set up in response to a letter written to the *Lancet* in February 1903 by Sir Lauder Brunton, Physician to St. Bartholomew's Hospital. The report, which appeared in 1904, suggested that much of the work of physical improvement which the committee recommended, should be left to voluntary organisations. In evidence Sir Lauder Brunton stated that in order to carry out any recommendations that might be made, the presidents and ex-presidents of the most important medical bodies in the three kingdoms had united to form a National League for Physical Education and Improvement.[15] Nevertheless, wide statutory powers were demanded to compel boys and even girls to undergo physical training. The committee thought that the State should train teachers of physical exercises, and that municipalities should provide gymnasia and instructors, and their main concern seems to have been with children of 14 and over who had left school. 'The Committee also think that the obligation should be laid on boys to attend continuation classes, in which drill and physical exercises should take a prominent place; and with a view to the encouragement of clubs and cadet corps, exemption from the obligation might be granted to all enrolled and efficient members of such organisations as submitted to inspection and conformed to the regulations qualifying them for public aid. By these means, without recourse being had to any suggestion of compulsory military service, the male adolescent population might undergo a species of training that would befit them to bear arms with very little supplementary discipline.'[15]   In essence their report, as far as physical training went, was a plea for military training without introducing conscription.

Public opinion generally was vocal on physical fitness although the support for veiled military training was far from unanimous.   Teachers were strongly opposed to such an idea and at the Liverpool Health Congress in 1903, Frederick Andrews, headmaster of Ackworth School, vigorously attacked it and pointed out the danger of all civilian teachers of physical training being ousted by the military authorities.[16]   The National Union of Teachers was on the same tack.

The *Manchester Guardian* conducted an open debate on national physical training in which two arguments were advanced repeatedly; the first, voiced by Winston Churchill, M.P., and John Burns, M.P., was that unless and until the problem of underfeeding was solved it was useless to compare the merits of different systems of physical training; the second argument, put forward by R. E. Roper, was that the basis of a national system must be Swedish drill, not English military drill, which was absolutely unsuitable and differed from the Swedish system as much as first aid to the injured differed from skilled surgery.[17]   It is difficult to assess the influence of this debate, but the fact is that during the next ten years from 1904 to 1914 the militarists lost ground, the Swedish system with modifications was adopted, and the development of physical education in elementary schools went hand in hand with other physical welfare services such as school meals and the medical inspection of schoolchildren.

Chapter 9. References

1 *Report of Departmental Committee on Playgrounds*, H.M.S.O., 1912, p. 56.

2 *Emergency Leaflet* CXXVIII, Rev. Canon Nunn, pub. Church Schools Emergency League, Manchester, June 1913, p. 23.

3 *Code of Regulations for Elementary Schools*, H.M.S.O., 1904, Introd.

4 *Hansard*, 15 July 1901, Vol. 97, Col. 387: and 26 May 1902, Vol. 108, Col. 5.

5 A. P. Graves, 'Physical Education in Primary Schools', *Contemporary Review*, June 1904.

6 A. P. Graves, *To Return to All That*, London, 1930, p. 288.

7 A. P. Graves, *op. cit.*, p. 289.

8 *R.B.E.*, 1906–7, pp. 24–5.

9 *Interdepartmental Committee on Physical Deterioration*, H.M.S.O., 1904: Evidence, pp. 13–14 and App. I.

10 *The Times*, 24 February 1903.

11 *National Physical Training. An Open Debate*, Ed. J. B. Atkins, London, 1904, p. 37.

12 *J.P.E.*, Vol. XLI, p. 36.

13 *Report of Interdepartmental Committee on the Model Course of Physical Exercises*, H.M.S.O., 1904, Col. 2032.

14 *Report of Royal Commission on Physical Training (Scotland)*, 1903, paras. 85, 165 and 176.

15 *Report of Interdepartmental Committee on Physical Deterioration*, 1904, Minute 2430 and para. 380.

16 *Ling Association Leaflet*, April 1904, Vol. I, No. 4.

17 *National Physical Training. An Open Debate*, Ed. J. B. Atkins, London, 1904, p. 151.

CHAPTER 10

Physical Training, Games and Medicine

UNDOUBTEDLY one powerful factor influencing the adoption of the Swedish system by the Board of Education was the increasing number of women teachers trained at the women's physical training colleges. In 1905 the Swedish system was being taught in twelve training colleges, thirty-seven high schools, forty private schools and nine smaller private schools.[1]   As a result of increasing support for the Swedish system, Colonel Malcolm Fox was sent to Sweden in 1907 with another inspector and their subsequent report was circulated to L.E.A.s.   In 1908 Miss L. M. Rendell was appointed the first woman inspector to supervise physical exercises.   An even more significant development was the setting up in 1908 of a medical department of the Board of Education under Dr. (later Sir) George Newman, who also had the oversight of physical training.   He almost immediately appointed three inspectors, Lieut.-Com. F. H. Grenfell, R.N. (later Captain Grenfell, D.S.O.), to supersede Colonel Malcolm Fox, Mr. Veysey and Miss Koetter. These three, together with Miss Rendell, formed the physical training inspectorate or the 'circus' as they were affectionately called by their more intimate acquaintances, for one of their early tasks was to tour the country organising demonstrations of physical training.   Commander

Grenfell even conducted classes for His Majesty's Inspectors at the Board of Education to try to give them some idea of the system of physical training that was to replace 'drill'.

The significance of Grenfell's appointment can only be fully appreciated after looking at his earlier career. In 1902 the last sailing ship vanished from the Navy and some form of physical training became imperative, to replace vigorous training aloft. A gymnastic department was created under Commander N. C. Palmer with Lieutenant F. H. Grenfell as his first assistant superintendent. They examined many of the current systems, including that used by the Army at Aldershot. They were dissatisfied with all of them. Palmer then visited Sweden and found what he wanted. On his return he set up a headquarters gymnastic school at Portsmouth where courses of training in the Swedish system could be given. Mr. Allan Broman, a Swede, who had previously worked for the London School Board, was invited to conduct the first course for sixty officers and men.[2] The naval gymnastic school was the first, and for many years the only, school in England where men were trained as teachers of Swedish gymnastics. (The Army did not adopt the Swedish system until 1907.) After some five years at the naval school, where he was a most inspiring teacher, Grenfell left the Navy to spread the gospel in schools. He started with preparatory schools and lectured wherever he could find an audience. He was joined by Lieutenant (later Commander) B. T. Coote, R.N., whose background was similar, and the two of them worked in harness. To improve their knowledge they decided to visit Sweden. They did this successively, the one at home helping the other financially out of his earnings. Subsequently, Grenfell took a post at Eton College and, after a short time there, was appointed H.M. Inspector of Physical Training in 1909. A Swedish basis for British physical education was then assured. Grenfell, moreover, firmly believed that physical education should be in the hands not of ill-educated N.C.O.s, but of educated and fully trained teachers, and he set about trying to give new dignity and prestige to his subject.

The supervision of physical training by the medical department of the Board not only gave the subject publicity—the annual reports of the chief medical officer, later published under the title *The Health of the School Child*, gave considerable space to physical training—but also certainly enhanced its prestige. The report for 1909 contained a justification of the Swedish system with its steady progression of exercises, its use of 'tables' in which movements followed one another in a recognised order and sequence, and its use of a word of command for each movement or part of a movement. In the same year a new syllabus was issued. The 1904 syllabus, as the Board admitted, 'had proved to be dull, tedious and monotonous',[3] and so the 1909 syllabus contained recreative exercises such as step marches, dancing and skipping steps and gymnastic games. Parts of this syllabus bore a remarkable resemblance to a Handbook published some years previously which Miss E. A. Roberts had been asked by the Ling Association to write. Some people felt that the Board had been guilty of plagiarism if not actual infringement of copyright.[4] However the identity of view between the Board and the Ling Association undoubtedly helped forward the Swedish system in England. A close examination of this syllabus shows a definite move towards therapeutic gymnastics and even a move away from the encouragement of games and sports which had been a feature of the Board's policy in 1906. The syllabus is divided into two parts. Part I consists of a number of short chapters on the general principles of physical training, and the application of physiology to exercises, with some paragraphs on the hygiene of physical training. After some aids to teaching, there follow seventy-one tables of exercises. Part I occupies 148 pages. Part II, that is, the remaining twenty pages, is devoted to appendices, one of which contains a few paragraphs on games. When we read that games are valuable for the enjoyment they bring, for their educational effect on the mind and character, for their encouragement of initiative, and further that games are valuable because 'children can learn in co-operation with others', we expect to find a fairly comprehensive treatment of games leading up to those national team games which are reputed to have played such an important part in developing our national character. It is a little surprising that the next three pages contain merely a brief description of such games as Fox and Geese, Leap Frog, Chase Ball and French Blind Man's Buff. In fact, no guidance whatever is given to teachers on team games, nor are they given any encouragement to develop those organised games to which the Board had given its blessing in 1906. Whatever lip service was paid by the 1909 syllabus to the educational value of games, the real drive was towards therapeutic exercises.

The syllabus also claimed to find a scientific basis for the exercises it prescribed, but it is difficult to see precisely what is the scientific basis for declaring that it is a fault if the fingers are separated in arms raising sideways, or if the hands are not in line with the arms in arms stretching upward. For all its general principles the 1909 syllabus was still influenced by the tradition of drill.

Swedish drill as practised in the early nineteen-hundreds was a rigid and inflexible system, and practitioners regarded departures from it almost as acts of heresy. Even the modest attempts of the 1909 syllabus to make the system more enjoyable were resented by some teachers. The *Journal of Scientific Physical Training* criticised the syllabus for straining after amusement and claimed that 'stress on the recreative side is always at the expense of due emphasis on the educational effect of exercise'.[5] The doctrine that education and recreation were opposed or incompatible was one that dogged the footsteps of physical education for several decades. Other points of discussion in the journal at this time were whether games could be played in corsets and whether the angle of the feet in standing to attention should be 90° or 45°. The lengths to which the tyranny of the Swedish system could go appeared in an article which stated that children should be discouraged from playing the violin because they could only do so in a 'bad position'.[6]

The therapeutic value of physical training had received special attention in the chief medical officer's report for 1909. He claimed that physical training raised a child's power of resistance to the onset of disease, and enabled him to overcome it more successfully if acquired. His statement that 'Tuberculosis, for example, can perhaps be avoided most effectively by increasing the resistance of the child to the attacks of the tubercle bacillus'[7] was in itself unexceptionable, but in its context could only give a false impression of what physical training could do and of what teachers of physical training ought to try to do. Naturally, remedial exercises for postural defects now received official encouragement, but by recommending corrective exercises for children suffering from malnutrition[8] the

Ia. Football at Rugby, *c.* 1870
Picture Post Library

Ib. Football at Stowe School, *c.* 1950
Radio Times Hulton Picture Library

IIa. Westminster Boys winning the race against Eton
at Putney, 1851
Picture Post Library

IIb. Girls of Gilliatt Secondary School learning to row
at Putney, 1968
Richmond and Twickenham Times Photographic Service

IIIa.
The Outdoor Gymnasium at Dartford Physical Training College, *c.* 1895
Physical Education Association

IIIb. Modern Dance, 1943
Keystone Press Agency and Physical Education Association

IV. The Government Gymnasium on Primrose Hill, 1848

Picture Post Library

V. Gymnastic Apparatus devised at Bristol, 1944

M.A.C. Engineering Co., Bristol

VIa. Massed drill in the yard of an Elementary School, 1906
Picture Post Library

VIb. Drill in a classroom of Townsend Road School, 1902
Picture Post Library

VII. Physical education at Upton County Primary School, Kent, 1951
Bexley Education Committee, E. Tudor Hart

VIII. Training in Winter Camping for Boys, 1961
The Times Copyright

medical department again overstated the case for therapeutic physical training.

Some modification of the official view of physical training became apparent in 1912, when the annual report
used the term 'physical education' for the first time.
Previously mention had been made only of 'physical
training', but in that year both phrases were used.
Chapter XV of the report was headed 'Physical Training',
but sub-headings referred to physical education in training
colleges and physical education in elementary schools, and
the tenor of the whole was less restricted than that of
previous reports.

It was perhaps not a coincidence that in 1911 the
National League for Physical Education and Improvement had published a pamphlet entitled *Organised Play at
Home and Abroad* in which R. E. Roper, then on the staff
of Eton College, had drawn attention to the contrasts
between State-aided and private schools and went on to
say that the recognition of games as a necessity instead of
a luxury in State-aided schools required more than the
provision of facilities. It involved a new mental attitude
to physical education. Specialised training was not sufficient. The teacher of physical education 'must above
all be an educational expert, able to conceive of the training of mind and body as a whole, possessing the wide
general knowledge demanded of specialists in other school
subjects; then, and then only, will the children of the
nation have a fair chance of a full education'.[9]

Official action to broaden physical training was taken
by appointing a departmental committee in 1912 to
inquire into the playgrounds of elementary schools. The
report revealed both the extent to which local authorities
and teachers had, on their own initiative, organised games

for schoolchildren and the appalling lack of playing space available. Birmingham had begun a scheme in 1910 to organise games on summer evenings in the city's recreation grounds under six teacher volunteers. In 1911 salaried organisers were employed, and in 1912 it was estimated that about 4,600 boys and girls attended at ten recreation grounds in densely populated districts.[10] Other schemes were in operation in London, Liverpool, Manchester, Preston and Norwich, but in some cases they depended for finances on voluntary contributions—the Evening Play Centres Committee in London had to raise £980 to keep open fifty playgrounds with 424,000 attendances—and in no place was more than a small fraction of the child population catered for. In Liverpool the fraction was estimated at one-sixteenth and in Preston one-tenth. The facilities for elementary schoolchildren were indeed bad. Reports from H.M. Inspectors revealed that 600 elementary schools had no playground at all and that a further 2,836 had playgrounds quite inadequate for recreation. The committee could not avoid comparing this state of affairs with the playing fields in preparatory and Public Schools and strongly recommended both *ad hoc* measures, such as co-operation between education committees and parks committees, to provide playing space, and also legislation to ensure adequate playgrounds and playing fields for new schools, and to fix a time limit for existing schools to conform to recognised standards.[11]

The suggestions for *ad hoc* measures were followed up by the Board, which in 1912 stated that field games should be used to supplement the physical training lesson, and by the beginning of the Great War the Board was holding up Birmingham and Manchester as shining examples of what could be achieved by co-operation between education committee and parks committee.[12]   Legislation for long-term measures had to wait until 1918.

In the pre-war period bills had been introduced into the House of Commons and the House of Lords to extend the scope of physical training, but they did not gain support and in some cases their promoters were most ill informed about what was already being achieved by the medical department of the Board of Education and by local authorities.   The bills revealed a concern among influential people about the physical welfare of the population and about the military preparedness of the country, but being piecemeal and badly constructed measures they were killed long before they could reach the statute book.[13]

The implementation of the policy inaugurated when the medical department of the Board was set up and an inspectorate was established would have been impossible without teachers in the schools who were able to interpret and apply the principles of the Swedish system.   The Board of Education, therefore, at the same time as it issued a new syllabus, turned its attention to the training of teachers.   Previously this work had been done by independent colleges, voluntary organisations and such local authorities as had held courses for their own teachers. Among colleges and voluntary organisations, the women's colleges, the Birmingham Athletic Institute and the Amateur Gymnastic Association, have already been noticed.[14]

Other bodies at work in the training or examination of teachers were the British College of Physical Education founded in 1891, the Gymnastic Teachers' Institute founded in 1897, and the National Society of Physical Education also founded in 1897.   These last three bodies aimed to develop a British system but in fact expounded modifications of the German system. There was intense rivalry between them and an attempt by them, together with the Ling Association of Teachers of Swedish Gymnastics, to amalgamate in 1905 in order to gain more definite recognition by the Board of Education, came to nothing. The British College, the G.T.I. and the National Society did come to a joint working arrangement and much later, in 1916, amalgamated to form the British Association for Physical Training. Meanwhile teacher training had passed out of their hands.

In 1909 the need for teachers was twofold, specialist teachers for training colleges and secondary schools, and non-specialist teachers for elementary schools up and down the country. It was this latter category that the inspectors and the Board attempted first to supply. In 1909 and 1910 the Board held vacation courses in hygiene and physical training in order to bring the two syllabi in these subjects to the notice of local education authorities and training colleges. But this was not sufficient to meet the demand for educated, as well as trained, teachers now that drill sergeants and professional gymnasts were regarded as unsuitable teachers for growing children.[15] In 1909, therefore, physical training was made a compulsory and examinable subject in all training colleges. This involved 80 colleges turning out 4,500 to 5,000 teachers a year. There was no examination yet for the 5,000 non-collegiate teachers nor for the 120,000 certificated and uncertificated teachers already in English and Welsh schools. Moreover, teachers who already held certificates of physical training awarded by the voluntary organisations were at a disadvantage since the Board did not recognise their qualifications. These organisations convened a Joint Board of Gymnastic Teachers to draw up a syllabus, conduct examinations and secure the recognition of the Government, but the withdrawal of the British College of Physical Education frustrated their efforts.[16]

The rivalry between competing organisations was one reason why they failed both to meet the need for a uniform qualification and to gain the recognition of the Government. A further and more serious obstacle was the lack of educational background of so many practising gymnastic teachers. This became serious in 1909, when the Board of Education initiated a new policy of raising the educational and social status of physical education. The same obstacle was brought into sharp relief when the Teachers' Registration Council was set up by Act of Parliament in 1907 and an attempt was made to formulate conditions for the registration of teachers of physical training. The difficulties in the way of achieving this were placed there largely by gymnastic teachers themselves, many of whom were not prepared to accept as a condition of registration as high a standard of general education as well as of technical training as was required of other teachers.[17] Eventually, in 1914, registration was permitted to all teachers of gymnastics who had had five years' teaching experience and were over 25 years of age. Requirements of training and attainment were postponed.[17]

It was largely to break the association between physical education and lack of education that in the Christmas holidays of 1912 a meeting was held to form the Physical Education Society. This was a society for men teachers and among its objects was 'to ensure that the general and special training of a gymnastic master should be such as to enable him to be a member of the educational staff of a school'.[17] The secretary of the new society was R. E.

Roper, who had now left the staff at Eton College for Bedales School and who was constantly endeavouring during the early years of the century to raise the status of physical education. Since one of his other objects was to secure the exclusive use of the Swedish system in the national system of physical education, any success which he had in raising the status of physical education tended to confine educational respectability to Swedish drill and Swedish gymnastics.

While voluntary organisations went their own way the Board of Education in 1909 initiated its own measures to equip intending teachers to give some physical training to their children, but progress was slow and far from satisfactory. An instructional circular was sent round to training colleges in 1911, but the *Report of the Chief Medical Officer* for 1912 stated that progress in the previous four years had been disappointing and that teaching was ineffective and dull instead of being bright and interesting. However, it was hoped to raise the standard of teaching eventually and to this end short courses of one month were held at various places in the summer. In 1912, Barry, Scarborough, Southsea and Falmouth all had courses and teachers were sent by their authorities to take part.

The supply of specialist teachers in 1909 was good and improving as far as women were concerned, but the supply of men specialists was almost non-existent. A few men had trained in Sweden; Roper, Grenfell and Coote were among them. In this country the facilities for training outside the armed services were meagre indeed. In 1905 Grenfell and Coote had announced their intention of running a one year's course in educational gymnastics in London for 'students training as assistant masters at Oxford and elsewhere',[18] but nothing seems to have come of it. The first course for training civilian specialists in educational gymnastics to be officially recognised by the Board was started at the South Western Polytechnic in Chiswick in 1908. It was under the direction of Lieutenant Braae Hansen from the Central Gymnastic Institute in Copenhagen, and its main purpose was to provide applicants for posts in training colleges now that physical training was a compulsory subject. The course was confined to gymnastics and the theory allied to it; outdoor games, swimming and dancing were excluded.

Two years later H. G. Junker started a course for English students at Silkeborg in Denmark. He had already held two holiday training courses for men and women students and was encouraged by the success of these to open a nine months' course in September 1910. The following year, in October 1911, Allan Broman opened his 'Central Institute for Swedish Gymnastics' for men students in Paddington Street, London. The building was new and included a gymnasium, dressing rooms, lecture rooms and a common room. Broman planned a two-year course and gave out that matriculation was a desirable qualification for intending students but not an indispensable one. In the same year a physical training college for women which had been opened in 1905 at Dunfermline was opened to men. These then were the only facilities for training men specialists in physical education until after the 1914–18 war. The comparatively small number of men who came from them did sterling work for the physical welfare of the children of this country and laid the foundations for the bigger structure that came after the war. Meanwhile the specialist colleges of physical training for women continued to send out a steady supply of teachers of quality whose contribution to the education of girls was not perhaps accorded the recognition which it deserves outside the secondary schools where it was made.

One way in which the quality of physical education in schools could be improved was through the appointment of full-time 'organisers' by local education authorities. Some cities had for many years had organisers or superintendents of physical exercises as they were called, but in 1909 there were still only forty-nine areas out of a total of 328 where an organiser was employed,[19] although teachers' classes were being held in as many as 100 areas. The Board officially encouraged local authorities to appoint full-time organisers, but as there was as yet no grant from the Treasury to meet even a part of the cost of their salaries, many authorities were slow to make the appointment.   Sheffield, however, was not among them. H. A. Cole was appointed Superintendent of Physical Training in 1913 and he was given wide duties in supervising work in the city's day and evening schools and in training teachers, pupil teachers, and students at the City Training College and at the University. Between Easter, 1913, and the end of 1914, 600 teachers in Sheffield attended short courses.   Mr. Cole's work and that of Miss McDowall, who held a similar post in Cornwall, were fully described in the medical officer's report for 1914 as a stimulus to other authorities.

Between 1900 and 1914 physical education in elementary schools had taken great strides forward. Military drill persisted in many places as a legacy from the past, but military training as official policy had been left in the ditch, and, armed with the 1909 syllabus of which nearly 100,000 copies were sold within a year of its publication,[20] inspectors, organisers and teachers marched along the road to therapeutic physical training. Some even had visions of a more liberal physical education beyond.

Chapter 10. References

1 *Ling Leaflet,* June 1905, Vol. 2, No. 6.
2 *Physical Training in the Navy,* by Gymnasticus, reprinted from *The Fleet,* London, no date.
3 *R.C.M.O.,* 1909, p. 174.
4 Barbara Whitelaw, *E. Adair Impey. Letters of Remembrance by some of her family and friends,* Guernsey Press, 1965.
5 *Journal of Scientific Physical Training,* November 1909, Vol. II, No. 1.
6 *Journal of Scientific Physical Training,* 1910, Vol. II, No. 2.
7 *R.C.M.O.,* 1909, p. 183.
8 *R.C.M.O.,* 1912, pp. 299–300.
9 *Journal of Scientific Physical Training,* 1912, Vol. IV, No. 12, 'Organised Play at Home and Abroad', N.L.P.E.I.
10 *Report on Organised Games presented to the Council by the Parks Committee,* Birmingham, 1913.
11 *Report of the Departmental Committee on Playgrounds,* H.M.S.O., 1912.
12 *R.C.M.O.,* 1915, p. 96.
13 *Hansard,* 14 July 1910, *H.L.* Vol. VI, 166, and 18 June 1912. *H.C.* Vol. XXXIX, 1500.
14 See Chapter 8.
15 *R.C.M.O.,* 1909, p. 184.
16 *Journal of Scientific Physical Training,* Autumn 1910, and Summer 1911, Vol. III, Nos. 7 and 9.
17 *Journal of Scientific Physical Training,* Vol. VI, pp. 3 and 11 and 41.
18 *Ling Leaflet,* July 1905, Vol. 2, No. 7, advertisement.
19 *R.C.M.O.,* 1909, p. 178.
20 *Hansard, H.L.,* 14 July 1910.

CHAPTER 11

Physical Education in
Secondary Schools, Old and New

IN the field of secondary education the 1902 Act
brought into effect a different dual system from that
which obtained in elementary education. Many old
endowed grammar schools which had previously had no
assistance from public funds were now 'aided' by L.E.A.s.
There also came into existence new secondary schools
built and 'maintained' by the municipal or county
councils. In their physical education the older grammar
schools had with greater or less success imitated the Public
Schools, some of which had themselves risen from the
status of local grammar schools. Games were played,
although often only by the better performers. There was
seldom any universal compulsion to play and the facilities
for games were usually less ample than those of Public
Schools, just as school funds were less ample. Many
schools secured the services of a visiting instructor to
conduct drill, and such gymnastics as were done were
modelled on the German system with the horizontal and
parallel bars. In the sister schools for girls, which only
grew up after the Endowed Schools Act of 1869 had
extended to girls the benefits of existing educational
endowments, the situation was somewhat better. Girls'
grammar schools were influenced by what was happening
in girls' Public Schools, and a number of the latter had by

the end of the century evolved comprehensive schemes of physical education including games, dancing and Swedish drill.[1] After 1902 new grammar schools were built out of public funds and they usually incorporated both playing fields and a gymnasium. In 1904 the Board of Education issued Rules for New Buildings and Equipment in Secondary Schools and in them provided for a gymnasium of unspecified size and a playground and playing field for cricket and football(boys), hockey and lawn tennis (girls).[2] A memorandum on physical training in secondary schools issued in 1911 stated that a gymnasium in which Swedish apparatus could be fitted was desirable and should measure not less than 50 feet by 25–30 feet.[3] A further memorandum issued in 1912 recommended a gymnasium measuring 60 feet by 30 feet and 16 feet high,[4] and these measurements were also given in the Building Regulations for Secondary Schools in 1914.[5] The Swedish apparatus to go in the gymnasium was also described in great detail. Very few existing schools had gymnasia even approximating to the standards laid down. However, the publication of the Board's recommendations and requirements indicated clearly the lines along which physical education was intended to develop. Nevertheless, as far as the programme itself was concerned schools were still left very much to their own devices. Although girls often had Swedish drill under a qualified teacher, the sad dearth of men teachers with any experience of physical education meant that the boys' grammar schools tended to follow the practices of the older grammar schools— haphazard games, and drill under an ex-army instructor.

Moreover, Colonel Malcolm Fox's policy of encouraging ex-army gymnastic instructors to seek posts in schools and of encouraging schools to appoint them continued under its own momentum. Schools found the Army Gymnastic Staff a rich source of supply, and the A.G.S. was naturally anxious that schools should continue to provide jobs for instructors when their military service was over.

When the medical department of the Board of Education was set up, physical education in secondary schools as well as in elementary schools came under its wing. However, although the code of regulations for secondary schools issued in 1904 had laid down that physical exercises were to be included in the curriculum,[6] the primary concern of His Majesty's Inspectors of Physical Training was with elementary schools, and little was done in the way of inspection or direction of secondary schools. The first serious attempt to influence work in secondary schools was made in 1911 in the circular on physical training in secondary schools signed by Dr. George Newman already referred to. The circular discouraged a number of contemporary features of physical education, such as the training of a limited number of pupils for gymnastic displays and the neglect of the rest, the emphasis on the disciplinary value of drill whether military or Swedish, and the use of horizontal and parallel bars, wands and dumbbells. On the other hand, the circular strongly encouraged therapeutic exercises throughout the school by means of the Swedish system, and considerable advice was given upon the application of the system. Games, which were much more of a practicable possibility for secondary schools than for elementary schools, were mentioned as desirable, but then immediately dismissed as being outside the scope of the memorandum.[7] It seems, however, that many schools preferred to follow the lead of the Public Schools rather than the policy of the Board. Inspection of fifty-three schools in 1912 showed that the Swedish system had not been widely adopted in boys' schools, that teachers were not efficient even in girls' schools, and that generally 'physical training had yet to win adequate recognition in a large number of secondary schools'.[8] On the other hand the Board was so anxious about the attention that games were receiving that in 1914 it prefaced its routine eulogy of the Swedish system with an official discouragement of organised games because they were inadequate and not systematic. Realising that the aided and maintained grammar schools aspired to reach but the foothills of greatness attained by the Public Schools, the Board pointed out that the Swedish system had been adopted by such famous schools as Harrow, Eton, Rugby and Clifton.

These schools were indeed experimenting with Swedish gymnastics, largely as a result of Grenfell's initial work at Eton. Grenfell's propaganda for the Swedish system had resulted in Canon E. Lyttelton, who succeeded Edmund Warre as Headmaster of Eton, inviting him to join the staff at Eton College in 1907. There he supervised the building of a new gymnasium on entirely Swedish lines and he conducted regular lessons for some of the junior forms. When Grenfell joined the inspectorate in 1909, he was succeeded at Eton by B. T. Coote and R. E. Roper. They were given additional forms to teach in the gymnasium during school hours. They also took voluntary classes and conducted remedial gymnastics. In 1912, Coote went to Harrow and developed a similar scheme there, while Roper went to develop physical education at Bedales. At Eton their posts were filled by A. E. Syson and F. D. Robinson. Syson had been a captain in the Royal Marines and an instructor at the naval P.T. school.   Both he and Robinson had just completed a year's course in Sweden, so that work along Swedish lines continued   When war broke out in 1914, most of these men rejoined the services and their work in schools fell into abeyance.

The significance of these appointments at Public Schools was that for the first time drill was taken out of the hands of N.C.O.s and was personally conducted by officers who were theoretically on an equal footing with the rest of the teaching staff.   Moreover, the drill that they taught was not mere military drill but Swedish gymnastics, in which they were fully qualified and of which they had wide experience.   They did have the services of N.C.O.s for teaching such activities as boxing and fencing, but they closely supervised the work.

Interesting as these experiments were, they did not significantly alter the pattern of Public School physical education.   Games and sports still remained the main focus of attention at these schools; moreover, they were organised independently of the gymnasium staff and there was never any possibility at this time of games, sports and gymnastics being welded into a single planned scheme of physical education.   Roper did in fact suggest developments along these lines,[9] but in 1912 he moved to Bedales —a progressive school where such a heresy had a considerably greater chance of being accepted.

Athleticism did not noticeably abate at Public Schools between 1900 and 1914, but it aroused increasingly strong criticism of the schools which fostered it.   Mack[10] has pointed out that until after the Liberal victory at the polls in 1906 there was no fundamental criticism of the Public Schools, that is to say none of their critics wanted them abolished or completely remodelled, and of the novelists who wrote about them between 1900 and 1909 all except Butler and Kipling were essentially defenders of the Public School system. Later, however, in the years immediately before the 1914–18 war critics of the Public Schools appeared not as reformers but as would-be destroyers. Bernard Shaw and H. G. Wells were among those and their shafts were directed particularly against athleticism. Games, which by this time were being justified as, among other things, preventives of masturbation, received a violent attack from Shaw in his preface to *Misalliance*, first published in 1914.

'A child has a right to finality as regards its compulsory lessons. Also as regards physical training. At present it is assumed that the schoolmaster has a right to force every child into an attempt to become Porson and Bentley, Leibnitz and Newton, all rolled into one. This is the tradition of the oldest grammar schools. In our times an even more horrible and cynical claim has been made for the right to drive boys through compulsory games in the playing fields until they are much too exhausted physically to do anything but drop off to sleep. This is supposed to protect them from vice; but as it also protects them from poetry, literature, music, meditation and prayer, it may be dismissed with the obvious remark that if boarding schools are places whose keepers are driven to such monstrous measures lest more abominable things should happen, then the sooner boarding schools are violently abolished the better.'[11]

Writers like Shaw might condemn Public Schools and their athleticism out of hand but none sought to explain and criticise the tyranny of games in such detail as H. B. Gray in his book *The Public Schools and the Empire*. He himself had been a schoolboy at Winchester and became headmaster of Bradfield College.   In his view games had become 'an insane cult—in Tacitean phrase, "a pestilent superstition" ' but he went on to ask why this had happened.   He found four reasons.   First, because of the constriction of much of school life, games had become 'an absolutely indispensable safety valve for the escape of steam in the overcharged human boiler'.   A second cause was the natural inclination of children to venerate physical rather than mental or moral qualities.   Thirdly, the competitive principle which was so heavily emphasised was comparatively innocuous when applied to games and at the same time was attractive to the boys.   Fourthly, games afforded 'the simplest solution of the problem how to make the existence of an unwieldy crowd of pupils compatible with the geographical limitations of the school premises'.

The influence of the 'games-mad' assistant master and of the Press had also played a part in encouraging the 'pestilent superstition' of athlete worship.   Gray heartily condemned athleticism and exposed the hollowness of physiological and ethical arguments that were commonly advanced in support of games and he even attributed professionalism in sport and the habit among the industrial classes of being spectators to the impetus given to games by the Public Schools.[12]

In spite of criticism no serious modification of the Public School system had taken place when war broke out in 1914.

A type of school that was greatly influenced by the Public Schools and had in fact been brought into being by them was the preparatory school.   Before Arnold went to Rugby as headmaster, this kind of school did not exist, but the raising of the minimum age of admission by Arnold to 12, the reform of the Public Schools, the heavy demand for places at them and the consequent competition to gain admission to them, made it necessary for some boys who would have gone straight to a Public School from home, to go to some other school first. They went, therefore, to preparatory schools at the age of 8 or 9, and stayed there until they went on to their Public School at 12, 13 or 14. The growth of these schools was encouraged by the institution of scholarship and entrance examinations in many Public Schools, and by 1900 they were a recognised feature of the English educational system. They were microcosms of the higher schools and to such a degree did athleticism project itself downward that not only was a lavish amount of time, space and energy devoted to games, but parents were apt to choose preparatory schools for their sons according to the quality of the cricket coaching; for, as one writer on these schools revealed, 'the fact is that skill in games confers the right of admission to the privileged circle, and it is only reasonable that a parent in his natural desire to secure for his boy a leading position should be alive to the advantages which an early and skilful training in games may be the means of winning him'.[13]

It would be wrong to leave this period between the Boer War and the Great War without mention of an organisation which was keenly interested in physical education, but had little use for either therapeutic exercises or for organised games. The early growth of the Boy Scout movement is best told in the words of its founder, Lord Baden-Powell. 'My idea of training boys in scouting dates from 1897 when I applied it to young soldiers in the 5th Dragoon Guards, having for years previously found the good of developing a man's character before putting upon him the dull routine training then considered necessary for a soldier.

'The possibility of putting responsibility on to boys and treating them seriously was brought to the proof in Mafeking with the corps of boys raised by Lord Edward Cecil there in 1899 and led me to go into it further.

'When I came home in 1902 I found my book *Aids to Scouting* being used in schools and by Boys' Brigade officers etc. for teaching boys. As this had been written for soldiers, I re-wrote it for boys (after having an experimental camp in 1907). I did not then intend to have a separate organisation of Boy Scouts, but hoped that the B.B. and Y.M.C.A. would utilise the idea. However, such a large number of men and boys outside these organisations took it up, that we were obliged to form a directorate to control it.

'The movement grew up of itself. In 1910 I had to give up the Army to take charge of it.'[14]

Baden-Powell was thoroughly opposed to drill as a form of training except as a final polish because it denied to boys the opportunities to shoulder responsibilities, to tackle difficulties and dangers, to shift for themselves and to dare from a sense of duty. For similar reasons he had little use for systematic physical training except six simple daily exercises. Instead he pinned his faith on troop games and above all on physical fitness through camping, hiking, climbing and other natural activities. Here was character training through physical activities which were quite different from the Philistines' team games. Scouting was a return to the old aristocratic barbarian pursuits of hunting and country sports, but with the difference that now these sports were opened up to all classes. The Boy Scouts and the sister organisation, Girl Guides, became national and then world-wide movements. In physical education they met a need that both the Swedish system and organised games had failed to meet, and they prepared the way for the great outdoor movement that took place in England after the war.

Chapter 11. References

1 See Chapter 8.
2 *Secondary Schools, Rules for New Buildings and Equipment*, H.M.S.O., 1904.
3 *Memorandum on Physical Training in Secondary Schools*, H.M.S.O., 1911. Circular 779.
4 *Physical Training, Memorandum on Gymnasium Equipment*, H.M.S.O., 1914.
5 *Building Regulations for Secondary Schools*, H.M.S.O., 1914.
6 *Code of Regulations for Secondary Schools*, H.M.S.O., 1904, Chap. 8.
7 Circular 779, *op. cit.*, Appendix D.
8 *R.C.M.O.*, 1912, pp. 300–2.
9 See Chapter 10.
10 E. C. Mack, *Public Schools and British Opinion from 1860*, Chap. VII.
11 G. B. Shaw, *Misalliance*, London, 1928, pp. xliv–xlv. First published 1910.
12 H. B. Gray, *The Public Schools and the Empire*, London, 1931, Chap. XI.
13 *Special Reports and Inquiries*, Board of Education, Vol. 6, 1900, pp. 348–9.
14 E. E. Reynolds, *Baden-Powell*, O.U.P., 1942, p. 137.

The Great War and
the Fisher Education Act

THE outbreak of war in August 1914 put an end to a period of steady development of social services. The event was attended by profound depression in many hearts, but by an outward show of excitement and by an anxiety on the part of almost everyone to do something for his country. The satisfaction of this desire would have resulted in such chaos that a slogan was quickly put around, 'Business as Usual'. S. P. B. Mais recalled a year later[1] what a hard injunction this was for schoolmasters. War was declared while they were on holiday and they were required in the midst of the excitement of wholesale recruiting and war fever generally, to return to their old routine of work and play.

In spite of business as usual, considerable disorganisation and some reorganisation of the country's life did take place and took place on an increasing scale as war dragged on. The school medical service and physical education suffered setbacks in common with other services, but such was the increase of public concern for physical fitness and so astute and energetic was Sir George Newman in harnessing this concern to the educational chariot that by the end of the war the prospects for physical education in elementary schools were probably brighter than they had ever been.

The advent of war was the occasion for renewed demands for military drill in elementary schools and even for the use of rifles in the course of physical exercises.[1] The Board of Education at once stated firmly that it had no intention of returning to the policy which it had finally abandoned after the Boer War, and that children of school age were too young for military training. 'Physical training in elementary schools,' said the Board, 'should not be less and cannot well be more, than a preparation for the more specialised forms of Physical Training which may properly be undertaken at a later age.'[2] The official syllabus, therefore, supplemented by organised games and swimming, remained the basis of physical education in elementary schools.

In maintained and aided secondary schools and in Public Schools military training was undertaken on a considerable scale through the medium of cadet corps and officers' training corps. Already by September 1915 there were fifty-eight cadet corps and ninety-one O.T.C.s in recognised secondary schools, and by September 1918, while there were still only ninety-two O.T.C.s, the number of cadet corps had risen to 106. Perhaps because of the widespread military training in secondary schools, the demand for similar training in elementary schools was not silenced by the official pronouncement of the Board in 1914. However, the introduction of military drill into the education of growing children was strongly opposed by the President of the National Union of Teachers. At the union's annual conference in 1916 he said that theretofore the attempts to introduce military drill into schools had been foreseen and he hoped the union would present their strongest opposition to such attempts. To introduce the military spirit into schools would be to give the Germans a greater triumph even than victory in the war.[3]   This attitude was supported by many of the physical education profession, and in 1916 Sir George Newman reiterated the official view that the Board of Education was not concerned with military drill or training, and that its task was to produce physically fit children and adolescents ready for military, industrial, or domestic duties as the case might be.

As the war progressed, the prospect of a direct invasion of the school curriculum by military drill, in place of other forms of physical education, became more remote, but the risk of infiltration was by no means remote.   In the House of Lords on 12 July 1916 Lord Haldane stated that he thought the nation would be very much better if we attended thoroughly to the physical side of education; he went on to say that he would like to see the Boy Scout system made an integral part of elementary school education up to 13 or 14, to be followed by cadet training in secondary schools for boys, and finally officers' training corps in connection with the universities.[4]   Certain education authorities had already encouraged and financed cadet corps and the *Journal of Scientific Physical Training* noted that in two cases school money formerly spent on gymnastics and games had been transferred to the cadet corps.[5]

A further and more insidious attempt at infiltration was suspected by the opponents of militarism when Mr. H. A. L. Fisher, President of the Board of Education, introduced his Education Bill in the House of Commons on 25 February 1918.   Clause 17 of the Bill provided for facilities for physical education, including school camps. Mr. Lees Smith asked whether clause 17 would make it possible to introduce military drill into school camps and obtained an assurance that such action would be contrary to the intention of the Government and any regulations for camps made by local education authorities would require the approval of the Board of Education.[6] In spite of this assurance, the debate in the House of Commons on 8 May showed that many people hoped to use clause 17 to obtain military drill for boys. Mr. Roper pointed out the dangers in the *Journal of Scientific Physical Training* and forecast that the shortage of civilian teachers would be used as an argument for putting the physical education of boys once more in the hands of the War Office. He urged the strongest resistance to such a move. So did a conference of the London Trades Council and other societies, which was organised by the National Council for Civil Liberties and took place on 18 May. A resolution was moved by Mr. W. C. Anderson, M.P., calling attention to the loopholes left in the Education Bill for the introduction of military training and militarist teaching by the War Office and declaring that all such devices for the militarisation of the rising generation were a menace to industrial freedom, to the safety of democracy and to the future good relations of the world. The resolution was seconded by Mr. Roper and, with two strengthening amendments, was carried unanimously.[7]

There was also a strong anti-militarist feeling in many working class organisations. A meeting of 700 delegates from such organisations held a meeting in May 1918 and recommended that 'continuation schools', which were a feature of the Fisher Act, should make ample provision for physical training, but that 'no drills of a military character should be permitted'.[8]

Some women specialist teachers were likewise opposed to giving physical education the form of military training.

The editress of the *Journal of Scientific Physical Training* asked whether military training could create any desirable qualities that could not be created by ample and varied physical training, and argued that if purely military exercise produced a sounder standard of health, more abundant intelligence, and higher ethical standards than physical training, it ought to be introduced into all girls' schools.[8]

As it turned out, clause 17 of the Education Act was never used to substitute military training for physical training, but the demands for military drill in schools would have been harder to resist, had there not been an alternative policy vigorously directed by Sir George Newman and the medical department of the Board, and energetically applied by organisers and teachers up and down the country.

This was the policy of therapeutic exercises supplemented here and there by games, dancing and swimming. It suffered considerable disorganisation at the beginning of the war. The two men inspectors, Commander F. H. Grenfell and Dr. C. Brehmer Heald, joined the forces and so did many men teachers. The training of men specialists came to a halt, Allan Broman's College in Paddington Street was turned into a hospital, and even the Army Gymnastic Staff was disbanded (only to be reconstituted later).[9]   Mr. Broman himself transferred his energies to recruit training and published *A Short Course of Physical Training* for the recruits of the new armies.   Men who had had any training in teaching physical exercises were induced to enlist by the promise of immediate promotion to the rank of non-commissioned officer, while teachers who were left in schools were asked to offer their services for recruit training in their own districts.   Even then the supply of recruits swamped the authorities, and women gymnastic teachers, who saw the physical training of recruits being neglected or done most inefficiently, made repeated offers of their services to the War Office. These offers were courteously but firmly refused. Nevertheless in three or four areas commanding officers made independent arrangements with women teachers for recruit training. It was reported from one district that 'the woman teacher's classes are very popular with recruits and her highly finished work has made so strong an appeal that, instead of her gymnasium being used as an overflow from the barrack square, the positions have been reversed'.[9] The reasons for her success in recruit training were probably somewhat more complex than this report implied. Women gymnasts were undoubtedly more in their element in the Almeric Paget Massage Corps, since their training had qualified them, not only in gymnastics and games, but also in massage. Mr. Almeric Paget, M.P., at the request of the War Office, had established a massage corps in September 1914, and many women began to leave their schools to join it.[10] The physical education of girls, therefore, as well as of boys, suffered from the depletion of school staffs. However, when the calls of the forces had been met, there still remained a large number of trained women in the schools, and women inspectors also remained at their posts. Although inspection of schools during the war was confined to infants' and girls' departments, the influence of women teachers was strong throughout the school system.

The upheaval of war was necessarily attended by serious disorganisation in schools, but there were certain compensations as far as physical education was concerned. In the first year of war the Board recorded: 'the wave of prosperity caused by good employment, high wages and the allowances made to the families of soldiers and sailors have had a marked effect on the general well-being of school children. In many areas they are better fed and clothed than ever before.' At the same time the number of rejections for the Army on physical grounds gave many people cause for anxiety. Sir George Newman was quick to see that this would be so and that a great opportunity for boosting the school medical service was at hand. In a preface to his annual report for 1913, which was published in October the following year, after war had broken out, he wrote: 'Under present circumstances no apology is needed for a Report which deals with what is now being done in this country for the promotion of the health of children. Whatever degree of success may attend the nation in the present European War, the cost in life must inevitably be heavy. Consequently, the question of the preservation of the rising generation, and care for its physical fitness and equipment, is of more than ordinary importance. Apart from the grave disadvantage that much of the value of the education of children will be lost unless they are physically fit both to profit by the instruction which they receive and to perform the industrial tasks which await them in the future, it is a matter of grave national concern to secure that physical unfitness and inefficiency in all its forms, due to ill health or lack of vitality, are reduced to the smallest possible dimensions.

'This is the task of the School Medical Service. In order that this national service may be adequate, it must fulfil the twofold purpose of providing treatment for the defective, and physical education for all children.[11] The following year he returned to the attack and pointed out that while it might appear at first sight that the present time was inopportune to extend and improve physical training throughout the country, yet the period of temporary disorganisation was a particularly suitable one in which to examine what was being accomplished by means of physical education and to make plans for the remedying of shortcomings and faults, plans which would be ready for adoption whenever it was possible to put them into force. If the whole question were shelved until after the war there would be a tendency to drop back into the old routine. The opportunity would have vanished and reform, when it did come, would be more difficult to introduce.[11]

The medical department, however, did not stop short at examination of the existing system nor at planning for the future, but pushed forward with immediate developments while there was still keen public support for physical training. Three lines of attack were developed: pressure was put upon local education authorities to appoint 'organisers' of physical training, extensive measures were taken to improve the quality of teaching in schools through vacation courses, and encouragement was given to physical recreation outside school hours through such organisations as the play centre movement. To a large extent the implementation of these policies was in the hands of local authorities and voluntary organisations, and although the exhortations of the medical department were not without effect, it was only when grants from the Exchequer were made available to meet additional cost, that substantial progress was made.

The *Reports of the Chief Medical Officer* for 1914 and 1915 described in some detail the good work that was being done by organisers in various districts, and urged the appointment of others. On 10 February 1917, *Circular*

976 was issued announcing that funds had been placed at the disposal of the Board, enabling them to pay grants in aid of expenditure incurred by local education authorities on the employment of competent persons to organise and supervise the physical training of children in elementary schools.   Within twelve months forty new organisers had been appointed.   By 1918, 51 authorities had made appointments and in 1920 there were 132 organisers working for 79 authorities out of the total of 316.

In at least one instance the Board of Education felt that the offer of grant in aid of expenditure on physical training was not enough.   On 25 March 1918 a letter was sent to the London County Council indicating that unless the whole scheme of physical training in London were revised and developed the previous level of grant might not be maintained and a full inspection of the subject would be carried out.   The L.C.C. already had in its employment one man and four women organising teachers of physical exercises, but the Swedish system had never been specially favoured by Thomas Chesterton, the late organising teacher, and it was not well developed in London schools.

As a result of the Board's letter the L.C.C. advertised for an organiser of physical education, received 305 applications and appointed the young Major A. H. Gem. As a result of his initial survey the Education Committee organised short courses for 5,000 serving elementary teachers and appointed five men and five women teachers to conduct the courses.   The L.C.C. also purchased from Allan Broman for £18,000 the Central Institute of Swedish Gymnastics which he had built in Paddington Street. Renamed the L.C.C. College of Physical Education the building became a central institution for the in-service training of teachers in physical education, and for the next forty years under Major Gem's direction the college, unique in Britain, had a very great influence on the physical education of a school population rising to nearly half a million. The Board of Education was satisfied and no more was heard of its threats of 1918.[12]

The increase in the number of organisers of physical education, many of them men, brought out into the open a divergence of view between men and women which sometimes amounted to open hostility. While there had been adequate specialist training for women since the beginning of the century, men had to seek courses abroad or at home which were inadequate in quantity if not quality. Many men appointed to organising posts at the end of the war therefore did not possess the professional qualifications of their women colleagues. The latter, jealous of their standards and their status, often resented and sometimes resisted the appointment of their men colleagues. They felt that a superstructure was being erected where no foundations had been laid. Major Gem's appointment was opposed at officer, committee and council level,[13] but his, like many other appointments of men organisers, proved abundantly fruitful for physical education.

One of the most important functions of organisers was to hold classes for teachers. Even before the war the Board had admitted that the chief fault of physical training lessons was their dullness; now, with many young men teachers in the forces, this fault was aggravated. Organisers could do much to improve the quality of teaching in their own areas, but many areas had no organiser. The Board, therefore, in 1915 offered 250 maintenance scholarships for teachers attending two approved four-week courses in physical exercises to be held in August at Barry, and at University College, Reading.[14] Scholarships of this kind were awarded each year until 1919. Vacation courses did something to compensate for the abandonment of ordinary physical training in the men's colleges, and they provided a reservoir of teachers who were at least familiar with some of the principles and exercises of therapeutic physical training. The existence of this reservoir made it more difficult for the militarists to plead that military drill was essential because of the lack of civilian teachers of physical training.

The third policy, which received first encouragement and then financial assistance, was the provision of play centres for the use of children after school hours. In London the play centre movement was associated with the name of Mrs. Humphry Ward and was started in 1897 with the formation of evening games classes at the Passmore Edwards Settlement. By 1915 there were twenty-one centres, each under a woman supervisor and each aiming to give children interesting evening occupations. Games, dancing and physical training were among the activities offered to children. In 1915 the medical department urged all local education authorities to consider what might be done by official or voluntary effort to set up play centres. The increase of juvenile delinquency was largely instrumental in leading the Board in January 1917 to make grants payable to cover up to half the cost of maintaining play centres.[15] The immediate result was a rapid increase in the number of centres until by the end of the war there were 254 centres being conducted by sixty-eight official and voluntary bodies.[16]

The encouragement and financing of play centres is of more than passing interest, because it indicates how far the official attitude to education had changed since the days of the Education Department. The Board of Education was now directly concerning itself not only with what children did in school, but also with what they did in their leisure time. This development was partly forced upon the Government by the war, by the absence of parental control when fathers were in France and mothers in munition factories and by the rise in juvenile crime, partly also by a growing social conscience and a general concern for the well-being of all children, no matter to what section of society they belonged. This trend continued after the war and profoundly affected the development of physical education.

During the war, the Swedish system spread far beyond school halls and playgrounds. Continuation classes for children over 14 were officially encouraged to use the Swedish system.[17] It was used extensively in the training of recruits, and it figured in a modified form in the recreational programmes organised for munition workers.[18] The extension of the Swedish system was naturally opposed by the champions of other systems. Lieutenant Müller, the author of *My System*, found space in the *Liverpool Express* in 1915 to deliver a reasoned and critical attack upon some features of the Swedish system, and he was only partially answered, in a technical sense, by his opponents.[19] Another challenge was made jointly in 1917 by the British College of Physical Education, the Gymnastic Teachers' Institute and the National Society of Physical Education. These bodies sent a deputation to Mr. Fisher at the Board of Education to urge the recognition and adoption of the British system of physical education in addition to the Swedish system.[20] The Minister deferred his decision until he had placed before him precise details showing exactly the principles and exercises of the British system. An official reply was contained in the Chief Medical Officer's report for 1916, which as usual was not published until late in the following year. The writer of the report admitted that no system was perfect and that some of the criticisms of the Swedish system were partially justified. He also examined the argument that the ideal scheme would be to take the best features of several systems and amalgamate them, and he rejected it out of hand on the grounds that the underlying principles of the Swedish and, for instance, the German systems were fundamentally different, and therefore no mixture was possible. As a choice of system had been necessary, Ling's system of exercises had been selected as the most suitable for adoption in the schools in this country, and would continue in use. Criticisms could best be met by modifying or supplementing the existing system rather than by introducing a different one. The Board of Education continued for many years to have a strong bias in favour of the Swedish system, or rather in favour of its own interpretation of that system, but arguments between champions of various systems were becoming less and less relevant as it became recognised that no single system of exercises nor any combination of exercises from different systems could, by themselves, provide an adequate programme of physical education. The movement to widen the scope of physical education was greatly accelerated during the war and the closed 'systems' which reached their zenith at the time of the Royal Commission's report in 1903 were, by 1915, on the decline.

The dullness of the Swedish system was a frequent criticism from the time of its first introduction into England, and it was freely admitted by the medical officer of the Board. His reports for 1909, 1911, 1912 and 1914 all admitted the dullness of many lessons based upon the syllabus. The usual remedy which he proposed was better teaching technique, yet the results remained far from satisfactory and in 1914 the chief medical officer reluctantly admitted: 'Even its most wholehearted supporters would admit that the Swedish system has certain shortcomings, and that there remains opportunity for research and experiment with a view to perfecting the exercises and their application, nor would anyone suggest that this should be the beginning and end of all physical training.' The remedy, however, was not found in substituting another system nor in further development along the line of formal exercise, but in the greater attention which was being paid to games and to those physical activities which made an immediate appeal to children and whose therapeutic effect was neither calculable nor obvious. In 1914 the medical officer not only stressed the importance of organised games, but he also welcomed the introduction into some elementary schools of scouting. In 1915 he again stressed organised games and gave special encouragement to open-air education, which included open-air classes, school journeys to the seaside or country-side, and holiday schools and camps. In 1916 he expressly stated: 'The position of play in a scheme of physical education has not yet received adequate attention in this country.' Of course play must be supervised for the best results to be achieved yet 'hunting Red Indians and stalking smugglers amid the bracken fern' was 'not to be undervalued'. It was a sad reflection upon physical education in England that when attempts were made in large munition centres to provide recreation for the girls employed it was found that they had 'never been accustomed to take

N

part in team games, or indeed any form of active exercise *for pleasure*'! The same discovery was made when troops in France were encouraged to play games behind the lines.

Annual reports continued to stress the importance of remedial treatment for specific defects, but physical education was now coming to embrace so many other activities that in 1915 the chief medical officer tried to clarify everyone's ideas by explaining how hygiene, school meals, systematic physical training and open-air education were all integrated in physical education as a whole.[5] The following year he further explained that physical training included (1) formal exercises, (2) play, games and sports, (3) training in rhythm through dancing and rhythmic exercises. This wide conception of physical education found expression in Mr. H. A. L. Fisher's Education Act of 1918. Clause 17 of the Act stressed the fact that social training and physical training were linked and it allowed local education authorities to provide, with the approval of the Board of Education:

(*a*) holiday and school camps especially for young persons attending continuation schools;

(*b*) centres and equipment for physical training, playing fields (other than the ordinary playgrounds of public elementary schools not provided by the local authorities), school baths, school swimming baths;

(*c*) other facilities for social and physical training in the day or evening.

An identical clause (para 86) was included in the Education Act of 1921.

Ample as these legal provisions were, the legislation was merely permissive. No legal obligation was put upon any authority or body to provide the additional facilities for physical education. That measure had to await another war and another Education Act, in 1944.

The reasons for the broadening of the official conception of physical education were numerous. The effect of new ideas and practices abroad was considerable. The playground movement in America strongly influenced our own play centre movement. The eurhythmics of Jacques Dalcroze, whose college was at Hellerau, near Dresden, but who also demonstrated and taught in England before and during the war, encouraged the development of rhythmical work in physical education, particularly that of girls and young children. The work of Madame Montessori in Rome and that of her disciples in England helped to foster a much more imaginative and informal approach to the physical training of small children. The chief cause of the increased emphasis on games and outdoor activities was correctly diagnosed by the chief medical officer when he wrote in 1917:

'The work of the Army Gymnastic Staff in England and in France during the war will undoubtedly have far-reaching results on the recreative side of physical training for children and adolescents as well as soldiers. The playing of games in a comprehensive and organised way for their mental and physical effect has never before been fully attempted as part of any scheme of physical training. The overwhelming success which has attended the general introduction of games behind the lines in France suggests that we have made far too little use of our national aptitude and love for games in the education and training of the young and as a means of wholesome recreation for the adult'.

Legislation could only provide the framework for the

picture, the detail had to be filled in by administrative action and by teachers in the schools. In 1919, therefore, the Board issued a new *Syllabus of Physical Training for Schools*. The change of title from that of its predecessor, the *Syllabus of Physical Exercises for Public Elementary Schools*, was significant of a broader content and a wider application. The arrangement of the new syllabus was similar to that of the old but the whole approach to the subject was less formal. A new chapter in the syllabus dealt specially with physical training for children under seven years of age and this section was also published separately. For infants the emphasis was still upon therapeutic exercises with specific effects rather than upon free activity, but the dictates of inadequate space, large numbers and untrained teachers could not be ignored and, within limits the new ideas on the teaching of young children were now applied to physical training in elementary schools.

The syllabus recommended many 'breaks' and 'general activity exercises'. The use of games was dealt with at some length. For the older pupils many games were suggested which might lead up to the national team games or were variants upon them suitable for the confined space of the school playground. To supplement this section of the syllabus, *Suggestions in regard to Games* was issued separately. The next year the Education Committee in London took a step of some significance. Now that facilities for games and swimming were being used for curricular as well as extra curricular activities the Committee decided to assume full and direct financial responsibility for hiring playing fields and swimming baths for secondary schools. Nine schools only were involved for playing fields and five for swimming incurring £343 in a year.[21] In 1966 the cost of hiring facilities for games and swimming for London children had risen to £125,000. Transporting them to and fro cost another £442,800.[22]

The work of the Board was strengthened when Captain Grenfell was released by the Admiralty at the end of the war and when additional men and women inspectors were appointed. For a short time immediately after the war there was a period of 'boom' in physical education as in other spheres, and the school medical service expanded. The number of organisers increased and official encouragement of games and camping continued. The cessation of hostilities made international communication easier and foreign influences were strongly felt. In Denmark Niels Bukh's work at the Folkshøjskole of Ollerup was already making its mark. Niels Bukh's methods were controversial in many respects, particularly in their use of passive stretching exercises, but they had a profound effect on men's gymnastics both in Denmark and in England. At the same time Elin Falk in Stockholm and Elli Björksten in Finland were busy 'feminising' Ling's gymnastics. Like Bukh they introduced more rhythmic movements into gymnastics. They emphasised, too, the psychological and aesthetic side of gymnastic training for women, they drove home the realisation that the conception of physical training as the development of a sound body which then had automatic and beneficial effects upon mental and spiritual life was inadequate, and that there was interaction between mind and body throughout life and physical education needed to take more account of this. By drawing attention to these Scandinavian developments in his annual report for 1920 the chief medical officer of the Board assisted their influence upon English physical education.

The post-war expansion of physical education naturally affected teacher training. The Board based the organisation of physical education on three groups of teachers, the class teachers with some familiarity with the techniques of physical training, but no advanced training, the specialist teachers who would work mainly in secondary and continuation schools, and organisers who would advise and help to train the non-specialists. The training of class teachers had gone on during the war through vacation courses, but had been abandoned in favour of military training in most of the men's colleges. After the war the vacation courses continued and the men's colleges resumed their physical training. The training of men specialists had come to a halt when war broke out. After it ended, Herr Junker's course at Silkeborg opened again and Allan Broman's College was taken over by the L.C.C. for short courses for London teachers. A large number of men had been trained by the Army Physical Training Staff, but the Board was reluctant to employ them in schools because of their inexperience in handling children and the brief and superficial nature of their Army training. The Board therefore made arrangements with the city of Sheffield first for a three months' course and then for a one year's course for certified teachers who had served on the Army Physical Training Staff. The supply of women specialist teachers was more satisfactory as their training had continued during the war in colleges at Dartford, Chelsea, Birmingham, Bedford, Battersea, Dublin and Dunfermline. The training of women gymnastic teachers, however, was still in private hands and the fees required by the colleges ensured a middle class clientele. Madame Österberg had offered her college at Dartford as a gift to the Board of Education, but her offer was declined by the

Cabinet because to accept would have involved too 'great a departure from established practice'.[23] However, in 1915 she handed over the college to a board of trustees which included Sir George Newman. A few weeks later, on the day the summer term ended, she died.

This remarkable woman, known as 'Napoleon' among her students, had trained some 500 students in the thirty years since she had founded her college. Her influence extended far beyond those who came immediately under her teaching, and the training at Dartford College was the prototype for the training of hundreds of students elsewhere. The number of women being trained in the Swedish system at various colleges had risen from fifteen in 1898 to nearly 150 in 1915. It was estimated by a writer in the *Journal of Physical Education* that the marriage rate was about twenty-seven per cent.[24] A rough calculation shows that there were about 1,350 women gymnastic teachers practising in 1915. They were conscientious and efficient. The Ling Association of Teachers of Swedish Gymnastics, which was the professional association of teachers trained at Dartford and at colleges inspired by Dartford, instituted its own diploma examination in 1901. Because the work of women teachers was in the main unobtrusive, its quality has sometimes been overlooked. While the bulk of sound teaching in schools was being done by women and while Dame Janet Campbell and the women inspectors were spreading new ideas from the medical department of the Board of Education, yet, when it came to action at the political or high administrative level, the limelight was stolen by men, whether by officers from the services like Captain Grenfell, or by medical men like Sir George Newman. The number of fully trained men teaching in the schools was negligible and the administrative superstructure of physical education rested on foundations laid by women teachers.

In spite of the uninterrupted training of women gymnasts, the demand for them after the war was so great that the Board started an experimental one year's course for women at University College, Reading,[25] and this was repeated each year until 1922.

The development, during the war years, of a broader conception of physical education, and the part played in this development by the experience of providing recreation for troops behind the line, have already been noticed. There were similar developments in the physical education of girls and the work of fully trained women gymnastic teachers. Women in factories, in transport and in auxiliary services did many tasks that had previously been done by men only, and in their recreations and sports they also emulated men. The Ling Association, which by 1920 was a well-organised body of fully trained women gymnastic teachers with an office and a paid secretary, had always taken a keen interest in the movement for women's emancipation and encouraged the development of games and sports. The association was open to men, but as the qualification for membership was full-time training for two years, the number of men who could and did join was very small. Women teachers, however, continued to preserve their interest in medical gymnastics, partly because massage provided an alternative career to teaching in schools. In 1922 the Ling Association made arrangements with the Chartered Society of Massage and Medical Gymnastics for all students at colleges recognised by the association to be examined by the Chartered Society. At the same time misgivings were expressed because the work of the educational gymnast was too much under the control of the school medical authority. The gymnasts felt that the tight administrative bond between themselves and the school medical service tended to keep them outside the pedagogic life of the schools. By and large they welcomed the opportunity to play and to teach more games, and so loosen the strings that tied them to the doctors. The movement in favour of games was not without opposition from representatives of an older school of thought. In 1922, the daily Press had a large number of letters on the danger of athletics for girls and women, and Miss Cowdroy, a high school head-mistress, wrote a letter to the *Lancet*[26] stating that 80 per cent of gymnastic teachers had breakdowns, that playing strenuous games produced a flat figure with undeveloped breasts, that athletic women suffered from nerves, heart trouble, rheumatism, suppressed menstruation and displacements, that they decried marriage, that their confinements were always difficult, that their children were often inferior, and that most athletic women seemed to have stifled what was finest in women—love, sympathy, tact and intuitive understanding. This was indeed a fine array of indictments prompted by strong emotions, and, although they were unsupported by statistical or medical data, they made sufficient appeal to the public at large to be a nuisance to games mistresses. The Ling Association felt it desirable to arrange a conference on games for girls to dispel the mists of ignorance and Victorian prejudice.[27] The chief medical officer of the Board also found it necessary to state that assertions that injuries and displacements resulted in girls who played games were not confirmed by medical men. He added that too few girls in secondary schools were being given an all-round interest in healthy games.[28] The Victorians were opposed by powerful enemies and by 1922 they were fighting a losing battle. In practice, tight lacing and croquet had already given way to the freedom of the gym tunic and the vigour of the hockey field.

The period from 1914 to 1922, then, was one of development and expansion for physical education in elementary schools and in girls' schools generally. No such development took place in boys' Public Schools. The experiments of introducing the Swedish system into the curriculum of Eton and Harrow and of appointing men of officer rank to conduct the work came to an abrupt end when the officers concerned returned to the armed forces at the beginning of the war. Only at Bedales, where Mr. Roper had gone in 1913 after leaving Eton, did the use of the Swedish system for boys at boarding school persist with any seriousness. Mr. Roper believed that the unnatural and sedentary life which children were forced to lead at school must have bad effects upon their growth and development unless specific measures were taken to prevent or correct them. This task was the function of physical education, and the tools to hand were the artificial exercises of the Swedish system adapted and applied to the needs of schoolchildren. Mr. Roper's book *Physical Education in relation to School Life*, submitted to Manchester University for a Master's degree and published in 1915, was a significant and scholarly attempt to work out in detail and to justify the therapeutic value of artificial exercises for schoolchildren. Bedales, however, was a 'progressive school' unaffected by the cult of athleticism and the games mania of the orthodox Public School.

Athleticism in the Public Schools underwent some modification when war broke out. Games were no longer the be-all and end-all of school life. Games gave ground to military training in the officers' training corps and the narrow loyalty to house or school made way for a wider patriotism. Nevertheless, the playing fields maintained great prestige if only because they were still regarded as the places where qualities of courage and leadership were instilled. Just because character and personality and physical courage seemed so much more important in warfare than book-learning, games, although no longer an end in themselves, were still regarded as important as means to an end—success in war. Paul Jones, a typical Public Schoolboy, whose wartime letters were published posthumously, wrote from the front, 'in my heart and soul I have always longed for the rough and tumble of war as for a football match'.[29] The romanticism of the early war years was idealised and popularised in the poems of Rupert Brooke, which were, in the view of T. C. Worsley, the expression of a death wish among Public Schoolboys.[30] The fact that, according to one authority, 20 per cent of all Public School men and 27 per cent of Harrovians in the war were killed[31] certainly bore testimony to the willingness of Public Schoolboys to sacrifice themselves for an ideal. Their keenness to enlist, their impatience when their despatch to the trenches was delayed, and the qualities which they displayed at the front silenced nearly all criticism of the institutions which had produced them.

By 1916, however, the mood had changed. The end of the war was still not in sight. S. P. B. Mais noticed that although boys still wanted to go to the front, the ardour of earlier years had disappeared and 'all the old problems of Public School life seemed suddenly to have sprung up again'.[32] In 1917 there appeared a novel about Public School life which was as sensational as any criticism that had previously been published. Alec Waugh wrote *The*

Loom of Youth when he had barely left school and the book was, therefore, full of topical interest. Moreover, the features of school life which he attacked most bitterly, athleticism and homosexuality, were in themselves sensational, and the latter had never had the attention devoted to it outside the schools, which it enjoyed within their walls. The tyranny of games was, however, in Waugh's eyes, the fundamental defect and was even responsible for much of the pederasty. Waugh's criticisms were closely related to issues outside the schools and to the widespread sense of frustration and dissatisfaction with the progress of the war. The cult of athleticism might have produced courage and self-sacrifice, but it had not produced imaginative leadership. Paul Jones, who thought that all would be well with his old school if the games were keen, had also written, 'The Englishman doesn't like thinking; if he did, he would not be the splendid fighting man that he is.'[33] It was just this unthinking attitude that Waugh abhorred, and the essence of his criticism was in his statement that 'Games don't win battles but brains do, and brains aren't trained on the footer field.'[34] Waugh's novel was a bitter criticism of Public Schools. A much more moderate and sympathetic book, written at about the same time, was E. F. Benson's *David Blaize*. While Benson admitted the existence in Public Schools of games mania and sexual irregularities, he threw no spotlight upon them but, instead, he emphasised ideals of loyalty and friendship which were prized by the chief characters in the book. Maddox, an older boy and David's hero, not only fought such things as smoking, cribbing, immorality and irreligion, but even the worship of athletics and contempt for literature.

The explosion which Waugh's and other writers'

criticisms seemed to forebode never took place. In the sphere of physical education some small attempts were made, after the war, to pick up the threads of therapeutic exercise where they had been dropped in 1914. Commander Coote addressed the Headmasters' Conference in 1919 on the physical effects of habitual attitudes in the classroom. Major A. E. Syson was appointed to succeed Commander Coote at Harrow and developed the Swedish system there, and in 1921 the schools' medical officers discussed the status of physical instructors. However, no general development of systematic physical education took place and, whereas the development of physical education in State-aided schools had the active support of the chief medical officer of the Board, the medical officers of Public Schools were by no means all dissatisfied with the *status quo*. Indeed Dr. Lemprière, medical officer at Haileybury College, maintained that the pendulum had already swung too far in the direction of contempt for mere muscle and for the drill instructors who produced it.[35] The broader conception of physical education which was gaining ground at the end of the war was the result of vision and initiative within the State-aided system of education, in girls' schools and in the armed forces. The Public Schools experienced little or no modification of their traditional attitude to games. Within their walls the prescription was 'the mixture as before'.

Chapter 12. References

1 S. P. B. Mais, 'The Public Schools in Wartime', *Fortnightly Review*, July 1915.
2 *R.B.E.*, 1913–14, p. 64.
3 *J.S.P.T.*, VIII, p. 54.
4 *Hansard, H.L.*, 12 July 1916.

5   *J.S.P.T.*, XI, p. 5.
6   *Hansard*, Vol. CIII, Cols. 456 and 1104.
7   *Ling Association Leaflet*, June 1918.
8   *J.S.P.T.*, Vols. IX, pp. 6–7 and X, p. 4.
9   *J.S.P.T.*, Vols. VII, p. 29 and VIII, p. 54.
10   *R.B.E.*, 1914–15, para. 40.
11   *R.C.M.O.*, 1913 and 1914.
12   London County Council, *Education Committee Minutes*, 10 March 1920 and 12 May 1920.
13   *London County Council Minutes*, 15 July 1919.
14   *Circular 910*, H.M.S.O., 1915.
15   *R.B.E.*, 1915–16, pp. 4–5.
16   *R.C.M.O.*, 1915, p. 97 and 1918, p. 165.
17   *R.C.M.O.*, 1914, p. 197.
18   *J.S.P.T.*, VIII, p. 1.
19   *Liverpool Express*, April and May 1915, quoted in *J.S.P.T.* VII, p. 1.
20   *Ling Association Leaflet*, July 1917.
21   London County Council, *Education Committee Minutes*, 10 March 1920.
22   Inner London Education Authority, Revenue Estimates for 1967–8, I.L.E.A., 216.
23   Jonathan May, *The Contribution of Madame Bergman Österberg to the Development of British Education*.   M.Ed. thesis, University of Leicester, 1967.
24   *J.P.E.*, Vol. XV, p. 79.
25   *R.C.M.O.*, 1918, p. 164.
26   *The Lancet*, 14 May 1922.
27   *J.S.P.T.*, Vols. XIII, p. 59 and XIV, p. 48.
28   *R.C.M.O.*, 1920.
29   Paul Jones, *War Letters of a Public Schoolboy*, London, 1918, p. 198.
30   T. C. Worsley, *Barbarians and Philistines*, London, 1940, p. 117.
31   A. H. H. MacLean, *Public Schools and the Great War*, London, 1919, p. 7.
32   The Nineteenth Century, January 1916, pp. 114ff.
33   Paul Jones, *op. cit.*, pp. 219.
34   Alec Waugh, *The Loom of Youth*, London, 1917.
35   Annual Meeting of Medical Officers of Schools Association, reported in *The Times*, 30 November 1921.

CHAPTER 13

Physical Education after the War

DISAPPOINTMENT and frustration followed close upon the heels of victory. The very severity of the terms of peace imposed upon the enemy was a boomerang. The success of the French in exacting as reparations more coal than they could profitably use had disastrous results on the British export trade. Every ship provided free by Germany to replace U-boat losses meant one less to be built in British yards. Towards the end of 1920 the rise in the number of registered unemployed became alarming. Between 23 October and 26 November the number rose from 344,000 to 520,000. By 8 January 1921 it was 859,000 and was still rising. By the end of the year it reached 1,885,478.[1] There had already been serious strikes on the railways and in the coal mines, and industrial unrest was widespread. The Government, seriously alarmed at the deterioration of the country's economic and industrial position, appointed a committee under Sir Eric Geddes to examine ways of cutting down expenditure to the tune of £100,000,000. In 1922 the 'Geddes Axe' fell, cutting off, not the full sum, but a sufficiently large portion of it to affect all the social services.

Physical education between the wars, therefore, has to be considered against a background of enforced idleness for many of the population, of mental and physical deterioration that went with it, of poverty and malnutrition. The cuts in the education service in 1922 were not as severe as had been recommended by the Geddes Committee, but their effect was felt in all branches of education, including physical education.   The training courses for men and women specialist teachers, begun after the war under the auspices of the Board of Education, closed down.   That for women at University College, Reading, ended in 1923 and the one year's course for men at Sheffield Training College ended in the same year 'for financial reasons'.   Thereafter until 1933, there was no college in England where men could obtain specialist training in physical education.   They had to go either to Scotland or to Denmark, where special courses were run at Silkeborg and Ollerup and, later, at Fredensborg for English-speaking students.

Naturally in time of retrenchment local education authorities were unwilling to embark upon capital expenditure on gymnasia, swimming baths, and playing fields, and because the relevant clauses of the 1918 and 1921 Education Acts were permissive and not obligatory, the provision of facilities hung fire in many areas.   There was an inclination too to cut running expenses, and the medical department of the Board was seriously alarmed lest organisers of physical training might be considered an unnecessary luxury.   Already in 1921 the number of authorities employing organisers had ceased to grow; in fact in 1921 there were 78 such authorities against 79 in 1920, but by 1923 there was a slight upward trend and the figure had reached 83.[2]   The line of approach taken by the Board and by the chief medical officer was to impress upon local authorities that physical education was a form of preventive medicine.   The annual report of the Board for 1921–2 stated: 'An efficient system of physical training is a potent auxiliary in the prevention of debility and disease amongst school children and is relatively inexpensive to maintain. The small expenditure involved, even in a large area, forms but a fraction of the cost which most Authorities willingly pay for their School Medical Service and the care of defective children, and it is reasonable to anticipate that if it is properly developed it will gradually afford relief from some of the heavy expenditure on other "special services". It is because experience has shown the real economy of prevention as compared with the expense of cure that the Board have asked Authorities to explore every other avenue of economy so as to be able, even in existing circumstances, to retain or appoint organisers of Physical Training.'[3] The chief medical officer also urged local authorities to cut other special services, such as play centres, and even ordinary services before curtailing physical training.[4]

There is little doubt that the close connection between physical education and medicine stood the former in good stead in the nineteen-twenties and enabled the Board to make more progress than would otherwise have been possible. Official policy continued to encourage a broad approach to physical education and drew attention to its function in training character as well as in producing physiological efficiency. Many teachers still tended to see no more in physical education than drill, while education authorities were 'too often deterred by the thraldom of an obsolete tendency to regard physical culture as a sort of trespass or encroachment upon the accepted and stereotyped form of education, what Huxley called the bookishness and "mass education" of the elementary school system'.[5] Games and swimming were officially encouraged, but progress was uneven up and down the country. Games and swimming were not easy to provide in urban areas, yet in some areas where the urban concentration was greatest and the problem of finding playing fields was most acute, the most ambitious schemes were launched.   In Sheffield by 1926 more than 90,000 children were being transported by tramcar each week to playing fields away from their schools.[6]   A similar scheme was started by the organisers of Birmingham in 1924, and during the next six years the Birmingham Education Committee purshased 216 acres of ground for playing fields and provided organised games for 23,500 schoolchildren.   As an experiment, classrooms were built on some of the fields to lessen the amount of school time spent in travelling to and fro.[7]   School games associations and inter-school leagues, which were often started by enthusiastic teachers out of school hours, also played their part in many areas, but still only a small proportion of elementary schoolchildren enjoyed organised games on a playing field, and it was a sad reflection on the state of the country that boys were prevented from playing football not only by lack of pitches but by lack of boots and shoes.[8]

Swimming had early gained official recognition as an integral part of physical education and by 1930 it was possible to say that 'Whatever else may be absent from the scheme for physical training in an area, swimming usually finds a place where facilities are available.'[9]   Real progress too was made with the modification of exercises to suit younger children.   Working to command and formal exercises gave place to play activities and the use of apparatus, such as attractive coloured balls and bands. The climbing frame and the 'junglegym' made their appearance in playgrounds, while the work of Dalcroze and Ann Driver resulted in the extensive use of music and natural movement for young children.

Camping too was an activity which was encouraged by the Board to mitigate the effects of urbanisation and slum dwelling, and in 1928 fifteen local education authorities were running camps for schoolchildren, apart from unofficial camps organised by individual teachers and voluntary bodies. The value of camping caught the imagination and in 1931 for the first time camping was included in the training of women specialist teachers. Chelsea College of Physical Education finished its summer term by spending two weeks under canvas by the sea.[10]

In spite of official encouragement of non-gymnastic activities, the assumption that physical education was a form of preventive medicine, and the training of specialist teachers in the Swedish system with its physiological basis, inevitably led to very strong emphasis being placed upon the therapeutic side of physical training. Of the eleven publications on physical education issued by the Board between 1919 when the revised syllabus appeared, and 1927 when the *Reference Book of Gymnastic Training for Boys* was published, only one, *Suggestions in regard to Games* (1920), was devoted to non-gymnastic activities. The emphasis of the others was on physical training in a restricted sense. The tenor of the annual reports of the chief medical officer in the twenties was also therapeutic and even the value of games and sports tended to be assessed on that basis. The teaching of the 'crawl' stroke in swimming to beginners was officially discouraged because it was 'not so correct physiologically as the breast stroke or the back stroke'.[11] Thus the dichotomy of physical education into training which was scientific and games which were recreative persisted.

A belief in the therapeutic value of physical training was perhaps stronger in the minds of teachers than in the reports and exhortations of Sir George Newman. It manifested itself in many ways, for instance in the large number of articles on therapy in the *Journal of Scientific Physical Training*, in the development of remedial or corrective exercises in schools, in the development of special exercises and activities for blind and deaf children, in the gradual loss of the idea of gymnastics as a sport and in such a trivial incident as the regulation issued by the Women's Amateur Athletic Association making all throwing events bimanual in order to avoid one-sided development. Above all, the enthusiasm for therapeutic gymnastics manifested itself in an intense interest in Scandinavian practices, in gymnastic demonstrations, and in an attention to 'posture' which in the thirties became almost fanatical.

Developments which had been taking place in Scandinavia during the war were given some publicity in the report of the medical department of the Board for 1920. At Easter, 1923, the Ling Association organised a professional visit to Denmark and Sweden, and in the same year there took place the first of many English-Scandinavian summer schools at Herne Bay. One of the organisers of this school, Miss Gladys Wright, was an ardent disciple of Frk. Elli Björksten in Helsingfors and did so much to foster her system in England that in 1934 she was awarded the Golden Cross of the Order of the White Rose of Finland by the President of the Republic, being the first Englishwoman to receive the honour.[12] Probably nothing did so much to foster professional and public interest in Scandinavian gymnastics as the visits to this country of Niels Bukh and his gymnastic teams. The first visit of his team was organised by the Ling Association in October 1927 and demonstrations were given in the provinces as well as in London. They met with enthusiastic audiences and accounts appeared in many London and provincial papers. Bukh was careful to distinguish his primary gymnastics from demonstration gymnastics but in his displays the former were hardly less impressive than the latter. Whatever the criticisms of members of the physical education profession—and there were many in England as in Denmark—the striking features of the Danish movements, their continuity, their rhythmic character, their emphasis on stretching and mobilising and their strenuousness, made a great impact on English teachers. Rhythm and continuity of movement almost ousted static positions from men's and women's gymnastics. An observer at the first demonstration could not believe that any series of violent exercises, however scientifically grouped, could advantageously be performed for some twelve minutes on end,[13] yet within ten years this had become common practice in men's gymnastics and simple rhythmical exercises crept even into the lessons in junior schools.[14] Demonstrations were not the prerogative of foreign teams. After the first post-war demonstration organised by the Ling Association in the Albert Hall in 1921 they were held frequently up and down the country, and helped to popularise the gymnastic side of physical education.

Posture had for many years attracted attention from the physical education profession, but it had never obtained quite such a degree of veneration as it enjoyed in the late twenties and the thirties. Perhaps it was Sir Arthur Keith's Hunterian Lectures on the Evolution of Man's Posture delivered in 1923 which gave new impetus to the drive for better posture. An abstract of the lectures appeared in the *Journal of Physical Education* and other articles on postural problems followed.   In 1932 the medical department of the Board took up the theme of posture and dogmatically stated 'the ultimate criterion of the success of any scheme or system of physical training is the carriage, mobility and equilibrium of the human body. If there is one test of the strength, tone and balance of the body it is posture, for this depends on the co-ordination of the muscles acting on the skeleton.   Good posture indicates health and soundness, bad posture the reverse.'[15] This dogma was the result of an investigation carried out by the department on some 1,600 schoolchildren to discover the frequency of postural defects, their relation to other physical defects and diseases, the best method for their detection and recording and appropriate methods of treatment.   The Board's investigations were not the only ones.   Dr. Hoffa was commissioned by the Ling Association to carry out a similar piece of work,[16] and numerous other investigations into posture were made by doctors and teachers in the schools.   They were all hampered by the fact that posture defied accurate measurement and statements about it depended ultimately upon the subjective assessment of the observer.   Because the postural tests which were applied were not usually themselves tested for validity and reliability, the precise percentages which were quoted for the incidence of this or that defect were hardly worthy of the serious attention which they received.   If the figures quoted were unreliable, attention was nevertheless directed to the undoubtedly large number of defects of foot and spine in schoolchildren which demanded treatment.   The physical education profession not only attempted to remedy these defects, but also became acutely posture conscious, and articles appeared in the professional journals on such topics as 'Posture and

Keep Fit Exercises', 'Motor Driving and Posture', 'Cycling and Posture'.[17] The Board of Education's revised *Syllabus of Physical Training*, too, contained a new section on posture. Posture in fact became the yardstick of gymnastics.

Two matters of particular importance for the medical department of the Board of Education during the nineteen-twenties and early-thirties were the reorganisation of elementary schools following upon the Hadow Report, and the neglect of physical education in secondary schools. The report of the committee under the chairmanship of Sir Henry Hadow was issued in 1926 entitled *The Education of the Adolescent*. The essence of the plan proposed in the report was to make secondary education the normal course for all children. Hitherto, children who did not pass on to secondary grammar schools at the age of 11 remained, with few exceptions, in elementary schools which were arranged in 'standards' from I to VIII to correspond with the years of age 7 to 14. The Hadow reorganisation, which was accepted in principle by the Board of Education, involved a break in school life for all children at the age of 11 +. Children would then proceed to post-primary schools or classes with a fresh organisation and curriculum. The syllabus of physical training which had been in use since 1919 was unsuitable for the new set-up, and a revision was undertaken. The new syllabus which appeared in 1933 was divided into two parts, one for use in junior schools for children under 11 years of age and a second for use in senior schools for children over 11. The exercises themselves had been overhauled; fresh exercises and revised methods of teaching were introduced 'with a view to the special encouragement of posture and flexibility of muscles and joints'.[18]   A large number of simple games were described and were intended to lead up to the more advanced field games. The programme of lessons and tables perpetuated a somewhat formal, gymnastic pattern of work but at the same time the inclusion of 'activity' exercises ensured plenty of free and vigorous movement in every lesson. The syllabus thus reflected trends in physical education which have already been noted and which by 1933 were to be seen in many schools in the more progressive areas.

While there had been a steady development of physical education in elementary schools since the beginning of the century and high standards were maintained in girls' schools, the same was not true of secondary schools for boys. Immediately after the war His Majesty's Inspectors attacked the problem of physical education in secondary schools; not only was there a dearth of trained men teachers, there was also a tradition of employing drill sergeants to take physical training wherever it was taken at all. The one year's course for men specialist teachers at Sheffield from 1919 to 1923 hardly touched the fringe of the problem and it ceased to run after 1923. In 1924, therefore, two of His Majesty's Inspectors, Major Syson and Captain Parker, conducted the first of several annual vacation courses for masters in secondary schools.[19] The members of this course founded their own Secondary Schoolmasters' Physical Education Association. Existing associations either were closed to them or did not cater for the social and educational self-consciousness of secondary schoolmasters. The Ling Association had been open to men since 1911 but the professional qualifications required for membership ruled out the almost untrained enthusiasts at Scarborough. The new association quickly grew in membership. By the end of 1926 there were 126 members and in 1930 there were more than 200.[20] In enterprise and enthusiasm this body made a contribution to physical education out of proportion to its size. In June 1925 it held its first annual conference and underlined the need for educated men to take up physical training. In September of the same year it published the first series of pamphlets, which were then issued twice a year until 1939. It issued its own certificates of attendance for the Board's vacation courses and in 1934 started its own Easter vacation courses at Mill Hill School. For President the S.S.P.E.A. secured first Sir W. H. Hadow, then Dr. L. P. Jacks, and Vice-Presidents were Dr. Cyril Norwood, headmaster of Harrow School, and Mr. M. L. Jacks, headmaster of Mill Hill School. A marked step forward in raising the status of physical education in secondary schools was taken when the Incorporated Association of Assistant Masters was persuaded in 1938 to discontinue the use of the word 'instructor' when referring to teachers of physical training.[21]

In spite of the work of the S.S.P.E.A., and H.M. Inspectors, progress in municipal secondary schools gave little satisfaction to Sir George Newman for many years. In 1929 he accused the schools of regarding physical training as an 'extra' to be cut down or excluded under pressure of examinations, he accused the physical training experts, women and men, who worked in the schools, of a lack of the 'missionary' spirit and outlook that characterised elementary school teachers, and he accused the authorities of failing to give encouragement and support.[22] The pressure of examinations in these schools was indeed great, if only because success in examinations brought to the pupils parity of opportunity with boys and girls at high schools and boarding schools. Physical accomplishments were naturally thought to be of minor importance. Teachers may have lacked the 'missionary' spirit but they did not enjoy the encouragement or support of area organisers as elementary school teachers did. In fact they themselves, although working in isolation, were specifically allotted some of the functions which organisers performed for elementary schools. Physical education remained unsatisfactory in most secondary schools, for boys at least, until specialist teachers trained at Leeds and Loughborough began to adorn their staffs in the nineteen-thirties.

The nineteen-twenties did, however, see the beginning of an offensive of ideas on physical education which in turn gave rise to some interesting experiments in schools and elsewhere. Many medical men had long been interested in physical training, but the problems of leisure and education for leisure, of enforced idleness and physical recreation stimulated a large number of eminent non-medical men to fresh lines of thought. One of the first of them to publish his views was Professor L. P. Jacks. In an address upon the Ethics of Leisure in 1928 he outlined the problem of the increase of leisure and the tendency to buy pleasure instead of creating it. His remedy was education for skilled performance in one of many lines of activity open to man.[23] He was soon exploring and explaining the opportunities of physical education to supply this remedy.[24] 'An unskilled body,' he said, 'is a thwarted body, and, because thwarted unhealthy. Thwarted bodies exist in millions and everyone represents a thwarted mind.'[25] This was not the language of medicine or of science but it was the kind of statement which appealed to the emotions of ordinary people. One of L. P. Jacks' great assets was the ability to express his theories in such telling phrases as 'man is a skill hungry animal',[26] and in the titles of his books *The Education of the Whole Man* (1931) and *Education through Recreation* (1932). The latter was particularly apposite as it exposed the fallacy of the current dichotomy of physical education into training and recreation. Probably none of Dr. Jacks' statements received so much publicity or attention as the one which he used to a group of Public Schoolmasters at Harrow in January 1935. He then declared that 70 per cent of the population were 'physical illiterates'.[27]

Lord Dawson of Penn was one of the most vociferous of the medical men who contributed to the offensive of ideas. His remarks at the opening of a new sanatorium at Epsom College in 1931 concerning a new and wider conception of physical education and the need for doctors to study it, were not only reported in *The Times* but also received the endorsement of a leading article.[28] The *Morning Post*, however, did not believe with Lord Dawson that the old-fashioned and corporate drill was mechanical and soul destroying. On the contrary it still provided one of the best examples of concerted action and an opportunity of teaching the discipline needed in all good team work.[29] Lord Dawson was undeterred by the diehards and from 1931 onwards was constantly entering the arena as champion of physical education.

At about the time that Dr. Jacks began his pronouncements on physical education a number of headmasters of Public Schools not only began similar pronouncements of their own but began to apply their theories in their own schools. Mr. M. L. Jacks, headmaster of Mill Hill School and son of Dr. L. P. Jacks, was strongly influenced by his father, but he was also impressed by a display of physical education for boys which was organised by the

Board of Education and supported by the S.S.P.E.A. and given by Mr. S. F. Rous (later Sir Stanley Rous), a master at Watford Grammar School. Shortly afterwards Mr. Jacks appointed to his staff Mr. G. W. Hedley, an Oxford graduate master who had attended the Board of Education's courses in physical education for secondary schoolmasters. Mr. Hedley was given the title of 'Director of Physical Education'. This was a great innovation in the Public School world and indeed no teacher in any English school had enjoyed this title before. Mr. Jacks set out the ideas behind this appointment in a letter to *The Times* in November 1931. A 'Physical Education Department' had been created and the director's duties were not only to supervise and carry out physical training, boxing, fencing, swimming and allied activities, but also to keep an eye on a boy's physical development and to guide it throughout his school life.[30] As yet, it should be noted, the director of physical education was not to have much to do with the major games of rugby, hockey or cricket. Mill Hill's games were run on traditional Public School lines and games coaching was therefore the preserve of the 'blue' and the county player on the staff. Drill too was still used, as it was in many other Public Schools, as a punishment for misdemeanours. Revolutions in Public School methods had never taken place overnight and did not do so at Mill Hill. Nevertheless, a real start had been made in working out the 'education of the whole man' and the influence of the physical education department at Mill Hil both upon the lives of the boys in the school and upon physical education in the country at large grew steadily during the next decade.

At Leighton Park School, a Quaker Public School at Reading, the headmaster, E. B. Castle, saw a definite relationship between physical education in school and the challenge of social problems outside.   On appointing a Danish trained master to take charge of physical education he said: 'We regard this as a definite part of our attempt to provide a physical and moral equivalent for the O.T.C. for whose absence we do not apologise.   On the contrary, we regard it as one of our duties to show that the school can develop *esprit de corps* and the spirit of service better by methods of scientific physical culture and by direct methods to train boys in the technique of social service than by any form of military training.'[31]

Here too was a pioneer appointment.   Appointments of a somewhat similar nature to that at Mill Hill were made at Harrow School and Gresham's School, Holt, while developments at Queen Elizabeth's Grammar School, Barnet, showed that, given a nucleus of enthusiastic and energetic masters, a live physical education department need not be the prerogative of Public Schools. Interesting experiments were also conducted at this time by Dr. Friend, the medical officer at Christ's Hospital, into rates of growth of boys at boarding school, and by Mr. Sutcliffe and Mr. Canham, masters at Lincoln School. The latter experiment was unique at this time in its application of recognised scientific, mechanical and statistical methods to an investigation of the effects of systematic physical training upon scholastic attainment.   Nevertheless, the developments in physical education in Public Schools during the nineteen-thirties were little more than isolated experiments and in 1936 there were still only 11 per cent of Public Schools represented on the Headmasters' Conference employing men who had been fully trained in a non-military college.[32]   Moreover, most of them were better described as gymnastic masters than as directors of physical education.   In the main the fortresses of athleticism remained unshaken.

The games and sports which boys and girls at Public Schools enjoyed on a lavish scale had long been used by teachers in elementary and other state aided schools in a more limited way.   In 1926, however, their use as instruments of social policy was encouraged at the highest political level.   The Prime Minister stated that 'the greater the facilities for recreation, the better will be the health and happiness of the people and the closer will be the spirit of unity between all classes' and his words were quoted and endorsed by the chief medical officer of the Board of Education in relation to physical education.[33]

An attempt to use games in this way had already been made in 1921 at the Duke of York's camp repeated annually for 400 boys, 200 from Public Schools and 200 from elementary schools who had by then, of course, left school and were working in industry.   The common denominator was found in games.

A comprehensive account of the development of sport and physical recreation is beyond the scope of this book but it is not possible to understand fully the changes in physical education which took place between the wars without a brief reference to some events which occurred outside the main stream of educational provision.   Local education authorities had already embraced within their programmes non-vocational classes for adults and young people who had left school, and these classes included physical education.   The London County Council re-organised its classes within Evening Institutes in 1913 and from the start their prospectuses announced classes in physical exercises or gymnastics; some of them included swimming and one or two included country dancing and

morris dancing.   Classes in physical activities grew in
number after the war.

Voluntary organisations such as the Y.M.C.A., the
Y.W.C.A., the Boys Brigade, the Scouts and the Guides
likewise expanded their programmes of physical recreation along with other activities.   New organisations also
came into existence.   Perhaps pride of place among them
should go to the National Council of Social Service.   It
was formally inaugurated in 1919 as a body of representatives from government departments, local government
organisations, national voluntary organisations and local
social service agencies.   Although not specifically concerned with physical education and recreation, the part
which it played in distributing private and public money
to other organisations, in overseeing clubs for the unemployed, in initiating such organisations as the National
Association of Boys' Clubs and Youth Hostels Association,
and in sponsoring 'Keep Fit' movements indirectly
affected many forms of physical recreation.

Three other organisations which came into being in the
nineteen-twenties deserve special mention because they
reflected current concern for physical education and two
of them at least heralded new trends in physical education.
They were the National Playing Fields Association, the
Youth Hostels Association and the Lucas Tooth Institute.

The N.P.F.A. was in part a product of the social
conscience which mass unemployment and the enforced
idleness of so many people were arousing.   Between 1921
and 1931 the number of registered unemployed only fell
below the million mark for two isolated months.   In the
early thirties it remained steadily above the two million
mark.   It was impossible to gauge the number of workers
on short time, but the distress and poverty, the frustration,

the physical and mental deterioration that went with unemployment were obvious and were accentuated from time to time by strikes and lock-outs.   The time was ripe, therefore, for a letter to the Press in April 1925 drawing attention to the lack of playing fields and the encroachment of towns and cities upon those that did exist.   The letter suggested that a central organisation be formed to meet the situation and it was signed by a number of influential people.[34]   So great was the response that in July a packed meeting was held in the Albert Hall and the National Playing Fields Association was formed under the presidency of the Duke of York.   An appeal was sent out asking for 'the financial help of every citizen who recognises the need for greater co-operative effort to give our young people a chance to play the game and not merely to continue as onlookers'.   In 1927 the Carnegie United Kingdom Trust assigned £200,000 to aid the purchase of playing fields after the Prince of Wales had appealed on behalf of the N.P.F.A.   The trustees claimed that their contribution together with the £60,000 supplied by the N.P.F.A. elicited at least £1,500,000 of other money and resulted in 800 playing fields comprising some 6,000 acres being made available to boys and girls in Britain.[35]

The Youth Hostels Association was of an entirely different order and came into being in 1930.   Hiking, which had long been a feature of 'scouting', came into fashion— and some disapproval—after the first world war.   The idea of youth hostels derived from pre-Nazi Germany where there were already 2,187 *jugendherberger* by 1928. Their purpose was to provide cheap accommodation and so remove the economic barrier of hotel charges from the way of impecunious young people in the vast conurbations. It was during the winter of 1929–30 that interested bodies met under the auspices of the N.C.S.S. and decided to form the British Youth Hostels Association. By the end of 1931 there were 73 hostels, 1,562 beds and more than 6,000 members. By 1939 the corresponding figures were 297, 10,689 and 83,417.[36] Many parties from schools used the hostels and this was one of the earliest signs of the development of outdoor activities as part of physical education which was to be such a marked feature of the scene later on.

The Lucas Tooth Institute was founded in 1913 when Sir Robert Lucas Tooth gave £50,000 to start a Boys' Training Fund. In 1925 a new gymnasium was opened in an old school in Tooley Street, London, and courses were held from then onwards to qualify young men to became instructors of physical training in boys' clubs and other youth organisations. The training appealed more to uniformed organisations than to the others and was symptomatic of the continuing interest in formal gymnastics and well disciplined physical training which military drill and the Swedish system had both incorporated in different ways.

Chapter 13. References

1   E. Wingfield Stratford, *The Harvest of Victory, 1918–26*, London, 1935, pp. 101–2.
2   *R.C.M.O.*, 1920, 1921 and 1923.
3   *R.B.E.*, 1921–2, pp. 76–77.   See also *R.C.M.O.*, 1928, pp. 37–8.
4   *R.C.M.O.*, 1921, pp. 21ff.
5   *R.C.M.O.*, 1928, p. 36.
6   *R.C.M.O.*, 1926, p. 83.
7   Report of City of Birmingham Education Committee, 1914–24 and 1924–30.
8   *R.C.M.O.*, 1926, p. 83.
9   *R.C.M.O.*, 1930, p. 78.

10 *R.C.M.O.*, 1928, p. 38 and 1930, p. 79.

11 *R.C.M.O.*, 1926, p. 90.

12 *Ling Association Leaflet*, January 1934.

13 *J.P.E.*, XX, p. 185.

14 *R.C.M.O.*, 1933, p. 48.

15 *R.C.M.O.*, 1932, p. 81.

16 *Ling Association Leaflet*, November 1934.

17 *Ling Association Leaflets*, December 1934 and March 1935 and *J.P.E.*, XXIV, p. 55.

18 *R.C.M.O.*, 1932, p. 79.

19 *R.C.M.O.*, 1923, p. 113.

20 *S.S.P.E.A. Pamphlets*, Nos. 4 and 15.

21 *S.S.P.E.A. Pamphlet*, No. 12.

22 *R.C.M.O.*, 1928, pp. 43–4.

23 L. P. Jacks, 'The Ethics of Leisure', *Hibbert Journal*, Vol. 27, p. 270.

24 L. P. Jacks, 'The Employer as Educator', reported in *The Times*, 17 June 1931.

25 L. P. Jacks, *Hibbert Journal*, Vol. 31, p. 217.

26 *The Times*, 17 June 1931.

27 *Ling Association Leaflet*, February 1935.

28 *The Times*, 5 and 7 October 1931.

29 *Morning Post*, 5 October 1931.

30 *The Times*, 7 November 1931.

31 *The Times*, 30 June 1930.

32 *Report of Physical Education Committee of the B.M.A.*, 1936, p. 9.

33 *R.C.M.O.*, 1926, p. 85.

34 *R.C.M.O.*, 1926, p. 84.

35 H. A. Mess, *Voluntary Social Services since 1918*, London, 1947, p. 177.

36 O. Coburn, *Youth Hostel Story*, London, 1950, pp. 1, 17–18, 52–3.

CHAPTER 14

Physical Training and Recreation

THERE was no clear break in the development of physical education during the nineteen-twenties and -thirties, but that development was so complex that it may be valuable at this point to pause and take notice of two events which were signposts showing both the road that had been travelled and the way ahead. The events were the institution of a diploma in the theory and practice of physical education by the Senate of London University in 1930 and the appointment of two additional men inspectors of physical exercises in 1931.

One of the two additional inspectors was a civilian, the organiser of physical education at Leicester; the other was an army officer. It was significant that this was the first occasion on which a civilian was appointed to be His Majesty's Inspector of Physical Exercises. The day had passed when the only source of men with sufficient education, training and experience to fill the post of inspector was the armed services. The chief medical officer of the Board, in his annual reports, had paid tribute to the excellent work done by organisers working for local education authorities. These men had considerable technical ability and wide administrative experience. In the circumstances it was not surprising that the appointment of a serving army officer raised a storm of protest from men organisers. The objection was not to the individual inspector, but to the principle of the appointment. A resolution of protest was passed at the annual conference of the National Association of Organisers of Physical Education and a deputation from the association was received by Sir George Newman and Mr. Wood at the Ministry of Health on 17 April.[1] The policy of training teachers to take the place of drill sergeants, initiated by Captain Grenfell and Sir George Newman some twenty years before, had now matured. Civilians were, henceforward, to exclude military and naval officers from the inspectorate, and physical education in schools was to be independent, not merely of military training, but even of direct military influence.

The institution of the London University Diploma of Physical Education was the achievement of sixteen years' hard work by women members of the physical education profession. From its inception the Ling Physical Education Association had been determined to maintain high professional standards. Membership was restricted at first to teachers who had been trained at colleges recognised and approved by the association. Only five had been approved by 1916, Dartford, Bedford, Chelsea, Anstey and Dunfermline. In 1904, however, membership was opened to teachers who passed the Ling Association's own diploma examination and a small number of teachers became eligible in this way. In 1916 the Ling Association refused to amalgamate with other physical education associations with a view to obtaining a charter for gymnastic teachers, because it saw that its own professional standards would thereby be lowered. In the same year, however, Dr. Janet Campbell of the Board of Education met representatives of the women's colleges to discuss the advisability of a common syllabus and a single examination and diploma for all colleges. There was also a move by the Bergman Österberg Union to persuade the Board of Education to undertake the examination of students and to grant Government diplomas. The Board of Education declined to act and the colleges found it impossible to agree among themselves upon a common syllabus and diploma examination. In 1918, therefore, inquiries were made about the possibility of London University undertaking to examine and grant degrees or diplomas to gymnastic teachers. It was not until 1927 that a formal memorial on the subject was presented to the Senate of the university, and not until 1930 that the Senate agreed to institute a diploma. The first examination for the new diploma was held in 1932. The high standard of work and training which had been jealously guarded by the women's colleges and the Ling Association was thus recognised. Furthermore, the close association with a university was a stimulus to these colleges, which, both socially and educationally, had been somewhat isolated from other educational institutions, and the new tie was much appreciated by them. There was still no college for training specialist men teachers of physical education in England, but that omission was soon to be made good. The starting of courses and the founding of colleges for men specialists was one of the three major developments of the next ten years. The other two were the propagation of ideas and the growth of popular movements to extend physical recreation.

During the nineteen-thirties the offensive of ideas continued with increased force, and with some gratifying results. In 1935 the education section of the British Association considered physical education and was addressed by Mr. M. L. Jacks, Mr. Rous, and other members of the physical education profession. The following year the report of the physical education committee of the British Medical Association appeared.   New books began to appear on the aims and objects of physical education such as *Physical Education for Boys* by G. W. Hedley and G. W. Murray (1936), *Movement and Thought* by R. E. Roper (1938).   Dr. Cyril Norwood, whose *English Tradition of Education*, written in 1929, described the function of games in some detail but made no mention of physical training, systematic exercise or the careful observation of boys' growth and development, made good the omission when he addressed the National Union of Teachers in 1934, and said: 'I look forward to a time when, just as a boy progresses from the first form to the sixth in mental accomplishments, so he will climb the ladder in physical fitness and accomplishments, and rise equally steadily from the low and undeveloped to the high and developed grades.   I do not mean that he will be trained for games, though such a training will help.   I do not mean that his body will be trained. . . .   I mean that there will be an enlightened attempt to educate him physically.'[2]   Other eminent personalities such as Sir Farquhar Buzzard,[3] Mr. Harold Nicolson,[4] and Sir Michael Sadler[5] began to appear on the physical education platform.   Much of what was said was in no way new, but some of the lines of thought which were developed were new and implied a change and even a reversal of current practices.   When the editor of the *Ling Association Leaflet* wrote: 'Correspondence lately in *The Times* from Sir Philip Devitt, Mr. M. L. Jacks, Headmaster of Mill Hill, and others, shows plainly the increased understanding of our aims among people whose opinion we value highly',[6] she was, perhaps, being a little self-satisfied.   The fact that neither of Dr. Jacks' books, *The Education of the Whole Man* and *Education through Recreation*, was reviewed in the *Journal of Physical Education* was an indication of the profession's interest in technical problems rather than in aims and objects. At the same time it is only fair to state that many members of the Ling Association and even some headmistresses had for many years been advocating a broader programme and a more enlightened conception of physical education than was recognised by educationists in general. Girls' schools could boast of much more efficient physical education than could boys' schools.

In the country at large, during the thirties, the fresh economic crisis in 1931 and the continuance and even increase of unemployment proved a stimulus to a number of mass movements in various forms of physical recreation. The Ministry of Labour strongly encouraged the provision of physical training at junior instruction centres for unemployed boys and girls,[7] but, in the main, the development of physical recreation was at first independent of Government action. In 1929 Miss Norah Reed, a teacher in Sunderland, visited Denmark and Sweden where voluntary gymnastics was already organised in a mass movement, and returned to Sunderland determined to embark upon a similar adventure with women and girls in the North-East. So began the 'keep fit' movement. 127 girls turned up for the first class and the numbers grew. The next winter there were nine classes running in various parts of the town, and attendances were about 500 per week. Soon a special class for mothers was started and then a 'keep fit' class for the 'over forties'. The classes lasted about fifty minutes and consisted of gymnastic movements with music. It would be difficult to analyse the reasons for the success of this movement, but the comment of a husband to his wife who attended a class—'If you are not any thinner you are certainly better tempered'—showed that the classes gave emotional satisfaction as well as physical benefits.[8] The movement quickly spread, not only to adjacent areas in Northumberland and Durham but to areas farther afield and in particular to Lancashire. In that county the depression in the cotton industry had resulted in a large number of unemployed women and girls. A 'keep fit' movement was started by the National Council of Girls' Clubs under the auspices of the National Council of Social Service. Similar classes were started up and down the country and by December 1934 it was possible to stage a display in the Albert Hall in which over 700 girls took part. The growth of a similar movement among men and its relation to unemployment was described by Mr. Major, the Warden of Carnegie Physical Training College, to the British Association in 1935. Men were naturally motivated differently from women in the 'keep fit' classes, and when physical training was introduced into men's occupational centres for the unemployed by the National Council of Social Service, the association of the phrase 'physical training' with memories of army service, and the suspicion that a disguised form of military training was being imposed upon them, caused some antagonism to physical exercises. However, less obnoxious titles such as 'recreative physical training' or even just 'physical recreation' came into use, and a programme of work which included swimming and some games, as well as simple rhythmical exercises and vaulting and agility, gained general acceptance. All kinds of premises were used for classes, from church halls to tram sheds. In 1934 camps for the unemployed were started on quite a large scale. Here again suspicion that they were being sent to 'labour or concentration camps' had to be dispelled before the scheme was successful. Leaders for all this work were trained in special courses organised by the National Council of Social Service.[9] Recreative physical training was not confined to classes for the unemployed, whether men or women. Just as the conception of social service in general changed from the idea of relieving distress to that of enriching normal life,[10] so recreative physical training came to be a recognised leisure pursuit for all, whether in or out of regular employment.

While the 'keep fit' movement was developing in the north of the country, private individuals and clubs were starting similar movements elsewhere. Margaret Morris who had been giving demonstrations of theatrical and remedial dancing for many years, devoted all her time from 1928 onwards to the development of Margaret Morris Movement. Another organisation, the Women's League of Health and Beauty, gained nationwide influence. The league was initiated by Mrs. Bagot Stack with a demonstration class at the Y.W.C.A. in Regent Street, London, in 1929, and ninety members were enrolled on the first evening. Mrs. Stack was a woman with very limited financial resources, but with a sound appreciation of what women wanted and with large ideas for the growth of her league. The title was devised to appeal to women's desire for glamour and the 'sparkle of necklaces'. Within a year of starting Mrs. Stack had staged a demonstration in Hyde Park; the next year she took and filled the Albert Hall, and by 1933 twenty-three league centres had opened and there were more than 30,000 members. By 1937, the league had enrolled 120,000 members. Mrs. Stack based her appeal not only upon the desire for physical beauty and well-being, but upon the growing hunger for peace and fear of war and strife. Her demonstration at the Albert Hall in 1933 included a mime symbolising the reconciliation of Capital and Labour and one of the expressed objects of the league was to further the cause of peace.[11]

By 1935 the growth of recreative physical training in many forms and under many different organisations had reached such dimensions that a national co-ordinating body was needed. In that year, therefore, the National Association of Organisers of Physical Education and the Ling Association co-operated to form the 'Central Council of Recreative Physical Training', an impressive body of men and women eminent in public life under the patronage of the King and Queen and Prince of Wales and the presidency of Viscount Astor. The Central Council was the brainchild of Phyllis Colson, who had qualified as a specialist teacher of physical education at Bedford Physical Training College. The initial financial backing was also provided by teachers since the two initiating associations were comprised of those who were or had been specialist teachers. While the council's general function was to co-ordinate and stimulate what was fast becoming a national campaign for more and better physical recreation, its immediate task was to undertake a survey of existing facilities and organisations so that definite proposals for future development might be laid before the trustees of various charitable funds. In the early months, too, the Central Council was busy compiling a list of volunteer men and women leaders, initiating training courses for leaders and organising demonstrations in London and the provinces. Before the end of the year there were over sixty classes in progress under the auspices of the council and requests for many more were coming in. However, for almost a year the council worked on very slender financial resources and relied for its work upon the energy and efficiency of its two volunteer secretaries, Mr. H. A. Cole and Miss P. C. Colson, and upon the help of countless volunteers among teachers and organisers. It was not until April 1936 that the council received its first grant of £1,000 from King George's Jubilee Trust and a further £1,000 from the National Playing Fields Association. A policy was then inaugurated of appointing travelling representatives to advise local bodies, arrange demonstrations and generally stimulate interest in recreative physical training throughout the country. In the early stages of the council's work the emphasis was upon a physical training approach to recreation. Such an approach was the natural outcome of the 'keep fit' movement, which itself was partly inspired by the popular gymnastic movements in Scandinavia; such an approach too was to be expected of a body inaugurated and staffed by members of the physical education profession whose training and experience had been largely in therapeutic gymnastics and who had been encouraged by Sir George Newman to regard themselves as practitioners of preventive medicine. Gradually, however, the long-standing interest of English people in games and sports asserted itself and physical training receded, until eventually, in January 1944, the central council changed its title from the Central Council of Recreative Physical Training to the Central Council of Physical Recreation.

The great development of recreative physical training in the nineteen-thirties was accompanied by the setting up of training facilities at long last for men specialist teachers. Here again, however welcome these developments were to the Government, the initiation of courses and the provision of facilities were left to local bodies or voluntary organisations. Carnegie Physical Training College in Leeds was made possible by the offer of £30,000 by the Carnegie Trustees for the building and by the provision of a site by the City of Leeds Education Committee. The college opened in 1933 and provided a one-year course in physical education for sixty students.[12]   In keeping with the general fashion, the approach to physical education at Carnegie was through gymnastics. A daily period of personal gymnastics and a daily lecture upon the theory of gymnastics together with afternoons spent on anatomy and physiology and teaching practice (of gymnastics) necessarily made the study and practice of the many other skills and techniques of physical education somewhat superficial. One feature of Carnegie College distinguished it sharply from the women's physical education colleges. The Board of Education had decided as early as 1930 that it was not desirable that physical education should be in the hands of those whose qualification was limited to physical training.[13]   The course at Carnegie College, therefore, was open only to those who had already obtained a teacher's certificate or a degree at a British university. The college thus gradually created a body of well-educated and technically efficient men whose absence hitherto had been a serious disadvantage and who now almost at once began to raise both the standard and the status of physical education in England. When the unabated demand for teachers and organisers later led to the opening of additional one-year courses at Loughborough College in 1935 and Goldsmiths' College, London, in 1937, these courses conformed to a similar pattern.

The initiative of Loughborough College in physical education was not restricted to a one-year course. The college included physical education courses in its summer school programme from 1932 onwards, and the course in athletics held in 1934 under the auspices of the Amateur Athletics Association, for which a coach was invited over from Finland, marked the beginning of a movement to study the techniques of many games and sports and to work out systematic ways of coaching them in schools and clubs. A more ambitious course was the three-year course which enjoyed the title of 'The School of Athletics, Games and Physical Education'. It was a specialist course, but being restricted to physical education it did not secure the recognition of the Board of Education and unlike all the other courses it did not survive the war.

Two factors of particular importance in the physical recreation movement of the early nineteen-thirties were the financial backing of great philanthropic trusts and the publicity given to physical recreation by the cinema, the wireless and the Press. The Physical Education Committee of the British Film Institute founded in 1933 supported the making of many films, including films illustrating the methods detailed in the 1933 syllabus and methods of recreative physical training. The wireless emitted a steady flow of appeals for money and of propaganda for physical recreation. Some of the written contributions to the movement made through the correspondence columns of *The Times* have already been described. News columns were also devoted to physical recreation and in 1938 the holiday course of the Ling Association was noticed in more than nineteen papers and provoked leading articles in *The Times* and the *Manchester Guardian*. [14] Little of the work done in physical recreation would have been possible without financial backing. Although the Women's League of Health and Beauty and some other

organisations depended, and flourished, on nothing but
their members' subscriptions, a large amount of other work
was only carried on with the help of the charitable trusts.
The trust deed under which Mr. Carnegie constituted his
United Kingdom Trust allowed wide discretion to the
trustees.   They were able, therefore, when the need arose,
to devote their funds to the cause of physical welfare, and
their gifts of £200,000 for playing fields in 1927 and
£30,000 for a physical training college in 1931 were the
largest of a number of gifts designed to help the physical
recreation movement.[15] The other two great trusts
which contributed substantial funds were King George's
Jubilee Trust and the King George Memorial Fund.
Both of them were made up of public subscriptions and
while the former, launched in 1935, was devoted to the
welfare of youth in general, and assisted physical recreation along with other causes, the latter, which was sub-
scribed after the death of King George V in 1936, was
specifically for the provision of playing fields.   In spite of
the work of the N.P.F.A. playing fields were still badly
needed.   By the end of 1935 the N.P.F.A. had assisted 908
schemes involving a total expenditure of £2,772,200.
Over twelve square miles of playing fields had been laid
down, yet on the Association's minimum standard of four
acres per 1,000 population, these facilities only provided
fields for about 2,000,000 people, less than 5 per cent of the
population.[16]

The government was not uninterested in the work of
the voluntary organisations and professional associations
in promoting physical education and recreation.   In November 1934, in the course of a speech at a dinner of the
Council of the British Medical Association, Sir Hilton
Young, the Minister of Health, had expressed the hope

that the medical profession would advise him how some advance might be made in bringing home the benefits of physical culture. The B.M.A. accordingly set up a Physical Education Committee, which issued a report in April 1936. The report gave a comprehensive survey of the provision of physical education and recreation. By the extensive use of questionnaires the committee was able to make such estimates as that 84 per cent of girls' secondary schools had gymnasia, that 750,000 amateurs belonging to clubs affiliated to the Football Association played football each Saturday, that 72 per cent of boys between the ages of 14 and 18 received no form of recreative physical training and that not less than 40 per cent of the population between the ages of 14 and 40 needed, but did not participate adequately, if at all, in physical recreation or training. In general the committee thought that the position in schools left much to be desired and that the arrangements for the continued physical education of persons no longer attending school were thoroughly unsatisfactory.[17]

The progress of physical education in elementary and secondary schools had certainly not been spectacular in the seventeen years following the end of the war in 1918. Nevertheless, the achievements of professional organisations such as the Ling Association and the Secondary Schoolmasters Physical Education Association, the influence of organisers engaged by local education authorities and of His Majesty's Inspectors, and the impressive growth of voluntary organisations in physical recreation outside the schools now prompted the Board of Education to give some positive encouragement and guidance to physical education.

The issue of *Circular 1445* 'Physical Education' on 13

January 1936 was the result of 'a growing concern for all that affects the physical welfare of the nation'. In view of the articles that were appearing in the Press about intensive physical training of the young in the fascist countries of Italy and Germany and a significant reference to them in the *Circular* it may be deduced that foreign as well as domestic affairs were influencing the Board of Education. *Circular 1445* did not confine itself to physical education in schools but indicated the ways in which the Board was prepared to help voluntary and statutory bodies in promoting physical education for those no longer at school.

Elementary schools were urged to have a daily period of organised physical activity, three for physical exercises, one for swimming and one for organised games or dance for girls. Local education authorities were reminded that they had legal power to provide playing fields for all school children and were encouraged to do so. The Board thought that the position in secondary schools was far from satisfactory. There were schools where only one period a week was given to physical training and where boys over 14 had none. The Board stated categorically that three school periods of normal length should be allowed for gymnastics and physical exercises in addition to the time allowed for games and swimming.

For 'persons no longer attending school' the Board realised that physical training alone was unattractive and advocated 'physical activities along with other allied activities'. However, classes wholly devoted to single games or sports were not approved.

The desire of the Board to link together the efforts of statutory and voluntary bodies in physical training and recreation is clearly brought out in the section dealing with the duties and qualifications of organisers of physical training engaged by local education authorities. The primary work of these men and women was to be in elementary schools but more than this—'He should in fact be the recognised guide and adviser for the community as a whole in matters relating to physical exercises and recreation, and his work should not be limited to Elementary Schools or even to Schools of any type, but should extend to young people, both employed and unemployed, who have left school. His services should be freely available to voluntary organisations and for coordinating their schemes with those of the Authority.'[18]

Circular 1445 was not without effect. By the end of the year forty-five more local education authorities had appointed organisers making a total of 169 and by the end of 1938, 249 authorities were employing 338 organisers. Another step forward was taken in *Circular 1450*, also issued in 1936, enabling local education authorities to provide clothing and shoes for physical training at public expense.[19]

The increasing provision of playing fields by local education authorities was another instance of statutory bodies following the lead of voluntary organisations, notably the National Playing Fields Association. During 1937, 159 new sites and 23 extensions to existing sites for playing fields were acquired by local education authorities of which 36 were intended to serve more than one school. Some authorities arranged for children to go to playing fields for a whole day and had built classrooms alongside the changing and showering facilities at the fields. In London it was hoped that by this means every child from 10 to 15 years of age would be able to play games on a grass field once a week.

The recommendations of *Circulars 1445* and *1450* were not enough to satisfy the growing concern for national fitness and in January 1937 the government issued a White Paper on Physical Training and Recreation. It was accompanied by the publication of technical handbooks, *Recreation and Physical Fitness for Youths and Men* and *Recreation and Physical Fitness for Girls and Women*, and by the setting up of a National Advisory Council for Physical Training and Recreation and twenty-two subsidiary area committees. These measures were followed by the Physical Training and Recreation Act passed in July 1937 and teeth were given to the whole scheme by the allocation of £2,000,000 to be spent over the following three years in the development of physical recreation. The National Fitness Campaign had moved some way from the physical training approach to recreation made by the C.C.R.P.T., and the meagre representation of the physical education profession on the National Advisory Council was attributed by the organiser for the L.C.C. to the very fact that in the public mind the profession was associated solely with knee bending and arm swinging.[20] At the same time the dichotomy of education into training and recreation persisted in the title of the Act. This dichotomy was further emphasised by Mr. Oliver Stanley, who moved the second reading of the bill. He felt it necessary to remind the House of Commons that the bill envisaged a scheme not only for physical training but for recreation; nevertheless he went on to stress the training and therapeutic side of the bill, claiming that wise scientific training given under proper instruction and with a scientific basis behind it could do much to remedy some of those minor and, indeed, major ills to which a highly civilised and industrialised society was liable. As usual when this argument was put forward, neither the ills nor the precise treatment to which they would respond was specified, nor was any objective evidence produced to support the claim. It was just as reasonable for some Labour members to argue, as they did, that when such a large proportion of the population was suffering from malnutrition, the minor and major ills of a highly industrialised society were more likely to be exacerbated by physical training than to be remedied by it. In default of objective data or scientific evidence, discussion along these lines was bound to be inconclusive. When the debate got as far away from the subject as the price of milk in Sweden, Mr. Deputy Speaker intervened.[21] Another line of attack upon the Government's policy was that the bill was designed to provide military training in disguise and some support was given to this idea by the coincidence of the bill with the rearmament programme. Some members of the House, like Sir Francis Fremantle, thought this was a point in favour of the bill, others thought otherwise.

Some of the most significant comments on the whole scheme were made by Mr. James Maxton and Mr. Aneurin Bevan. Mr. Maxton's argument was that the emphasis on health was a mistake. Health should be a by-product rather than the objective of the scheme. Boys should play football and girls tennis because they liked it, not because it was a national duty or a substitute for medicine. Mr. Bevan took the same line in the debate on the second reading of the bill. He said: 'I think the desire to play is a justification in itself for playing; there is no need to seek the justification of national well-being for playing, because your own well-being is a sufficient justification. The idea that you must borrow some justification for playing is one of the worst legacies of the Puritan revolution.'

Mr. Bevan also made another criticism of Government policy on physical training. He maintained that the Government was pushing physical training on the masses because it was easier and cheaper than providing the facilities and the playing fields which the upper and middle classes already enjoyed. 'This idea that you must get all the boys and girls in rows, like chocolate soldiers, and make them go through evolutions, is a miserable substitute for giving them sufficient playgrounds in which they can play their own games in their own ways.

'I know that what I am going to say is sheer heresy and that I may call down on my head the wrath of many people, but I would abolish precise and formal physical training in schools. I would provide some other means of recreation.'[22]

In spite of criticisms, the bill was welcomed by the physical education profession and the country at large. Most people were more interested in the opportunities and funds which this new legislation offered than in the motives that had prompted it. Application for some of the £2,000,000 made available soon came from clubs and organisations and duly passed through the National Fitness Council under the chairmanship of Lord Aberdare to the finance 'Triumvirate' under Sir Henry Pelham.

By March 1939 789 offers of grants had been made amounting to £1,468,302, but in fact only £532,982 had actually been spent when war broke out in 1939 and of this sum £152,957 had gone on salaries and administrative expenses, so that actual financial help received by organisations in the field was not as great as might have been expected.[23]

Another significant development which was assisted under the national fitness scheme was physical education in the universities. Speakers had for many years been urging British universities to pay more attention to the physical education of students and to provide for the study of the subject on a level with academic subjects.[24] As early as 1926 Dr. Adami, Vice-Chancellor of Liverpool University, had advocated the appointment of directors of physical education at every British university. Scottish universities were first in the field with the creation of departments of physical education. The department at Edinburgh, set up in 1930 under Colonel R. B. Campbell, found its way into the report of the University Grants Committee for the period 1929–30 and 1934–5, and the committee advocated the provision of physical training facilities in all universities. In 1937 the National Union of students issued *Student Health* and therein reviewed facilities for physical education. At only four places in England and Wales were there any regular courses of physical training open to students as a whole, and it was estimated that only 25 per cent of students outside Oxford and Cambridge took part in any games.[25] The report urged both the appointment of directors of physical education and the provision of gymnasia, swimming pools and administrative offices. In 1938 it was announced that by an arrangement made between the National Fitness Council and the University Grants Committee £200,000 had been made available for capital expenditure on facilities for physical education at universities. Out of this fund as well as from private benefactions some of the facilities recommended in *Student Health* were provided in English provincial universities, and before the war supervened, directors of physical education had been appointed at Liverpool, Leeds, Manchester and Birmingham Universities.

At the end of July 1939, there was a mass pilgrimage of gymnasts to Sweden to do honour to P. H. Ling, the founder of Swedish gymnastics, and to take part in a great gymnastic festival. The Lingiad, as the festival was called, was perhaps a not inappropriate finale to a period of steady development of physical education with its emphasis upon therapeutic gymnastics. The very appearance of the British contingent at the opening ceremony revealed the pattern of the physical recreation movement in this country. The massed teams from Germany and Denmark and Sweden, each more than 1,000 strong, marched into the stadium at Stockholm uniformly dressed with their national flag or emblem upon their chests. The various little troupes that made up the great British contingent preserved their identities. One girls' team wore white divided skirts and red cardigans, another wore plain white dresses, this group of men wore white flannels and blue blazers, that group wore white shorts and vests, some were adorned with Union Jacks, some with their college emblem, some had no emblem at all. This motley crowd, who had to be placed in the very centre of the stadium in order to avoid wrecking the symmetry of the whole display, showed how the physical recreation movement in Britain grew up with a minimum of central direction and a maximum of local effort and individual initiative operating through voluntary organisations. The teams had hardly returned from the Lingiad to their own countries when war broke out. In England there was an immediate mass evacuation of schoolchildren from the towns, the National Fitness Council ceased to function, the Grants Committee made no more grants, and general mobilisation threw physical education into the melting pot.

Chapter 14. References

1 *J.P.E.*, XXIII, p. 105.
2 *J.P.E.*, XXVI, p. 57.
3 *S.S.P.E.A. Pamphlet*, No. 27.
4 *Op. cit.*, No. 29.
5 *J.P.E.*, XXVI, p. 147.
6 *Ling Association Leaflet*, June 1937.
7 *R.C.M.O.*, 1933, p. 53.
8 *J.P.E.*, XXV, pp. 165–71.
9 *J.P.E.*, XXVII, pp. 127–9.
10 H. A. Mess, *Voluntary Social Services since 1918*, p. 2.
11 J. A. Cruikshank and P. Stack, *Movement is Life*, London, 1937, *passim*.
12 *R.C.M.O.*, 1932, p. 80.
13 *R.C.M.O.*, 1931, p. 82.
14 *Ling Association Leaflet*, March 1938.
15 *J.P.E.*, XXIX, pp. 148–52.
16 *J.P.E.*, XXVIII, p. 57.
17 *Report of the Physical Education Committee of the B.M.A.*, London, 1936.
18 *Physical Education*, Circular 1445, H.M.S.O., 13 January 1936.
19 *Clothing and Shoes for Physical Training*, Circular 1450, H.M.S.O., 20 October 1936.
20 *J.P.E.*, XXX, p. 33.
21 *Hansard, H.C.*, 7 April 1937, Cols. 201–30.
22 *Hansard, H.C.*, Vol. CCCXX, Cols. 116–17: Vol. CCCXXII, Cols. 252–7.
23 Civil Appropriation Accounts 1937, 1938 and 1939, H.M.S.O.
24 See Sir William Milligan, M.D., in *Ling Association Leaflet*, July 1917 and R. E. Roper, *J.P.E.*, p. 32.
25 *Student Health* pub. National Union of Students, 1937.

CHAPTER 15

Danger and Movement

THE outbreak of war in September 1939 was accompanied by a much greater disorganisation of education than the same event in 1914. The risk of aerial bombing in 1939 had caused elaborate plans to be prepared for the evacuation of school children from what were considered to be dangerous areas and these plans were put into operation two days before war was declared. In the evacuation areas schools were closed and in the reception areas schools and homes had to cope with a huge influx of children and teachers. Only in 'neutral' areas was the work of schools anything like normal.

Evacuation was the first but not the least blow to physical education. Gymnasia and swimming baths were requisitioned for rest centres or first-aid posts; Manchester, for instance, was left with a few plunge baths and no swimming baths. Mobilisation too was more rapid than in the previous great war; and although at first men over 25 were 'reserved' the call up of younger men teachers and the transfer of some women teachers into the armed forces threw a sudden burden upon the physical education service.

The war also saw a steady deterioration and diminution of equipment, whether apparatus like footballs or of personal equipment like shoes and clothing and towels. As in the previous war the civilian training of men specialists in physical education ceased. Of course the community took emergency measures to deal with the immediate disruption. A scheme of priority allocation of shoes, clothes and equipment to be shared by the children did something to mitigate the worst effects of these shortages. When men teachers went to the forces often older men and, in some schools, women took over physical education from their colleagues on active service. Vacation courses continued and some local education authorities ran special lecture demonstrations to help women and older men to cope with physical education. Nevertheless standards of performance and standards of hygiene which had been built up so laboriously over many years inevitably fell.

Outside the schools physical education and recreation was also disrupted. The National Fitness Council closed its doors on 30 September 1939 but in its place the government set up a smaller National Youth Committee and in November issued a circular *The Service of Youth*, thus giving a name to the new drive for the provision of leisure time occupations and for the general well-being of adolescents. This well-being was not considered merely in terms of physical recreation but physical recreation did seem important enough for the War Office to sanction, in 1940, the release from the army of qualified physical education specialists who were prepared to return to their posts and help in youth service, and whose employers were prepared to have them back.[1] Many teachers thus returned to civilian life, and these men, without the status conferred by rank and uniform, did unobtrusive but invaluable work in physical education.

From December 1941 all boys and girls were required to register at 16, and at the registration interview were encouraged to join some youth organisation. New pre-service organisations grew up and attracted large numbers of boys and girls into their ranks. The desire to be ready for military service in the forces and for civilian service in the civil defence organisation was met by the Central Council of Recreative Physical Training in its 'Fitness for Service' campaign. The C.C.R.P.T. had at first been told by the Board of Education to close down along with the National Fitness Council through which it received its grant. All the staff were actually given notice but the officers of the C.C.R.P.T. refused to abandon their work without protest. They gained a reprieve in order to work mainly for the 14–20 age group, and physical training was thereupon conducted in public parks and playgrounds throughout the country. Fitness for Service indeed provided the answer to the question 'Fitness for What?'—a question which had been prompted by the National Fitness Campaign and had never been satisfactorily answered. Now all difficulties of logic were resolved in the immediate tasks of surviving and winning the war.

The urgency of the immediate tasks had the paradoxical effect of stimulating long-term plans for the more distant future and not for the first time in the history of educational legislation. The Boer War had been followed by the Balfour Act of 1902. The 1914–18 war had not ended when the Fisher Act became law in 1918. The 1939–45 war saw the Butler Act reach the statute book in 1944. It was as if the military and naval disasters abroad, the bombing at home and the knowledge that so many of those in the prime of life were being destroyed made people feel that it was more than ever necessary to plan a better future for the children. Similar concern was aroused by the revelations of evacuation. The appalling conditions of home and school under which many children had been growing up could no longer remain hidden or ignored. *Our Towns*, a survey produced by a group of women in 1943, was a close-up of black spots and created a great stir. A quotation epitomises the mood of the time, 'A group of poverty-stricken children was seen standing on the kerb. "They don't look much, do they?" said one housewife to another. "Well, anyhow," replied her companion, "that's what England always falls back on!" '[2]

The 1944 Act then was a response to this mixture of disillusion and aspiration. It provided the legal and administrative framework for significant developments in physical education as in education generally. The abolition of fees for all secondary schools other than independent and 'direct grant' schools meant that secondary education for all was a real possibility and, as far as physical education was concerned, the earlier distinctions made between the programmes for boys and girls of 11–14 at senior elementary schools and boys and girls of the same age at grammar schools had no longer any justification. The raising of the school leaving age to 15 which followed the passing of the Act meant that more mature forms of physical education had to be thought out for the additional year at school. Section 53 of the Act replaced the permissive clause 8b of the 1921 Act and put a specific duty upon all local education authorities to provide adequate facilities for recreation and physical training. The act also replaced the Board of Education with a Ministry of Education and transferred to the Ministry the functions of the National Fitness Council and Grants Committee which had been set up by the

Physical Training and Recreation Act of 1937, thus involving the government more intimately than ever with the leisure pursuits of the community at large.

The administrative machinery was remodelled in other ways too. The regulations prescribing standards for playing fields issued in 1944 specified half an acre for every fifty pupils in a primary school and five acres for a one-form entry secondary school rising to fourteen acres for a three-form entry school.[3]   The Boards Memorandum on planning and equipping gymnasia produced in 1939 had already adumbrated gymnasia measuring 70 feet by 40 feet to replace the recommendation of 60 feet by 30 feet, but the war and emergency rebuilding immediately afterwards delayed the implementation of this proposal for some years.

A most significant administrative change was made in 1945 when His Majesty's Inspectors of physical education ceased to be within the purview of the school health service and were absorbed into the general administrative side of the Ministry.   This change meant that they were responsible to the senior chief inspector instead of having direct access to the chief medical officer.   It was doubtless true, as the report of the chief medical officer said, that physical education was by that time regarded not even as a subject of the curriculum but as a fully accepted aspect of education.[4]   The administrative change, however, prepared the way for a decline in official interest in the therapeutic element in physical education and a decreasing emphasis on the medical value of physical exercises.   The change was accepted not without regret by some H.M.I.s who had greatly appreciated the close association of the medical branch with their work.   However the pedagogical changes in physical education which were already taking place and were to gather momentum after the war did not find their inspiration or basis in medicine and the new administrative arrangements probably made for their smoother and more rapid development.

The arrangements for the training of teachers were also altered after the publication of the McNair Report in 1944. In 1937 the government's White Paper on Physical Training and Recreation had given the establishment of a National College of Physical Training as one of the measures to be taken at once.[5] The McNair Committee took an entirely different line. It stated that the subject of physical education was too often regarded as special when the one thing required was that it should be regarded as a normal subject. The committee therefore was at pains to integrate the training of teachers in physical education even more closely with the training of other teachers. They did not go so far as to recommend the abolition of the existing specialist colleges for women but said that they were justified only provided that neither staff nor students were segregated from the main service of training. At the same time the Committee formally recommended that teachers of physical education should not be distinguished from teachers of other subjects in the matter of recognition, salary, and eligibility for promotion to posts of special responsibility or Headships.[6] After the war therefore the women's specialist colleges all in time were brought under the new university institutes of education, which took over from the Joint Examination Boards' responsibility for the initial training of teachers. One-year specialist courses for men were opened at York, Exeter, Cheltenham and Cardiff in addition to those at Leeds and Loughborough. When in 1960 the two-year period of initial training for all teachers was increased to three years it became necessary to incorporate the supplementary year of specialist training in the three-year course of general training. Accordingly certain general colleges were designated by the Ministry to organise courses for specialists in physical education. Such students would pursue their general training and study another subject as well as physical education, but colleges with a designated physical education 'wing' were to have preferential treatment in the allocation of facilities. With their comparatively large number of physical education students they could also justify the appointment of a larger specialist staff than would otherwise have been possible. There were 17 'wing' colleges, ten for men and seven for women. Although some of the physical education 'wings' were at mixed colleges there were no mixed 'wings' so that the training of men and women specialist teachers of physical education was intended to remain separate and distinct. The women's specialist colleges of physical education, which were not general colleges, continued to offer their three-year specialist courses much as before.

There was one institution where men and women were able to study physical education together and on an equal footing from 1946. The University of Birmingham accepted physical education as a subject which might be studied as one with others for the general degree in the Faculty of Arts, at first without honours but later with full honours classification. No other university followed this lead. There was another respect in which the University of Birmingham remained unique. During the war all students had been required to take a course in physical education in their first year as a part of the fitness for service campaign. When the war ended the senate allowed this requirement to stand. With expansion in the number and variety of courses from camping to ski-ing and gymnastics to judo it became possible to interpret the requirement very liberally. Courses in more than twenty activities came to be offered. It was clear, however, that the University would not have imposed this requirement *de novo* in peace-time. Again no other university followed suit.

While changes in the legal and administrative framework of education were being made during and immediately after the war, even more radical changes were taking place in the content and method of physical education. In the early months of the war the Board of Education and His Majesty's Inspectors made strenuous efforts to maintain physical education in the form which it had come to take in the nineteen-thirties. One Memorandum on Physical Education for the schools in war-time issued in January 1940 stressed the importance of regular periods of physical exercises, games, dancing and, where facilities permitted, swimming and showed how the 1933 Syllabus might be adapted for use by schools in 'evacuation areas'.[7] A second Memorandum issued in September 1940 dealt with such problems as the replacement of 'men teachers of physical training' by retired teachers, by women gymnastic teachers and by training through short courses those who were over military age. Throughout the Memorandum emphasis is laid upon the danger of injury and strain to boys in the hands of untrained teachers, 'Teachers who have not been trained to take exercises on apparatus and who have no real understanding of the technique of these exercises should not attempt to teach them. If incorrectly taught and performed they tend to develop faulty posture, or, where this is already present, to increase its ill effects;

more seriously still they may cause undue strain and possible injury.' Again, 'To avoid the possibility of strain special care must be taken to adapt exercises from these groups (dorsal, abdominal and lateral trunk exercises) to the capabilities of the class.' And again, ' "standing by" for all exercises in which there is the possibility of accident, e.g. vaulting and agility, must be strictly enforced.'[8]

Meanwhile in the armed services a different form of physical training was being developed which was to have a far-reaching influence on physical education especially in primary schools. The penetration of the Maginot line of defensive forts, the defeat and subjugation of France and the miraculous evacuation of the British Army from the beaches of Dunkirk brought home to everyone that the war could not be won, nor could defeat be avoided without taking risks, in training as well as in combat. In the army basic fitness was still regarded as important and was produced by formalised exercises of the Swedish pattern but in addition combat training and commando training were developed to produce battle fitness. Logs, ropes, nets, walls, ditches, mounds, fences, and all manner of natural and invented obstacles were used to induce a mental attitude as well as a physical ability to overcome every obstruction whatever the hazard.

Obstacle training had long formed a minor element in army training. *The Manual of Physical Training* issued in 1931 had a chapter upon it, but the obstacles were attacked and surmounted on word of command and the illustrations showed men mounting a wall wearing neat white trousers. From being a minor element, obstacle training became in 1940 of supreme importance and the whole approach was made tougher and fiercer; denims and battle dress were worn instead of long white trousers. The training proved remarkably enjoyable.

The moment at which this vigorous form of physical training made a significant impact upon schools can be located in 1943 when local authority organisers and His Majesty's Inspectors of Physical Education used the occasion of their annual conference held that year in York to visit the physical training headquarters of Northern Command. There they saw a demonstration of the training as it had been pioneered and developed by officers and non-commissioned officers of the Command. At once several of the visitors were struck by the possible application to primary schools in terms of both activity and apparatus. The first to put the idea into practice was Miss Catherine Cooke, organiser for Bristol. There, by the beginning of 1944 one experimental net had been erected over a pole, eight feet high in an infants' playground and parallel ropes were installed in a junior hall at a somewhat higher level than those seen at York.[9] Other climbing apparatus was devised and improvised and set up in many primary schools in Bristol and elsewhere. In Essex the traditional wooden Swedish apparatus provided the inspiration for new portable climbing and agility apparatus for junior schools. By 1947 Darlington, Manchester, Somerset, Oldham, Southampton and Halifax had all devised special apparatus to satisfy the basic need for free and individual practice of climbing, hanging, heaving, and balancing skills. The variety and the unknown potential of these pieces of apparatus demanded a new teaching technique. For a time it was the children who were showing the teachers what could be done. The appeal of personal and individual discovery of solutions to physical problems was strong to children and teachers.

R

Formal groupings and words of command leading to uniform class activities were gradually abandoned in favour of directions or suggestions which every child could interpret in his or her own way and according to his or her own capacity.

There was naturally some concern expressed about the risk of accidents. They did not occur. Mr. E. Major wrote, in November 1943, after the visit of organisers and inspectors to Northern Command—'The excessive practice of the "Safety First" doctrine during the period 1919–1939 has nearly resulted in a major tragedy for this country during the past four years. It has been necessary for the Army, especially since Dunkirk, to modify the safety first principle in training. . . . The interesting thing is that the large increase in accidents which was forecast has not materialised.'[10]   In Bristol schools an investigation on accident proneness in 1951 and 1952 showed that only three out of a total 313 were caused by climbing apparatus and two of those had happened during use against orders.[11]

The content and method of physical education were also influenced from an entirely different source, namely dance.   Even before the war there had been some searching for principles of movement which were not inextricably bound up with anatomy and physiology.   Some progress in the search had been made in Austria and in 1938 Margaret Streicher wrote an article, 'The Principles of Human Movement', for the *Journal of Physical Education*. She classified movement under (1) Locomotion, i.e. walking, running, jumping, clambering, climbing, crawling, swimming, gliding and wriggling; (2) Movements with objects, i.e. pulling, pushing, lifting, dragging and throwing.   (Here she insisted that real objects such as sticks, ladders and baskets for dragging must be used.) (3) Educational movements such as the artificial exercise of knee bending.[12]

It was not, however, the principles of movement enunciated by the Austrians which caught the imagination of English teachers but principles enunciated by the protagonists of modern dance. One consequence of this choice was that portable apparatus was eschewed and such movements as pulling, lifting, dragging and throwing were mimed instead of being performed in real situations, and the educational emphasis was placed on creativity rather than functional practice.

Two schools of modern dance had evolved during the early 20th century, one in America and one in Central Europe. In America Isadora Duncan, Ruth St. Denis and Ted Shawn had translated classical dance into a modern idiom and had found accomplished exponents in Martha Graham, Doris Humphreys and Charles Weidman. In the English *Journal of Physical Education* in 1939 it was claimed that in Isadora Duncan's work there were no fixed rules or set techniques but that the body was an instrument for movement as an expressive idiom. 'The contemporary dance form affords an excellent physical and functional training of the whole body with an immediate goal and purpose for such training.'[13]

It was, however, the central European Dance which was demonstrated at the Easter holiday course of the Ling Physical Education Association in 1940. Principles of tension, relaxation and *schwung* were illustrated leading to an improvisation and development of the theme 'Inexperience' to Gustav Lind's 'Valse Impromptu'.[14] A number of teachers were experimenting with Central European Dance and next year in April in response to inquiries the Ling Physical Education Association held a conference on Modern Dance. The Association's leaflet reported that the real inspiration of the conference lay undoubtedly in the contributions made to it by Mr. von Laban and Miss Ullman. Laban was stated to have cultivated consciously the recreative and regenerative side of free dancing which at one time he hoped would rejuvenate civilisation. The conference requested the Board of Education to promote Modern Dance in schools.[15]

In November 1941 Louise Soelberg, who, like von Laban, had been formerly in the Ballets Joos, explained Modern Dance in the *Journal of Physical Education*. Movement was spelt with a capital letter. She claimed that modern dance opened up an enormous field of observation of the structure and function of the human body and above all developed the whole personality through creative activity.[16]   Louise Soelberg had been running the Dance Centre in London with Leslie Burrows since 1936 and von Laban had also been working here from 1938. Lisa Ullman had come from Essen to Dartington Hall in 1934 and there had been working with a group from the Ballet Joos. It was, however, in 1940 that Laban's modern dance first broke upon the physical education profession. Thereafter it gathered to itself an increasing number of women teachers, lecturers, organisers and inspectors whose devotion to the cause and to its inspirer verged at times on fanaticism.

There was still considerable interest in the medical side of physical education. In 1942 for instance there was an extensive inquiry into the effect of gymnastic training on childbearing. It transpired that there was no effect.[17] Increasingly, however, modern dance featured at courses short and long and at conferences. The Modern Dance Summer School organised annually by von Laban and Miss Ullman at Moreton Hall provided a focus of interest and training. In 1943 Mrs. Sylvia Bodmer and Miss Ullman started the Manchester Dance Circle and in their first year gave thirty-four practical sessions and eight lectures. The following year an article in the *Journal of Physical Education* entitled 'The Art of Movement and its Significance in our Times' indicated the wide claims being made by the enthusiasts for Modern Dance.[18]

The wider the claims became the more sceptical and antagonistic were the men specialists. The emotional atmosphere became tense and rational discussion of the potentialities and limitations of Modern Dance became almost impossible. For this reason perhaps, hardly anyone put pen to paper on the subject from 1944 until 1950 except von Laban himself. His book *Effort*[19] published in 1948 was largely concerned with movement in industry but *Modern Educational Dance*[20] published in the same year giving sixteen basic movement themes and the rudiments of free dance technique and space orientation provided the technical skeleton upon which women teachers could hang their new concept of physical education. The word 'educational' was inserted between 'modern' and 'dance' by Laban because, when modern dance sessions were advertised in Manchester, people turned up in evening dress. So modern dance became modern educational dance.

In 1946 the chief medical officer of the Ministry of Education recorded that experiments in modern dance which had started in girls' schools during the war continued on a larger scale in Manchester, Sheffield, Middlesbrough and many other centres. He commended its high value in developing feeling for and understanding of 'movement'.[21]   Henceforth 'movement' was the key to the official evaluation of physical education just as 'posture' had been in the nineteen-thirties. The term movement, and phrases incorporating movement such as the art of movement, movement training, movement education came to be used more and more in place of dance as those who championed the new cause extended the scope of their claims upon physical education. Lisa Ullman opened an Art of Movement Studio in Manchester in 1945. A one-year supplementary course for teachers was asked for by the Ministry of Education in 1947 and in 1949 the Ministry formally recognised the studio. The studio was formally approved again in 1954 after it had moved to permanent headquarters in Addlestone, Surrey, in 1953.

Acceptability of the art of movement to the Ministry was no guarantee of acceptability to specialist teachers. In 1950 many women and almost all men were antagonistic to the wide claims, and the methods employed in schools by the converted. So wide became the gulf between men and women that in 1950 the Ministry organised a course on Current Problems in Physical Education for women only thereby underlining the difficulties involved in open discussion at this time.

In 1952 and 1953 the Ministry issued *Moving and Growing*[22] and *Planning the Programme*[23] Parts I and II of 'Physical Education in the Primary School' which was to replace the *Syllabus of Physical Training for Schools* issued in 1933. These books brought together the two main influences upon physical education in schools over the previous ten years, obstacle training from the army and movement training from centres of dance and the Art of

Movement Studio. Laban's terminology was not mentioned except to be abandoned,[23] and whatever physical activity could not be classified as games, swimming, movement as an art, dance or dramatic movement was still labelled as 'P.T.' a term used to cover the 'grammar of movement'. Nevertheless both in the text and in the illustrative photographs the influence of Laban as well as of the new climbing apparatus was clear to see.

The functional, anatomical and physiological approach to gymnastics was restated with force by Mr. A. D. Munrow in his book *Pure and Applied Gymnastics* in 1955. The growing tendency for the art of movement to oust functional gymnastics and indeed other activities from physical education left three questions to be answered in Mr. Munrow's view.

1 Was it claimed that this work was a fundamental approach to all forms of skill?

2 Was the pursuit of skills such as hockey, athletics and tennis to be curtailed, extended or untouched by the introduction of movement training?

3 In a programme based almost exclusively on movement training was it reckoned that the general gymnastic effects of mobility, strength and endurance could be disregarded?[24]

Two developments in physical education on the functional side at this time were important. Circuit training was devised by G. T. Adamson and R. E. Morgan at the University of Leeds to attract students and motivate them to carry through their own individual programmes of physical exercise. Before long it was widely adopted by boys and men first in Britain and then in many other countries. Weight training and the use of progressive resistance exercises similarly grew in popularity for the measurable and almost inevitable improvement in performance which resulted from them.

The years of war and immediately afterwards was also a period in which games and sports were greatly extended and when outdoor activities such as canoeing, sailing, climbing and outdoor adventure in general were introduced for the first time. When in 1944 the Central Council of Recreative Physical Training changed its name to Central Council of Physical Recreation, the event attracted little notice. It was, however, significant of a new social attitude to physical recreation which became more clearly defined in the fifties and sixties. In 1948 the chief medical officer of the Ministry of Education noticed that there had been a gradual extension of physical education in secondary modern schools to cover such activities as lawn tennis and hockey for girls and canoe making for boys.[25] This extension was helped by the development of coaching schemes by some governing bodies of sport especially the Amateur Athletic Association. The Amateur Swimming Association and the Football Association had long had schemes to help schools and spread their expertise among teachers and others. In 1947 the A.A.A. appointed first one and then four national coaches and the Ministry of Education undertook to pay a proportion of their salaries. Similar facilities were offered to other bodies. These coaches spent much of their time and energy in coaching teachers, with a consequent extension and improvement of track and field athletics and of other sports in schools.

One campaign for physical education which had considerable publicity during the early part of the war was the 'County Badge' scheme. The scheme was inaugurated and fostered in Britain by Kurt Hahn, who had been forced by the Nazi regime to leave his progressive school in Germany. He started a school on similar lines at Gordonstoun in Scotland and instituted a badge to be won for achievements in the basic physical skills of running, throwing, jumping and swimming, and in expeditions and projects requiring moral as well as physical qualities. From the school the programme spread outwards to the surrounding county of Morayshire and the Moray County badge was instituted.

The idea of extending the scheme to the nation at large appealed to a number of men eminent in public life, and in the summer of 1939 articles and considerable correspondence upon the County badge scheme appeared in *The Times*. The outbreak of war stimulated rather than damped down propaganda for the County badge, but the scheme was applied in only a few schools and in one county, Hertfordshire, where it did not have general support. Nevertheless, propaganda for the scheme played its part in the outdoor movement of the war and post-war years, and doubtless helped to encourage the participation of boys and girls and young men and young women in more adventurous and resourceful outdoor sports such as camping, mountain walking and rock climbing. To foster such activities and 'to present conditions necessary to give opportunity for self discovery' two 'outward bound schools' were set up at Aberdovey in 1941 and Eskdale in 1950 under an Outward Bound Trust. One hundred years earlier the team games of football and cricket were regarded as the principal educational instruments for training character. By 1955 adventurous activities in open and rugged country and at sea were regarded as the best means of developing courage, initiative, co-operation and leadership.

Chapter 15.   References

1 *Hansard*, 17 October 1940.
2 *Our Towns, A Close Up*, Women's Group on Public Welfare, Oxford, 1943, p. 111.
3 *Regulations prescribing standards for school premises*, H.M.S.O., 1944.
4 *R.C.M.O.*, 1948–49, p. 16.
5 *Physical Training and Recreation*, Cmnd. 5364, H.M.S.O., 1937.
6 *Teachers and Youth Leaders*, Report of the McNair Committee, H.M.S.O., 1944.
7 *The Schools in Wartime*, Memorandum No. 11, *Physical Education*, Board of Education, 1940.
8 *The Schools in Wartime*, Memorandum No. 23, *Physical Education (2)*, Board of Education, 1940.
9 Catherine Cooke, 'Experimental Work on Physical Education at Bristol', *Childhood and Youth*, July–September 1950, Vol. 4, No. 3.
10 E. Major, 'Army Physical Training and its possible Postwar Influence', *J.P.E.*, Vol. XXXV, 1943.
11 Catherine Cooke, 'Accidents in Schools' in *Mother and Child*, Vol. 28, No. 8, November 1957.
12 *J.P.E.*, Vol. XXX, No. 91, 1938.
13 *J.P.E.*, Vol. XXXI, No. 94, 1939.
14 *Ling Association Leaflet*, Vol. 39, No. 5, May 1940.
15 *Ling Association Leaflet*, Vol. 40, No. 5, June 1941.
16 *J.P.E.*, Vol. XXXIII, No. 100, November 1941.
17 *Ling Association Leaflet*, Vol. 47, No. 7.
18 *J.P.E.*, Vol. XXXVI, No. 108, 1944.
19 R. von Laban, *Effort*, London, 1948.
20 R. von Laban, *Modern Educational Dance*, London, 1948.
21 *R.C.M.O.*, 1946–47.
22 *Moving and Growing*, H.M.S.O., 1952.
23 *Planning the Programme*, H.M.S.O., 1953, p. 16.
24 A. D. Munrow, *Pure and Applied Gymnastics*, London, 1955.
25 *R.C.M.O.*, 1948–9.

Reports, Committees and Councils

THE historical assessment of recent events is very difficult, perhaps impossible. The history of physical education between 1955 and 1968 is especially difficult to write for a number of reasons apart from the nearness of events. There were great changes in the structure and organisation of secondary schools and at the same time changes in teaching technique involving coaching methods in games and sports as well as the teaching of non-competitive activities such as dance and gymnastics and the development of movement training and the art of movement. Activities within the physical education programme proliferated to include thirty or forty different games, sports or recreative activities. This proliferation was partly the result of and partly the cause of a blurring of the distinction between education and recreation. The latter had been largely the responsibility of voluntary organisations. Local authorities now became not merely the great providers of facilities for sport and recreation, which they had been for many years, they also became employers of teachers and coaches in recreative programmes in evening and day classes for youth and adults in a great variety of games and sports in clubs, schools, colleges, institutes, swimming baths and parks. Voluntary organisations, too, became inextricably tied up with statutory bodies. The governing bodies of sport received grants from the national government to aid their coaching schemes and then hired out their coaches to local education authorities and colleges of education to reap further payment from public funds. The Central Council of Physical Recreation expanded its activities year by year and drew an increasing amount of revenue from the Ministry of Education. State aid for sport gradually increased and eventually touched some parts of school sport. The international implications of physical education and sport also became matters of interest and of public policy. The history of physical education therefore became so closely interwoven with the history of sport and recreation that the different threads are difficult to distinguish and impossible always to separate. This chapter, however, will not attempt a comprehensive history of sport, physical recreation and education, but will indicate first some developments in physical education in schools and then give a brief account of the committees and councils which were set up during this period—of which there were many—and the reports which they issued. In this way some of the more important elements in attitude and policy affecting physical education may be noticed.

In the nineteen-forties and early fifties movement training and the art of movement had aroused great enthusiasm amongst many women teachers and a number of His Majesty's women inspectors of physical education. It had also aroused suspicion even when it first appeared as modern educational dance and therefore claimed only a part of the physical education programme. When, however, movement training was dressed in the guise of the mother of all physical education it aroused opposition from those who felt that there must be a time when children grew up and when for instance swimming, football and even gymnastics could leave home, exist in their own right and cease to be movement training. It also aroused opposition from those who felt that aesthetic criteria which properly determined the art of movement were not the only criteria or even the most important criteria in physical education. The critics were not convinced that functional efficiency, emotional stability, social adjustment and leisure skills would develop naturally from the art of movement alone.

One point of interest that emerged in the nineteen-fifties was that the new teaching method of allowing and encouraging children to explore and discover for themselves was not necessarily identified with Laban's enunciation of movement themes, still less with his terminology. A large amount of credit for demonstrating this fact must go to men organisers in Lancashire, Mr. A. Bilborough and Mr. P. Jones. Having developed in their own schools the theory of more and less limitation in directions given to boys and girls in the gymnasium and therefore more and less freedom in interpretation by boys and girls, they offered the results of their experience to a wider public through the annual school of physical education at Blackpool organised by the North Western Counties Physical Education Association. 'Movement Training (Men)', first appeared in the prospectus in April 1958.[1] Their book on *Physical Education in the Primary School* (1963)[2] set forth their methods in greater detail. Movement training may have thereby become corrupted in the eyes of purists but it was also more widely adopted by teachers in primary and secondary schools. There were many other variants of the teaching method as teachers experimented with their own classes of children.

A second distinction which was made was that between

dance and gymnastics.   For a time the art of movement seemed to embrace both or to make the distinction irrelevant, or at least make gymnastic apparatus unnecessary.   In 1951, however, the programme of the Ling Association Easter course showed two parallel sessions, 'basic movement leading to gymnastics' and 'basic movement leading to dance'.[3]   Nevertheless the confusion remained for a number of years.   The issue was pinpointed by Christine Roberts in the Ling Association *Leaflet* in June 1958.   It had been claimed that the full range of movement experience was only possible when one was free of apparatus and this kind of movement led naturally to creative dance, yet most teachers were unwilling to abandon the use of gymnastic apparatus and felt that there were occasions in the gymnasium when there was room for either mechanical skill or expressive movement. Was the same terminology applicable to both aspects of movement and were the same techniques of teaching and standards of judgement to be used?[4]   Both teachers and children were often confused on this point.   A considerable amount of thought and discussion was going on, however, to differentiate between dance and gymnastics within movement.

In 1946 Ruth Morison, a tutor at I. M. Marsh College of Physical Education in Liverpool, had abandoned the Swedish system of gymnastics and tried to apply Laban's principles of movement to gymnastics.   In 1956 she produced a small booklet showing how Laban's basic concepts of space, time, weight and flow could be applied to gymnastics with and without apparatus.   The booklet was entitled 'Educational Gymnastics'.[5]   In 1960 Miss Morison wrote in more detail on Educational Gymnastics for Secondary Schools.   The distance that had been travelled in thought since the Board of Education's memorandum on the schools in war-time (Chapter 15) and the differentiation within the general concept of movement which was taking place in 1960 are exemplified in one quotation from Miss Morison's booklet. 'There is no set method of progression in this form of gymnastics, no definite starting point or step by step progress to the goal as there is in learning to swim or to play a game. . . . Everyone works in her own time and as all are doing different things no one is conspicuous. . . . Each can learn to assess her own powers and launch out to her own limits but no one will be pressed beyond her limit or be compared disparagingly with others.'[6]

At the infant stage it was neither necessary nor desirable to differentiate very much. 'Movement Education for Infants', therefore, which was the title used by women inspectors of physical education in London for their guide for teachers, could cover the whole programme of physical education for children of this age.[7]   At the primary stage swimming, minor games and even major games of football, netball and cricket could be separated from movement training. A distinction also came to be made between expressive movement, sometimes involving percussion and music, and educational gymnastics often called modern educational gymnastics. 'Educational Gymnastics' was the title of the London guide for teachers in junior and secondary schools.[8]   In secondary schools modern educational gymnastics involving climbing and vaulting apparatus came to be fairly clearly distinguished from modern educational dance, although Laban's principles and often his terminology were applied to both. In boys' secondary schools educational gymnastics with its freedom of interpretation for boys and teachers was further differentiated from competitive gymnastics with its stereotyped work determined by the apparatus and exercises prescribed in international competition.

Clarification there had been, but a number of questions still remained unanswered in 1968. Was 'movement' co-extensive with 'physical education' either in name or in content? Did 'movement' or 'physical education' differ significantly and fundamentally for boys and girls, men and women? Was 'movement' an art or a science or both? It had frequently been pointed out that if 'movement' was in fact co-extensive with 'physical education' its study at the level of professional training of intending teachers must cover the findings of physiology in human performance, of psychology in the acquisition of physical skills and of Newtonian physics, especially the laws of motion. It was indeed at the level of professional training that the lack of clarity and unity was most apparent. The syllabuses for the teacher's certificate within the Institute of Education of the University of London for 1967–8 included five on movement and physical education namely Art of Movement, Art and Science of Movement, Physical Education (Women), Physical Education (Men) and Physical Education (Men and Women).

Meanwhile the Art of Movement studio was clear and definite in offering courses in movement as a creative art. Lisa Ullman was aware that the laws of motion and the findings of the biological sciences could not be entirely disregarded but was equally emphatic that terms such as weight and space and time could well be used in a non-Newtonian way. Laban died on 1 July 1958 but a trust had been set up and under this trust Lisa Ullman continued to direct the Studio, offering, in conjunction with Trent College, a joint course in general education and the art of movement which would give successful students the status of 'qualified teachers'.[10]

The tradition of therapeutic physical education with a medical basis died away except in a few places. At Marlborough College, far from dying away it was further developed by G. W. Murray. Particularly good use was made of circuit training and weight training to provide for the physical education of boys with postural defects, poor physiques and physical handicaps.[11]

The first of the mid-century reports on education to appear was the Crowther Report issued in 1959.[12] It was concerned with the age group 15 to 18 some of whom were still in full-time education while some were at work. The sixth forms at English schools had a long tradition of specialisation and the report laid great stress upon the use of 'minority time', that was the part of the curriculum not devoted to the main examinable specialisms. The complete separation of those who were studying arts subjects from those who were scientists was regretted. Physical education was recommended as one of the common elements which should be taken by arts and science specialists together. Art, music and religious education were the other common elements. There had been a tendency in schools for examination pressure and physical lethargy on the part of some adolescents to cause the omission of physical education from the curriculum of the sixth former.

The majority of boys and girls over 15 were not at school. Sir Geoffrey Crowther found that they dropped many of their interests and hobbies when they left school. There was evidence that participation in physical recreation was more widespread and more persistent than some other active pursuits but the percentage of boys playing

s

games three years after leaving school was depressingly low. The committee recommended compulsory part-time education for all young persons of 16 and 17 who were not in full-time education and stated that the development of their physical skills should form an element in the curriculum.

The committee felt too that the experience of Outward Bound Schools and of the Duke of Edinburgh's Award Scheme should be recognised and used. The former was noticed in the previous chapter; the latter was launched by the Duke in 1956. It was based on, and similar to, the Fourfold Achievement of the County Badge Scheme and the Moray Badge Scheme which the Duke himself had experienced as a boy at Kurt Hahn's school at Gordonstoun. Each boy had to satisfy certain conditions in fitness, community service, pursuits and an expedition test. In 1958 a similar Award for Girls was instituted. By 1966 it was estimated that well over 100,000 boys and girls between the ages of 14 and 20 were taking part,[13] some through their schools, some through clubs and voluntary organisations and some through their places of work.

The adventure and expedition elements in the Duke of Edinburgh's Award Scheme fitted in particularly well with a trend of the times. The Outward Bound Trust had started its work to promote these activities during the war. After the war the Central Council of Physical Recreation ran courses and opened mountain centres in Wales and Scotland. In 1951 Derbyshire Education Committee opened White Hall Outdoor Pursuits Centre for students mainly from Derbyshire Schools. Many other local education authorities followed suit even those far removed from mountainous country. Schools in the

Midlands and even the South East were sending boys and girls to Wales and the North to stay in simple accommodation or to camp in the hills and carry out easy or strenuous expeditions. In the sixties some schools were organising expeditions for exploration and survey to places as far afield as Jordan, Svartis in Northern Norway and Lapland. Canoeing trips in summer and ski-ing courses in winter in Norway or the Alps became a commonplace. The assimilation of outdoor pursuits into the physical education programmes of so many secondary schools was a remarkable feature of the post war years.

In 1960 the Wolfenden Committee issued its report under the title 'Sport and the Community'.[14] The origin of the committee is referred to elsewhere in this chapter. The report itself was concerned mainly with physical recreation outside school. Nevertheless it could not avoid reference to the Ministry of Education since it was that government department which had been administering grant under the Physical Training and Recreation Act of 1937. Just because there was a public impression that there was a lack of interest on the part of the Ministry in sport and physical recreation the Committee recommended the setting up of a Sports Development Council with £5,000,000 per annum to distribute. The government did not accept this advice but in 1963 did assign to Lord Hailsham, a senior minister, the responsibility of co-ordinating the aid given to sport and recreation by different government departments. A change of government in the following year led to the setting up in 1965 of an advisory sports council under the chairmanship of Denis Howell, M.P., Parliamentary Undersecretary of State in the Department of Education and Science.[15] The Sports Council made a number of far-reaching recommendations from its inception. Among them was the recommendation that competitors representing their country in international sporting events should receive financial aid from public funds. This recommendation was implemented and the arrangements extended to schools' national teams as well as to full national teams. All the activities of the Sports Council impinged to some extent upon physical education in schools and colleges, but of particular importance was its strong recommendation that facilities for physical education in schools and other educational establishments should be planned for joint use by the school and the community. Unfortunately neither administrative nor financial arrangements at central and local government level made this recommendation easy to carry out and progress in the next two years was slow.

Lady Albemarle's committee on the Youth Service reported in 1960, the same year as the Wolfenden Committee.[16] The attitude of the Albemarle Committee to physical recreation was unequivocal.

'There are powerful reasons why provision for physical recreation should be improved. First because sports and physical activities generally are a major leisure time interest in the lives of the adolescent boy and girl. Secondly because this interest is unrelated to academic ability or manual skill; it cuts across the stratification of society, the incidental effects of which we have deplored. Thirdly, because there is evidence that work and their present leisure activities fail to satisfy the increased physical energies of many young people. Physical education at school has become much more challenging and more comprehensive in scope than it used to be; yet planned physical education stops as soon as young people leave school.'[17]

The issue of the report was followed by an immediate allocation of funds to provide facilities for physical recreation for youth, part of the 'blood transfusion' which the committee had recommended.   Probably the quickest results and the greatest value for money came from flood-lighting existing playgrounds and constructing new ones.

'Half Our Future' was the title of the report of John Newsom's committee set up to advise upon the education of pupils aged 13 to 16 of average and less than average ability.[18]   It was issued in 1963.   The committee was concerned about the lack of facilities for physical education and inadequate staff particularly in down-town schools, and recommended generous community centre facilities on the spot or round the corner rather than playing fields and sports facilities miles away.   They were also concerned with the reluctance of many boys and more girls to take part in any of the physical activities which were offered to them.   The image of athletic grace and physical well-being did not seem reconcilable with their notions of adult interest and fashionable good looks.   The committee was slightly baffled but did feel that the inclusion of courses in activities which were more easily organised than team games might overcome some of the reluctance.   Some local education authorities had man-aged to achieve some success in this way.   Large com-prehensive schools which were entitled by the number of pupils to the equivalent of three, four or even five gym-nasia substituted a swimming bath and a sports hall for two of their gymnasia.   Local squash courts, skating rinks, cycle tracks, golf courses and even horse riding establishments were used to provide introductory courses in adult recreations for older boys and girls.

The Newsom Committee also pointed out that mentally

able children had a disproportionate share of places in sports teams representing their schools and that the least able mentally were also the least successful in achieving selection in representative teams.   A subsequent survey of comprehensive schools confirmed this discovery.   It was disconcerting to find that sport or, more accurately, competitive sport was not a great leveller of academic grades, but the importance of non-competitive activities in physical education was even more obvious than it had been.

Next in chronological order came the Robbins Report on Higher Education.[19]   Its relevance to physical education was in its recommendations on the training of teachers.   The committee made specific mention of 'specialist colleges often of high quality, that train women teachers of physical education or domestic science', and recommended that their future should lie in gradual enlargement of scope and subjects covered so that they could expand their teaching of general subjects without sacrificing their standards in their specialisms.

The most far reaching proposal was that some students at training colleges, now to be called colleges of education, should be enabled by means of a four year course to take a Bachelor of Education degree.   The course would cover professional training and academic study.   There were protracted discussions within universities and colleges about the registration and admission of students to such a degree and about the maintenance of the universities' traditional standards of study, teaching and attainment. Where the college course involved a subject which was covered by an existing university discipline and department no special difficulty existed.   However, only one university, Birmingham, had previously accepted physical education as an academic discipline, the rest found it difficult to approve courses and ensure adequate standards of teaching and attainment. However, by 1968 most university institutes of education had accepted physical education as a subject which could be offered for the B.Ed. degree.

Children and their Primary Schools, the report of Lady Plowden's committee appeared in 1967.[20] It drew attention to the poor state of primary schools and made a number of proposals for reform and aid. The report added, 'Yet not everything costs money. Some of our recommendations call mainly for changes of attitude, understanding and knowledge in individual teaching.' In particular the committee stressed that 'finding out' should replace 'being told'. In physical education in the primary school the revolution in teaching method and 'new emphasis on building up a child's resources in movement', which was begun during the war, had already done much to make this substitution a reality.

In one respect the Plowden Report revealed a profound change in the concept of physical education that had taken place since the introduction of the Swedish system under the medical department of the Board of Education. Special surveys had shown that about 30 per cent of the population had foot defects which had originated in childhood. The task of prevention was laid by the committee upon chiropody and remedial exercise clinics. No mention was made of any contribution that could be made by physical education in school.

One committee which had had no chance to make an impact by 1968 was the physical education committee of the Schools Council. This Council was established by the government to advise upon curriculum development.

By its constitution a majority of its members had to be serving teachers. In 1967 a subject committee was appointed for physical education.

An area of physical education which was barely touched upon by any of the foregoing reports was that of adults in evening and some daytime classes organised by local education authorities. There was a great expansion of such classes in the post-war years. In London alone there were in 1966–7, 4,700 classes in some sixty different physical activities meeting once a week and this figure represented an increase of 1,400 over the total number of classes for 1960–1.[21] Increasingly physical education provided by local education authorities was seen to embrace all ages and almost every available form of physical recreation. Outside the realm of the statutory bodies voluntary organisations, governing bodies of sport and, above all, the Central Council of Physical Recreation were in the mid-20th century pursuing an ideal of sport for all which broke down or took no notice of social and educational distinctions which had been such a feature of physical education and recreation fifty years earlier. The change was reflected in the title 'Sports Council'. The National Fitness Council had died in 1939. No one wanted resurrection of the council or the name. By 1965 sport and physical recreation were considered to be self justified and did not need the support of a drive to national fitness. The setting up of the Sports Council therefore in that year represented far more than a change of name. It indicated that sport and recreation were of political, social and educational importance in their own right.

The international involvement of Britain in physical education grew rapidly from 1952 and at first did so despite opposition for the government. In that year the

seventh session of the Unesco General Conference author-
ised the Director General to make inquiries with a view to
submitting detailed proposals for action by Unesco to
assist in the development and improvement of athletic
sports for educational purposes. The U.K. delegation
did not consider that the time had come to inquire into
the place of sport in education. In 1954 the U.K.
delegation again voted that nothing should be done.
Nevertheless Unesco went ahead and in 1956 published
the results of its inquiries under the title 'The Place of
Sport in Education'.[22] There was no contribution from
the United Kingdom.

When the Minister of Education was questioned in the
House of Commons on the failure of this country to co-
operate with Unesco in this project his reply was that it
was not practical or worth while enough. He also said,
'On the other hand I have read the report and while it is
interesting, I must point out that the English idea of sport
is such that the English do not like professional professorial
discourses on sport. At the same time, I can see that there
is some rather interesting information, perhaps, for some
countries which are backward in education matters.'[23]

Meanwhile interest in international aspects of physical
education and sport was growing in the country at large.
In 1952, the year in which Unesco first debated sport the
Olympic Games took place in Helsinki. Britain's only
victory was in an equestrian event. One bitter comment
in the press was that our only gold medal was won by a
horse. A group of lecturers at Birmingham University
who had themselves had some experience of international
sport set to work and reviewed the situation in a booklet,
Britain in the World of Sport, published in 1956.[24] This in
turn stimulated the C.C.P.R. to set up in 1957 a committee

under Sir John Wolfenden to examine factors affecting the development of games, sports and outdoor activities in the United Kingdom and to make recommendations.

In 1957, too, the International Association of Physical Education and Sports for Girls and Women held a congress in London which both provided a shop window of what was going on in Britain and also showed that as a profession women teachers were anxious to play their part in international affairs. For the men the 1958 President of the British Association of Organisers and Lecturers in Physical Education became a vice-president of the International Council of Health, Physical Education and Recreation when it was established in 1958 as a branch of the World Confederation of Organisations of the Teaching Profession.

A third International organisation had been conceived in 1956 during the Olympic Games in Melbourne. A group of sportsmen and teachers had felt the need to bring together the two worlds of physical education and sport and to bridge the gaps between nations and continents. The International Council of Sport and Physical Education was formally constituted under Unesco at Rome in 1960 at the time of the Olympic Games. Its president was the Right Honourable Philip Noel Baker, M.P., who had represented Britain in two Olympic Games and who had later been awarded a Nobel Prize for his work for disarmament and peace.

The energy and activities of individuals and professional organisations had by 1960 shown that they were ahead of the government in wanting to become involved in the internationalisation of physical education and sport. They had also in 1958 forced the government to take notice of their attitude. In that year they organised a British

Commonwealth Conference on physical education and sport in South Wales at the time of the British Empire and Commonwealth Games which were held at Cardiff. Representatives of both Her Majesty's government and opposition were invited to address the conference and did so.

The government itself became involved willy-nilly in international physical education when the Council of Europe, which was an intergovernmental organisation of eighteen European States and the Holy See, decided to discuss and report on physical education in 1962. In 1963 the Commonwealth Relations Office agreed to meet a small deficit which had been incurred as a result of participation in the Commonwealth Games held at Perth in Western Australia in November 1962, and the Ministry of Education had already financially aided a non-governmental delegate to attend the physical education conference which was held in Perth immediately before the Games. From that time onward succeeding governments financially assisted British representation, both at international sporting events and at international conferences on sport and physical education.

In retrospect many profound changes in physical education can be seen to have taken place since 1800. The Swedish system had come and gone. Drill had given place to therapy and therapy to self discovery and body awareness. The yardsticks of 'sharp obedience, smartness, order and cleanliness' had been replaced first by 'posture' and then by 'movement'. 'Being told' had become 'finding out'. The role of character training had passed from the team games of Tom Brown's schooldays to the expeditions of the Duke of Edinburgh's Award Scheme. The Public Schools remained intact for those who could afford the fees—and entrants were not lacking

—but the games and sports of Matthew Arnold's Barbarians and Philistines had almost all become available to his Populace.   There was still culture and anarchy and the latest in the long line of prophets who had warned of the dangers of overdoing competition were the Plowden committee and Edmund Leach in the Reith Lectures for 1967.[25]   Nevertheless after a century and a half competitive sport continued to be a strong and vital element in physical education.   When, in 1966, the world football cup was won in England by England the victory gave great satisfaction to a nation whose traditions and education had been steeped in games and sports for many generations.

Chapter 16.   References

1   *The Leaflet*, Physical Education Association of Great Britain and Northern Ireland, Vol. 59, No. 1, Jan.–Feb. 1958.

2   A. Bilborough and P. Jones, *Physical Education in the Primary School*, London, 1963.

3   *The Leaflet*, Vol. 52, No. 1, Jan.–Feb. 1951.

4   *The Leaflet*, Vol. 59, No. 5, June 1958.

5   Ruth Morison, *Educational Gymnastics*, Liverpool, 1956.

6   Ruth Morison, *Educational Gymnastics for Secondary Schools*, Liverpool, 1960.

7   London County Council, *Movement Education for Infants*, 1963.

8   London County Council, *Educational Gymnastics*, 1962.

9   University of London, *Regulations and Syllabuses for the Teachers Certificate 1967–68*.

10   Art of Movement Studio, *Prospectus*, 1967.

11   G. W. Murray and T. A. A. Hunter, *Physical Education and Health*, London, 1966.

12   *15 to 18*, Report of the Central Advisory Council for Education, England, H.M.S.O., 1959.

13   Peter Carpenter (Editor), *Challenge*, London, 1966.

14   *Sport and the Community*, Report of the Wolfenden Committee on Sport, C.C.P.R., 1960.

15 *The Sports Council, A Report*, H.M.S.O., 1966.
16 *The Youth Service in England and Wales*, Cmnd. 929, H.M.S.O., 1960.
17 *Op. cit.*, para. 196.
18 *Half Our Future*, A Report of the Central Advisory Council for Education, England, H.M.S.O., 1963
19 *Higher Education*, Cmnd. 2154, H.M.S.O., 1963.
20 *Children and their Primary Schools*, A Report of the Central Advisory Council for Education, England, H.M.S.O., 1967.
21 P. C. McIntosh, *Sport in Society*, London, 1963.
22 *The Place of Sport in Education*, Unesco, 1956.
23 *Hansard* quoted in *The Leaflet*, Vol. 59, No. 3, April 1958.
24 Members of the Staff of the Physical Education Department of the University of Birmingham, *Britain in the World of Sport*, London, 1956.
25 Edmund Leach, *Men and Learning*, The fifth of the Reith Lectures in *The Listener*, 14 December 1967.

The Bergman-Österberg Physical Training College

by JONATHAN MAY, M.Ed.

MEETING in London in 1899, the International Congress of Women concerned itself with a review of the progress made so far by women throughout the World in the professions.[1] A substantial part of the Congress was given over to the general position of women in education. One report dealt with opportunities in England for women to train for teaching. Although the speaker gave a comprehensive review of the various institutions offering opportunities for women to enter teaching and included some rather modest and subsequently abortive schemes, she made no mention of the work being done at Dartford by Madame Bergman-Österberg. Instead, the final report of that particular section of the proceedings was given by Madame herself on her methods and her college. This might reasonably be taken as an indication that Madame Österberg was, at the time, considered, by her peers, to be leading perhaps the most significant development in the field of teacher education for women.

Martina Bergman had originally been brought to England in 1882 by the School Board for London to introduce Swedish Gymnastics to its girls' schools and departments. Had her work with London, until 1887, been her only contribution to physical education in this country, she would still have ranked amongst our leading teachers of physical education; but in the final event, it turned out to be merely one of her considerable achievements.   However, at the latest in 1885, she determined to devote herself to the health and welfare of young women of her own 'middle class', and to the provision for them of a new profession, in physical education.

> 'Is it not funny,' she subsequently recalled, 'that you here in England think that what is good for the poor cannot be good for the rich?   By that time I found that I had completed my task; the teachers I had trained would train others, and my work had received many flattering remarks of approval.   But the system had become identified with that of the poor; that was the difficulty.   Because, if it was good education for the poor, it could not possibly be the same for the rich.   However this argument did not impede me for long.   I built the College and Gymnasium in 1885 and since then have been steadily working to improve the development of women of the upper and middle classes.'[2]

Still employed by the School Management Committee of the London School Board, Martina Bergman (she married a schoolmaster from her native Sweden in 1886), quite without backing, financial or otherwise, bought, in fact, a detached house in Hampstead, 'Reremonde', 1 Broadhurst Gardens, and built a gymnasium in the garden.   This became the first fully fitted Gymnasium in the country, but nevertheless included in its equipment German apparatus.   Here perhaps we have a clue to the methods of this remarkably far-sighted woman.   Although she had come to this country to bring 'Ling' gymnastics to our schools, she at no time concerned herself solely with Swedish Exercises. At Hampstead, she added German vaulting to her programme, and continually experimented with apparatus of her own design. At the International Health Exhibition at Olympia in 1884, she had advocated the use of games in programmes of physical education and had recommended to the London School Board subsequently that they develop playgrounds to include facilities for games such as tennis and squash. For the Hampstead students, she acquired a games field at Neasden, and added tennis and cricket to her curriculum. Swimming was added as soon as the new Hampstead Baths across the road from Reremonde opened. Apart from these substantial innovations, the course was much the same as the one Martina had followed a few years before at the Royal Central Gymnastic Institute in Stockholm. Theoretical studies included Anatomy, Animal Physiology, Chemistry, Physics, Hygiene and Theory of Movement. Practical subjects were, Games; Swimming; Dancing, waltzing and national dances, mainly Swedish; and Gymnastics.

'Each movement—the march or the double, the jump or the vault, the knee flexions and extensions, the backward and forward bends, the boom or horizontal bar exercises; the various exercises connected with the 'Ribs' a series of wooden bars at each side of the gymnasium, the sinuous winding in and out of the horizontal ladder—all consist of simple initial movements gradually growing and developing into the perfect exercise. Here the muscles of the legs are being used and there the muscles of the abdomen, here those of the flanks and there those of the arms.

T

No one is jerky, though several are rapid; indeed, I was much struck by the rapidity with which many movements were performed. Time was another feature, and it was well marked at the beginning and end of several exercises by a simultaneous stamp of the feet on the floor. There is grace in a skilful act, and although the object of the training is not grace but health, many of the evolutions that I witnessed were exceedingly graceful. Some of the older students performed a series of gymnastic feats, of which I have some personal experience with an ease and absence of apparent effort which really astonished me. Here it is that Ling's system is so much in advance of any other. The graduation of the exercises is so delicate and so regular that at last very difficult movements of the body are performed, with or without apparatus, with what is real ease.'[3]

The students initially were few and standards high. Fees of thirteen guineas per session meant that applicants were of necessity from well-to-do families and selection was extremely careful, sometimes even ruthless. Candidates were attracted by means of guaranteed employment upon completion of training at a salary of not less than £100 per annum. Students found wanting in any way were instantly removed from College at any stage during the course. Although an end of course open day allowed studies and practical work to reach a suitable climax, the telling examination for a Bergman-Österberg Diploma was in practical teaching. Students often taught in schools throughout London, but practice was regularly provided within the gymnasium with visiting children under the direct supervision of Madame herself.

Initially, Madame Österberg undertook most of the lecturing duties, helped by an unqualified assistant and a variety of part-time male specialists. The first of the assistants was Margaret Stansfeld who was awarded a certificate after one year at the Gymnasium. The men helped with the games, German vaulting and Dancing, but were replaced by Madame Österberg's own students, often direct from College, where this was possible. This was an attempt to guard against a possible dilution of standards.

At first the students wore the blue merino dress favoured by the Central Institute for practical subjects. However, Madame took a particular liking to a tunic designed and worn by Mary Tait, one of her students. After a trial period, the tunic was adopted by the College, and students were exhorted to secure its general use in schools in subsequent years. In this way the influence of the 'Österberg Girls' was felt throughout the World as the 'Gym Slip' was adopted internationally.

Side by side with the training of teachers, Madame Österberg offered courses in massage and remedial gymnastics at her College, for private patients, and many of her students entered private practice when they left College, to open their own clinics or health homes.

Although the application of rigorous standards kept numbers down initially; as the reputation of the college grew, even temporary accommodation at 5 Broadhurst Gardens proved inadequate and new premises became a desirability. With the approach of the new railway line this became a necessity, and in 1895 the decision was made to transfer the Bergman-Österberg Physical Training College to a new site in Kent between Bexley and Dartford on the edge of Dartford Heath. The new house, Kingsfield, had been the home of a wealthy solicitor and possessed extensive 'pleasure gardens'. It was generally agreed that it represented the ideal situation for such a college. Much greater scope than had been available in Hampstead existed for physical education. A running track was laid on the lawn, and hard tennis courts and a cricket pitch were added. The ballroom was converted into a gymnasium, and Swedish apparatus was also installed in the woods within the grounds, making an out-of-doors gymnasium.

> 'And she took me to see the out-of-doors gymnasium, explained to me the mysteries of the rib stools, and showed me some of the exercises of the Ling System, all of which are designed with a view to the proper development of the muscles, and to the acquirement of graceful movements. Here all through the summer, whenever the weather is suitable, the girls go through their exercises in their quaint costumes, wearing no hats, drinking fresh air, training their bodies to be as near perfect as possible for each individual student. After the most casual glance one cannot fail to be struck by their erect carriage, their free and graceful manner of walking and running.'[4]

Madame Österberg had herself introduced the American game of Basketball to her Hampstead College and to this country. Her students developed Netball from it. It was found to be ideally suited to the grounds of a country house and flourished in the new setting. Hockey was introduced during the first term at Dartford. Some of the students, namely, E. Peesey, H. Williamson, E. Impey and B. Marriage, passed on this new game they had learned in their own progressive schools. Lacrosse, too, was added to the games programme soon after the turn of the century. From that time, the Dartford students were prominent at the highest levels in the various games played by women in Britain. C. Lawrence and M. Hankinson, E. R. Clarke and E. Adair Impey, for example, were key figures in the establishing of national governing bodies for women in Hockey, Lacrosse and Netball respectively, and in general the Österberg Girls were to play, collectively, a role in women's sports not unlike that of the A.P.T.C., through the years, in the corresponding areas for men.

Dancing continued to thrive at Dartford, on the same lines as before. Before she died, however, Madame Österberg had sent a member of her staff to Hellerau in order to bring back the methods of Dalcroze, further evidence of the forward looking approach of the pioneer even in the last days of her career.

In other ways too, the work of Hampstead was continued and extended. Students offered medical gymnastics and massage in a local cottage to local adults and children. These clinics continued until 1964. The children were welcome in the college to join classes in educational gymnastics, and the students also ran classes in the local drill hall for children from Dartford schools. For the small numbers of students, there was ample provision of practice in the Wilmington Board Schools near by. Classes in gymnastics were also undertaken at the South Darenth Hospital, where mental patients enjoyed the welcome visits of 'Madame's Girls'.

'Madame's Girls' are still remembered today by many Dartford people with impressive affection, despite the fact that their only contact with the world around their college was through their teaching or their frequent bicycle rides to local shops or beauty spots.

Otherwise, theirs was very much the life of the college.

> 'They were never out of her mind, and when she brought back pottery and pictures from Italy or elsewhere, it was for thought of what might interest them. Her whole effort of taste in the college was for their sakes. She was proud of the old students at re-union and grieved over them if overworked or worried, when she would do everything possible to improve their working conditions.'[4]

However, discipline was severe. 'Napoleon', as Madame was called by some of her students, would demand, 'If you cannot control your legs, how can you control your class?', or 'How can you keep your children in order if you cannot keep your hair tidy.' 'No student of mine,' she would admonish, 'ever says, "I cannot".' Every back straightened when she entered a room, each student conscious that the slightest shortcoming would be instantly noticed. Two things may be said about this rather harsh discipline about which many anecdotes have been written. Firstly, the imposing Principal had the personality to carry off these methods, a personality which has meant that many successful and able women still obviously love her, half a century after her death. Secondly she had an oft stated purpose in ever pressing her students.

> 'I have only two years in which to make fine women of you. Not a moment can be wasted. Remember, my dears, it does not matter how good you are, you will never be good enough for the profession you have chosen.'[5]

Certainly the work of the college was remarkably

successful. The students were in great demand when their training was complete.

'They go literally everywhere. Some are snapped up by the great American colleges where Ling is already known, and they simply have to carry forward and amplify work that others have begun. Others find work to hand among their kith and kin. Wheresoever, in fact, the physical status of womankind is capable of being raised there are to be found one or more of the teachers whom Madame Österberg has trained. They constitute, collectively, the "little yeast" that, in time, so many people think will leaven the whole lump.'[6]

As early as 1906, Madame herself was demanding a three-year course for training her specialists, grants for them whilst they trained, and the development of physical education to include 'the whole gigantic range of outdoor and indoor games' and dancing of an aesthetic kind. Her students were much in the same mould, and some were instrumental in the development of a whole system of specialist colleges on the Dartford mould. Stansfeld at Bedford, Anstey in Birmingham and Adair Impey at Chelsea are the best known of these. Österberg herself had introduced her methods to every school board schoolgirl in London in a little over five years. From 1887 her students introduced them to girls' schools of another kind throughout the English speaking world. The practical course in training teachers to specialise in physical education long survived her. The practical course examined for Teachers Certificate, Advanced Art and Science of Movement in 1968 comprised Gymnastics, Swimming, Games, Dance and Athletics. This was, in general terms, the field developed in Dartford before Madame died in 1915. The games examined were exactly the same played by those pioneers, netball, hockey, cricket, lacrosse and tennis.

Madame Österberg's foremost distinction was in the development of physical education for girls and women, but her influence on men teachers and doctors was significant. It was also felt in the British armed forces.[7] Indeed it was she who really laid the foundations upon which the structure of Swedish physical education in English schools was built during the first forty years of the 20th century.

Appendix A.   References

1 Reports of the Inte. .ational Congress of Women, 1899.
2 M. Österberg, *Professional Women on Their Professions*, 1891.
3 A. Montefiore, *Educational Review*, March 1892.
4 *Kingsfield Book of Remembrance.*
5 *Kingsfield Book of Remembrance.*
6 C. L. McCluer-Stevens, *The Windsor Magazine*, 1899.
7 Jonathan May, M.Ed. thesis, University of Leicester, 1967. *The Contribution of Madame Bergman-Österberg to the Development of British Education.*

Physical Education at Mill Hill School
1929–1939

by G. W. HEDLEY and G. W. MURRAY

ORGANISED physical training began at Mill Hill School in 1885 when a new gymnasium was opened. At first the work was done by ex-service instructors. It consisted of morning drill periods for all and afternoon club practice in gymnastics on 'German' apparatus, and boxing for the enthusiasts. Senior and junior gym VIIIs and boxing teams of a high standard were regularly produced.

In 1922 M. L. Jacks was appointed headmaster at the early age of 28. A Unitarian by religion, liberal and humane, international in outlook and progressive in education, he was encouraged by the governors to reform and develop the school. Personal experience of the rigours of prewar public school athleticism,[1] together with his efforts to provide something better for his troops when in rest billets, had convinced him that a wider and more appealing curriculum would be needed if the subject was to contribute anything of real value to school life. Although Jacks had a shrewd idea of the kind of results which he desired he had little knowledge of how to achieve his aims until the demonstration by Mr. S. F. Rous at Watford supplied a starting point.[2] It also supplied a check, for he realised that the type of work which he had seen could not be applied to Mill Hill by the elderly sergeant-instructors being employed at that time.   Regretfully the ideas were laid aside.

Then, in the spring of 1929, Sergeant Peters was killed in a road accident.   Immediately Jacks approached a young man whom he had met at Watford and who was in charge of physical training at Haberdasher's Aske's school at Hampstead, to ask if he would welcome the chance to help launch a pioneer experiment in physical education.   G. W. Hedley was an ex-officer who had done an advanced course in physical training at Aldershot. He was also an Oxford graduate and had attended vacation courses in physical training organised by His Majesty's Inspectors.   Aged thirty and with varied school experience he was considered by Jacks to be well equipped to help him clarify his ideas and to implement them at Mill Hill.   These ideas were revolutionary and far-reaching. They can be summed up as:

> (1) To substitute for the current inadequate notions of physical training an intelligently conceived system of physical education in every school.
>
> (2) To create a recognised Department of Physical Education which would have a rank equal with that of other departments such as classics and mathematics.
>
> (3) The Director or Head of this department to be an university graduate.
>
> (4) Physical Education Departments to be established at universities and physical education to be studied there along with established academic subjects.
>
> (5) The term physical education to include educational gymnastics, voluntary training and competitive gymnastics, minor games and sports inside and

outside the gymnasium, corrective and remedial treatment.

(6) The director's brief to cover promotion of the physical development of every boy in the school, especially the less skilful, the weak and the unstable, and liaison with the school doctor, the form masters and the house masters.

(7) Massed drill or grouped P.T. to be replaced by form gymnastics timetabled in school periods.

In May 1929 Hedley started, with the new title and freedom to create his own department. The governors actively supported the venture and equipped the gymnasium lavishly with modern apparatus of Swedish type. Later the gymnasium itself was extended to ninety feet in length and squash courts were built against an outside wall.

The work in school periods was given the name 'Educational Gymnastics'. It was based on the current Board of Education's system of Swedish strengthening and mobilising exercises, Danish rhythmic work, vaulting, agility and simple games or breaks.[3] For this syllabus boys in the lower and middle school came twice each week, those in the upper school once. In the early afternoons the gymnasium was oriented to help the games organisation by providing fitness and skill training sessions or recreative gymnastics. On the three half-holidays club activities of gymnastics, boxing and fencing were organised in the later afternoon. This type of programme was a practical expression of Jacks' belief that physical education could and should play a greater part in boys' lives, for instance by skill training in place of aimless road runs, by the opening of club activities to the mediocre and the weak and by the provision of corrective exercises for those in need.

After a year's intensive effort in the gymnasium attention was turned to outdoor activities. In addition to swimming and lifesaving, cross-country running and track and field athletics were developed. All of them were in poor condition. Proximity to London made it possible to secure the services of visiting specialist coaches, but it was clear that time was needed to organise and supervise such a varied programme and to ensure co-operation with other masters and other interests. So, to relieve the director in the gymnasium, an ex-Quartermaster R.N. P.T.I. was made available to take some of the afternoon sessions of fitness training and to help with boxing. Next the house gymnastic competitions were reformed to test three distinct types of work. Gymnastic competitions with other schools increased in number. For each boy a Health Book was provided which showed termly changes in physical data and some health records with space for reports by the doctor and the director. Thus parents and housemasters were kept informed.

After three years' work a report was submitted on the original aims of the experiment, the progress achieved and what remained to be attempted. So pleased were the governors that this report was printed and privately circulated while the headmaster wrote a review of the situation for *The Times*. This in turn focused the interest of some leaders in medicine and education on the physical welfare of youth. Meetings were held, a number of visitors came to Mill Hill, there was a good deal of press publicity and, before long, the school found itself in a position of national significance in the development of the subject.

At about this time a new concept of physical education was being worked out at Queen Elizabeth's, Barnet, which was geographically close to Mill Hill. (See Appendix C.) Jacks arranged for the two masters in charge of physical education to meet and he encouraged them to develop their ideas together. This they were happy to do since it was apparent that their views on physical education and the content of their work were similar. Furthermore they both attended a private course in London with R. E. Roper who inspired their subsequent work.

Thereafter they worked together, attended courses, visited schools and training colleges, spoke at meetings and developed their work in schools. In 1935, with the help of a studentship from the Board of Education, they spent six weeks of study leave in Scandinavia and their report was accorded the unusual honour of publication.[4] Previously, in 1934, the Secondary Schoolmasters' Physical Education Association had established their annual Easter courses at Mill Hill and thus brought many teachers into touch with the school.

Experience of these courses and of the work at Mill Hill and Barnet indicated that the system of physical training advocated by the Board, while greatly superior to the earlier concept of drill, was still far too narrow and that the prevailing divorce of the gymnasium from games and sports was a profound error. Physical Education should be made an integral part of the curriculum with close co-operation between the academic and physical education staff and provision should be made for remedial treatment through liaison with doctors. These ideas were canvassed among colleagues and were published in a book.[5]

In July 1935 Hedley left Mill Hill en route for His

Majesty's Inspectorate and was succeeded as director of physical education by Murray. His tenure of this post was marked by consolidation rather than expansion. The earlier success had generated some hostility among certain games-playing traditionalists, in the school and the country, who felt that the experiments should be contained lest the established patterns of school life be impaired. More important, the deepening economic depression of the thirties caused a drop in numbers so that financial difficulties combined with political anxiety to discourage further adventures. For these reasons it was decided to concentrate on improving the services offered within the existing framework.

In this era inter-school gymnastic competitions were based upon the educational gymnastic programme. Parallel and horizontal bars at Mill Hill had been put in the loft, and the school was not defeated in one of these new gymnastic competitions throughout the decade. A particular contribution was made in the remedial field. Also, special coaching and individual programmes of exercise were introduced for the weak or unskilful boys. The collection of physical data was reorganised and analysed each term to reveal both group and individual trends in growth. The provision of an outdoor swimming pool in 1936 made possible an extension of the aquatic programme. For athletics, working parties of boys constructed additional facilities and field events received special attention from visiting coaches, both amateur and professional. Franz Stampfl was among them. General standards rose and some striking successes were achieved in schools' meetings at national level.

During this period perhaps the most important contribution made by the school was extramural. Initial success, combined with the reputation of M. L. Jacks, brought many visitors and many inquiries. To reduce the ensuing correspondence a comprehensive report was written. It was introduced by the headmaster. It was published in 1937 and was widely distributed. The school supplied evidence to many committees and gave much private help to politicians, government officials, public bodies and leaders in medicine and education. There was also a steady stream of inquiries from other Public Schools as well as from state-aided schools.

The S.S.P.E.A. courses multiplied and the association grew in influence. Under the guidance of S. F. Rous it began to foster research projects in schools and to press for the acceptance of the new conceptions of physical education as opposed to those of physical training. At this time Dr. G. E. Friend of Christ's Hospital and Dr. F. W. W. Griffin of the Lucas Tooth Institute became asociate members and gave strong medical support, forging a link with the Medical Officers of Schools Association. In 1938 and 1939 the Easter courses featured an 'advanced course' on which practical work was replaced by consideration of the wider aspects of physical education. These were directed by R. E. Roper aided by a group of specialists. That they were oversubscribed is evidence of their value. They offered a forum and a type of work unobtainable elsewhere at that time. At the course in 1934 P. A. Smithells read a paper on the incidence of fatigue in schoolboys and the value of compiling physical data to reveal personal variations and group trends. In discussion other speakers offered evidence to suggest that there were wide differences in the physique of boys attending different types of school and that variations in growth between term-time and school holidays indicated exposure to different pressures.   In September 1936 a small anthropometric study was launched to investigate the problems.   Fifteen schools of different types took part with a total of more than 8,000 boys.   Growth measurements were taken nine times a year until December 1939 but the results could not be analysed until 1947.[6]

Unfortunately all this work at Mill Hill as elsewhere came to an abrupt halt in September 1939.   The school was evacuated to St. Bees where a programme suitable for restricted facilities in difficult conditions was devised. Staff, including the director of physical education, joined the forces in 1940.   The boys carried on by themselves with minimum guidance for the duration of the war. That they brought back with them so much is, perhaps, the best tribute to all that had gone before, but the pioneer work in physical education at Mill Hill School was over.

Appendix B.   References

1   Arnold Lunn, *The Harrovians*, London 1913, and Alec Waugh, *The Loom of Youth*, London, 1917.
2   See Chapter 13.
3   *A Reference Book of Gymnastic Training for Boys*, H.M.S.O., 1927.
4   G. W. Hedley and G. W. Murray, *Physical Education in Denmark and Sweden*, H.M.S.O., 1935. Educational Pamphlet No. 104.
5   G. W. Hedley and G. W. Murray, *Physical Education for Boys*, Methuen, London, 1936.
6   G. E. Friend and E. R. Bransby, 'Physique and Growth of Schoolboys', *The Lancet*, 1947, II, p. 677.

See also:

G. E. Friend, *The Schoolboy, A Study of his Nutrition, Physical Development and Health*, Heffer, Cambridge, 1935.
F. W. W. Griffin, *The Scientific Basis of Physical Education*, London, 1937, Oxford Medical Publications.

F. W. W. Griffin and J. K. McConnel, *Health and Muscular Habits*, London, 1937.

L. P. Jacks, *The Wider Possibilities of Physical Culture*, in 'Education of Today', ed. E. D. Laborde, Cambridge, 1935.

M. L. Jacks, *Education as a Social Factor*.

M. L. Jacks, *Physical Education* (Nelson Discussion Books), London, 1938.

G. W. Murray, *Physical Education in the Curriculum* in 'Problems in Modern Education', ed. E. D. Laborde, Cambridge, 1939.

R. E. Roper, *Physical Education in Relation to School Life*, George Allen and Unwin, 1917.

R. E. Roper, *Movement and Thought*, Blackie, London, 1938.

P. A. Smithells, *Physical Education*, in 'Mankind in the Making', ed. T. F. Coade, Peter Davies, London, 1939.

P. A. Smithells, *R. E. Roper*, in 'Nine Pioneers in Physical Education', Physical Education Association, London, 1964.

U

APPENDIX C

Physical Education for All: First Principles and Practice

by K. L. WOODLAND

formerly Coordination Master, Queen Elizabeth's Boys Grammar School, Barnet

WHEN in 1932 Queen Elizabeth's School abandoned its old Elizabethan building in the centre of Barnet and moved to new accommodation built by the Hertfordshire County Council on the playing fields at the edge of the town, it acquired among other things maintained school status and a gymnasium. P.T. lessons and the sergeant's drill were no more, and were superseded by a new subject with the new name of 'physical education'. In fact it was more than a subject, it was a department of the school embracing all the activities which went on outside on the playing fields or inside in connection with the gymnasium or the medical room and the specially appointed School Doctor. There was also a Director of Physical Education, G. W. Murray, a young master who had already been at the school several years, whose promotion to the new post was an inspired choice of the Headmaster, E. H. Jenkins, who in only his second year at the school had shown a remarkable genius in selecting his staff.

G. W. Murray was making a big impact on what was then a small country grammar school with his tremendous drive and enthusiasm, his wide interests, particularly in drama and music, and his outstanding games prowess. But he had another unsuspected asset which he brought to bear on his new task, which enabled him in a few years to develop an entirely new conception and treatment of physical education, and make the Department a Mecca not only for specialists in the subject (from the senior H.M.I. downwards) but also for leaders in medicine, sport and education from this country and abroad; and this was a formal medical training received before he came into education, allied with extensive and influential family contacts with the medical world. Attendance at a Board of Education holiday course run by H.M. Chief Inspector for Physical Training, F. H. Grenfell, brought him in touch with current thought and ideas; and it was here that he heard R. E. Roper lecture on a new concept of 'physical education', which had nothing to do with 'drill' or 'training' but set out *to assist the development and integration of the growing organism which makes up each individual child.* 'Body is a structure and mind is a function,' wrote Roper, and the two must develop together. 'Physical education . . . is a piece of creative integration which each individual must achieve for himself.' Murray at once realised the great significance of Roper's theories and their wider implications for education, and they provided the philosophical basis for the new physical education at Queen Elizabeth's.

In the Department the individual needs of the 320 boys were always the first consideration. The simple aim was to help each one to develop a sound and healthy body (which he might hope to maintain throughout his adult life) with a sound and healthy mind functioning in it. This inevitably demanded a close working relationship between the academic and physical work of the school.

Roper had estimated that in any school at any time some 40 per cent of the pupils would require special attention to their individual needs, which might reveal themselves sometimes externally as a fault in movement or carriage, or sometimes in the classroom as a change of attitude to the work. It was necessary that each boy should know that his personal difficulties would be a prime concern of the Department, and the new Director therefore gave up the various controlling positions he held in the school games system, to make himself available at any time out of school hours for boys who wanted his help. He had to establish and maintain individual records, physical, medical, academic, and particularly records of height and weight changes, for (again as Roper had shown) a variation in the height/weight ratio was often the first warning sign of lowered vitality, and this in turn might bring about some physical trouble such as flattening of the foot-arch, or a decline in the level of the boy's class-work (since the mind needs a healthy body in which to function), or even some moral delinquency, or perhaps all three. Noting deviations from the normal in the pupils in his charge was every master's responsibility, and in this way almost the whole staff was drawn into the work of the Department.

But a major concern was still the provision of a range of physical activities, based in the gymnasium and extending over the playing fields, wide enough to meet the varied needs and interests of the boys but not so wide that any of it had to be unsupervised and uncontrolled. Sending the class out for a run round the roads, which seems the stand-by of many p.e. specialists today, was never countenanced, not solely because of the harmful effect of hard metalled roads on the delicate structure of immature feet but because of the impossibility of knowing what each boy was doing and what effect it was having on him. While the

Director was, of course, in charge in the gymnasium, other masters had full responsibility for the various games. The three who organised rugby, cricket and junior games (later athletics also) formed with the Director a kind of managing board for the Department, and the whole-hearted co-operation of the first of these, J. A. Strugnell, who a few years later became Second Master in the school, ensured general acceptance and success for the venture. Two periods in the gymnasium were augmented by two outside games a week, rugby in the winter, cricket and athletics in the summer. The school had then (and still has in 1968) Wednesday afternoon for games with lessons on Saturday morning, and by making small pitches for small boys and using some of them twice over it was possible to have all the boys playing on Wednesdays and again on Saturdays. The boys in their first year of rugby spent their time learning handling and scrumming, and playing short games in teams with three or five forwards and four or five outsides; at cricket there was group coaching in batting (with dummy bats), fielding and bowl-ing as well as ordinary games. The next three years' groups (to 15) played in a series of 'junior games', labelled from 'A' down the alphabet as far as was necessary. They were graded not so much according to age as to ability, size and speed, so that every boy could find satisfaction in playing in a homogeneous group at his own level of competence. Rugby proved most suitable, offering scope as it does for all physical types, where even the slow and unco-ordinated boy can be doing something useful for his side merely by being in the right place attempting the right thing at the right time. The lowest junior games played not more than 10-a-side, and only 'A' Game played regularly a full fifteen. Athletics in the late spring and summer was mainly an activity for the seniors, especially those for whom cricket no longer held any interest. It too offered scope for a wide range of physical types, and when in grading for competition height and weight were taken into account as well as age the interest was very keen. All boys who opted for athletics were required to do something on the track as well as in the field, and track walking proved invaluable as an alternative to running, especially for those with poor carriage, lack of co-ordination or slowness in movement, and incorrect leg or foot action which often had caused flat feet. Juniors were given a little athletics in the summer, mainly intended to teach them a relaxed and economical running action.

All these games were supervised and coached, and at one time twelve of the sixteen masters at the school were regularly taking them. A separate card index was kept for games, the card having one line for each term on which was put the letter of the game in which the boy had played and the master's comment on his play. It was patent to all that the games were not team-building nurseries for the talented, but were an important aspect of physical education, and that the boy's personal level of achievement was a matter of equal significance whether he played in 'A' or 'J' Game. Masters with little or no previous knowledge of rugby or cricket or athletics were able to learn how to teach the boys in the lowest games, apparently to their mutual advantage. When athletics was first introduced in 1932 half a dozen masters voluntarily divided the various events among themselves, and set about learning the techniques to such good effect that by 1939 when the war came the school was regularly winning the L.A.C. Schools Championships, and its reputation for a high all-round standard of athletic performance was country-wide. Guidance was sought and obtained on a voluntary basis from the outstanding experts of the time, including F. A. M. Webster, A. H. G. Pope, J. E. Lovelock, and later F. F. L. Stampfl. Yet the foundation remained equal coaching for all, regardless of standard and potential.

The Director always had his list of cases, perhaps fifty or more, compiled from his own observations and from reports received from other masters, mostly boys who were doing exercises (at home or after school in the gymnasium) to correct lordosis or hallux valgus or some other physical defect which they had temporarily developed. Many things which came to light in the Department required reference to the boy's parents and doctor, sometimes a psychiatrist. With all this it was still possible on games afternoons for the Director to assist as one of the junior games' coaches, and in the summer term he was often able to walk round and look in at the various games going on, discussing the play and the players with the masters taking them. In this way the wide-reaching interest of the Physical Education Department was made apparent to all.

The feeling of well-being and confidence which came with the possession of a healthy body and the knowledge of how to use it soon brought a marked change in the general bearing and carriage of the boys as they moved about the school (and the town). Anyone who has lived and worked in such a community is aware at once on encountering a crowd of normal boys elsewhere of the significance of L. P. Jacks's phrase 'physically illiterate'. Here the occasional round-shouldered, the flat-footed, the tired and weary singled themselves out from the rest and

soon came to the notice of the Department.   Of the boys
who attended Queen Elizabeth's in the decade before the
war not all derived a lasting benefit from the physical
education, though all were influenced by it while they
were there.   Some owe a great deal, and know they owe a
great deal, a lifetime's physical contentment perhaps, to the
help they had; others probably went away and succumbed
to some of the many natural shocks that flesh is heir to;
but few can have failed to gain some little satisfaction and
advantage from the experience and knowledge acquired in
their Barnet schooldays.   The war dispersed for ever the
masters who worked in the Department, but those who
are alive and remember know that with the passing of
this phase of physical education for all something of real
value has been lost.

Index

313